COMPUTERS AND BUREAUCRATIC REFORM

Computers and Bureaucratic Reform

THE POLITICAL FUNCTIONS OF URBAN INFORMATION SYSTEMS

KENNETH C. LAUDON
Center For Policy Research, Inc.
and
John Jay College
of
The City University of New York

A WILEY-INTERSCIENCE PUBLICATION

JOHN WILEY & SONS, New York · London · Sydney · Toronto

Library of Congress Cataloging in Publication Data:

Laudon, Kenneth C   1944-

    Computers and bureaucratic reform.
    "A Wiley-Interscience publication."
    Bibliography: p.
    1. Electronic data processing—Public administration.
2. Local government—United States—Case studies.
3. State governments—Case studies. I. Title.

JS344.E4L38   353.9'028'54   74-9750
ISBN 0-471-51840-9

Printed in the United States of America

10 9 8 7 6 5 4 3 2 1

TO MY PARENTS

KENNETH A. AND LEONE M. LAUDON

Foreword

Ken Laudon's book deals with one of the most important issues of our time: how we reassert the primacy of our values over technological and productive and administrative powers whose dynamics we often do not understand and do not control. If we are to guide these powers, to make them work to our priorities rather than being subject to their whims, "needs," and vested interests, several key changes will have to occur. Political mobilization of those hereto excluded will have to take place; corporate power will have to be reallotted; new definitions of self will have to evolve.

Laudon focuses his attention—and study—on one essential facet of this development: the electronic extension of our mind, consciousness, and capacity to communicate, hence ultimately, control. If the industrial revolution expanded our muscle power but contributed much less to the development of our mental capacities, the postmodern era, which may be said to have started in 1945, aims to catch up on this level, through the development of new, nationwide real-time communication networks, automation, and above all, the introduction of the computers.

But these "second order" or review and control tools (which guide the first layer activities, the "performance" ones) are not really accepted; they require changes in institutional arrangments in the human guidance mechanisms. Laudon's study provides compelling data and analyses to show how difficult, fortuitous, indeed often self-defeating, such efforts are. The factors Laudon's study points to on the level of knowledge (information theory), political overlay (the overbureaucratization and lack of professionalism in local governments), and political base or "underlay" (the lack of political mobilization, or "will") are all significant, not just in the cases he studied. The author correctly concludes from his data that the main block is political, not technological. This also suggests that in a changed polity a somewhat modified "second order" technology could go a long way to remedy many of our domestic problems, which, Laudon shows, it is not now helping to curtail.

AMITAI ETZIONI
Professor of Sociology
Columbia University
and Director of the Center
for Policy Research

Preface

This study investigates the role of advanced information technology in the reform of four state and local government bureaucracies in the United States. Information technology—the use of computer storage and information transmission devices—is seen as affecting the distribution of a critical bureaucratic resource, information. The study focuses on two consequences of the redistribution of information: the level of centralization and the degree of resistance to reform. In addition, the research focuses on the implications of information technology for the origination and administration of new social policies.

The principal findings of the study are that levels of centralization and resistance due to reform are primarily the product of political and bureaucratic forces, not the result of inherent technological requisites. The process of technological innovation thus appears as a political process characterized by conflict and compromise among the parties involved. Several models of technologically induced bureaucratic change are outlined, and their various social consequences are discussed.

The social policy implications of information technology in public agencies are found to be rather conservative. Contrary to our expectations the use of computers in the public sector has tended to strengthen the grip or traditional social policies and appears to lessen the perceived need and public demand for fundamental reconception of social policies in diverse areas such as police, welfare, and health. A detailed analysis of the various groups and interests responsible for the development and design of public sector information systems is undertaken to understand how and why this occurs.

The book is divided into three parts. Part One deals with the historical and theoretical concerns that guided the research effort. Part Two presents case studies and reflects the issues outlined in Part One. Part Three assesses the political and historical impact of computerized information systems on public decision making.

Several chapters in Part One may be skipped over lightly by professional data processors. Chapter 2 briefly defines the basic elements of modern computer systems and presents certain terms used throughout the book.

Academic and other readers not familiar with computer terms should read Chapter 2. The remaining chapters in Part One review previous research efforts (Chapter 3) and develop a sociological theory for understanding the origins and development of information systems (Chapters 4 to 6). Chapter 4 may be especially interesting to data processors as an examination of the administrative reform movement in which they played an important role during the 1960s.

The case studies presented in Chapters 7 to 10 focus primarily on the social and political factors that shaped the development of computer information systems. Readers interested in technical descriptions of hardware and software are referred to the system description appendices following each case study.

The materials and documents for the research were collected between 1968 and 1971. In 1968 the author began work with Professor Alan F. Westin (Department of Government, Columbia University) who was then working under a grant from the Harvard Program on Technology and Society on a study of the impact of information technology upon public decision making. When I joined the project, Professor Westin had already collected public documents on more than 100 information systems in state and local governments. From these systems approximately ten were selected, on the basis of whether they were indeed operational systems and other considerations, including length of operation and sophistication of design and concept. From this group of ten, four cases were selected for in-depth analysis. The next two years involved a series of site visits at these locations, with occasional side excursions to nearby installations.

This book would not have been written without the support of the Harvard Program on Technology and Society between 1968 and 1971, and the Center for Policy Research between 1971 and 1973. The Harvard Program and its director, Emanual Mesthene, provided support to Professor Westin and myself during the period of data collection and initial analysis. The Center, through its director Amitai Etzioni, provided both clerical and intellectual assistance and encouragement to revise my doctoral dissertation for publication.

My primary intellectual debt is to Professor Alan Westin, who convinced me in the course of four years that the technology used by government to store and process information about its citizens is an important social issue, therefore an important sociological issue. With his encouragement and enthusiasm I managed to learn the art of sleuthing through county court houses, police agencies, welfare bureaucracies, and newspaper files for bits and pieces of information required for our story. In countless dialogues during the course of the research Professor Westin's keen understanding of the legal and political forces which shape local bureaucracies contributed immeasurably to interpretations and conclusions I have reached. At several points in the research when masses of documents and interviews challenged the writer's ability to synthesize, Westin's personal encouragement and liberal gift of time kept the work proceeding.

A second major intellectual debt is owed to Amitai Etzioni (Department of Sociology, Columbia University) whose theoretical acumen helped forge fragments of information into a coherent whole. The apprentice graduate student typically finds himself with enormous quantities of data but lacks theoretically interesting questions. Insofar as this work asks interesting questions it is in large part due to Amitai's insistence on the primacy of formulating good questions the art of which is not widespread. One focus of this book is directly attributed to Etzioni's influence, namely, how can a society shape emerging technologies to fulfill its conscious needs rather than merely react to social and technological change? Most of this book focuses on the social and political forces which are in fact shaping the use of a major new technology, computerized information systems in the public sector. Neither of these questions would have been broached without Etzioni's previous published work and his personal support.[1]

Many others participated directly in the intellectual work of this book, especially the members of my dissertation committee at Columbia: Alan Silver (Sociology), Stephen Unger (Engineering), and Samuel Sieber (Sociology).

Of course none of these souls who gave of their time and energy are responsible for the final product. That is the author's burden.

KENNETH C. LAUDON

New York, New York
May 1974

---

[1] For a full discussion of the general conditions necessary for societal guidance see Amitai Etzioni, *The Active Society* (New York: Free Press, 1968), especially Chapters 8 and 9, which deal with the role of societal knowledge and information.

Acknowledgments

I wish to thank the following sources for permission to publish copyrighted material.

Edward Hearle and R. J. Mason, *A Data Processing System for State and Local Government*. Reprinted by permission of Prentice-Hall, Inc. Englewood Cliffs, N. J., © The RAND Corporation.

James Q. Wilson, *Varieties of Police Behavior*. Reprinted by permission of Harvard University Press, Cambridge, Mass., © 1968.

Daniel Bell, *The Coming of the Post-Industrial Society*. Basic Books, Inc. New York. Reprinted by permission of Basic Books, Inc., © 1973.

Richard Hofstadter, *The Age of Reform*. Reprinted by permission of Alfred A. Knopf, Inc., © 1963.

"Program Budgeting for Police Departments," *The Yale Law Journal*. Reprinted by permission of The Yale Law Journal Company and Fred B. Rothman and Co. from the *Yale Law Journal*, Vol. 76, p. 823.

Elizabeth Drew, "HEW Grapples with PPBS." Reprinted by permission of *The Public Interest*, No. 8 (Summer 1967), pp. 9–29, © by National Affairs Inc., 1967.

Contents

COMPUTERS AND BUREAUCRATIC REFORM

PART **ONE**

ONE

Technology and Bureaucratic Reform

Social crisis is the crucible of societal innovation. In American political history these innovations have entailed alternatively changes in political structure or changes in the administrative machinery of government. The former is commonly referred to as political reform, the latter we shall call bureaucratic reform. These two responses to periods of national trial have molded together the Populist and Progressive strains in America.

This is a study of bureaucratic reform in the 1960s—a period of intense moral and political questioning that produced, like other similar eras, innumerable proposals for political change and modest suggestions for improving the body politic, releasing fervent calls and hopes for a radical democracy. The 1960s was also a period of rapid technological development in computers, and many of the innovations came to be associated with bureaucratic reform. This is hardly the first time in American history for a new technology and bureaucractic reform to become linked, but the closeness of the relationship is new.

In the decade of the 1960s rapid technological improvements in computers, giant production and marketing firms, politicians of all sorts and sizes, and key administrators of certain public bureaucracies combined to produce some far-reaching and long-term changes in public bureaucracies, especially at the local level. These changes are of sufficient magnitude to be called "bureaucratic reforms."

We examine a type of bureaucratic reform that is largely unheralded. These efforts have escaped the scrutiny of informed publics, even though more monetary resources and manpower have gone into them than into the more politically oriented reforms of the antipoverty programs of the 1960s. Most scholarly and public attention in the 1960s focused on the controversial political reforms of the period, ignoring changes in other spheres of public life.

The bureaucratic reforms we consider do not mobilize large numbers of citizens; whereas the kinds of values that clothe bureaucratic reforms are quite traditional, they are different from earlier reforms utilizing the same or similar values. The reforms we describe are of low visibility, originating from the "top down," not the "bottom up"; they are sponsored reforms rather than populist reforms.

For all their invisibility, the bureaucratic reforms we describe are established and ongoing. For the most part they were initiated by well-financed and powerful private corporations in pursuit of the expanding, lucrative "civilian" computer market of the early 1960s. Such plans were enthusiastically received and often naïvely ballyhooed by elected politicians looking toward the next election; they were expectantly supported by state and local civil servants seeking "nonpolitical" solutions to what some politely called "the problem of delivering urban services" and others characterized as the complete breakdown in the ability of public urban bureaucracies to deliver welfare, education, police, and health services to those most in need.

The array of established social forces behind the bureaucratic reforms we describe contrasts vividly with the ragtag group of intellectuals, activists, minority leaders, and dilettantes who formed the base of the antipoverty projects of the 1960s. And although the poverty program has been eased from the national agenda, the bureaucratic reforms we describe were just the beginning of a still continuing process of change.

COMPUTERS AND BUREAUCRATIC STRUCTURE

Previous research on technological change and organizational structure has been devoted mainly to the impact of various and limited kinds of *automation* on status relationships within an industrial setting. Rarely have these innovations involved major changes in the so-called core technology of an industrial operation.

In this research we study a kind of automation that differs significantly from the usual kind of industrial automation. First, computers automate not an industrial operation or process, but the processing of information itself. Second, ours is a unique setting for observing the impact of information automation. For the public bureaucracies we study, information is both a primary output and a core technology. The impact of computers on bureaucratic structure is potentially comparable to the impact of mass production on industrial organization.

THE PROBLEM

The central problem we address is defining the relationship between bureaucratic change and a new technology of information processing. Observers of public and private bureaucracies have suggested that the introduction of information technology causes these organizations to become more centralized, often leading lower level participants to resist central controls made possible and efficient by electronic computers.

Our research began, naïvely perhaps, with the question, What is the impact of this new information technology on bureaucratic structure? In the course of the research I came to realize that the more fruitful question is, rather, How does social structure shape the use of information technology? Specifically, how does bureaucratic structure shape the critical decisions that inform the design, the avowed purpose, and the utilization of a major new technology? What social and political values intervene between the development of a technology and its widespread use? How do various conflicting groups of differing relative strength and perspectives alter the utilization of a technology, and ultimately its social consequences? In short, our central problem is to analyze the factors that shape the social organization of a new technology.

THE TECHNOLOGY: COMPUTERS

Without exception, the development of computers has been in response to well-articulated need by scientists and laymen. Demand precedes realization. These demands have been made by astronomers with better things to do than arithmetic in the process of testing their hypotheses and producing tables on celestial motion, by mariners too seasick to accurately calculate their longitude, by mathematicians who would rather formulate general descriptions than explicit predictions, and, most notably in the modern period, from the requirement of artillery gunners in the World Wars I and II to find their targets. All these situations have shared one characteristic: the tedious task of arithmetic prevented men from adequately attaining their goals.[1]

The development of the computer is often portrayed as simply a response to a demand for greater speed of calculation. This is deceptively true: speed of calculation has increased enormously. Behind this truth lies another more important reality, however. Speed for its own sake is hardly impressive. Speed is important because it allows men to do things they otherwise would not have done, for lack of will, time, or energy. The development of computers signifies not just an increase in speed of calculation but offers as well a quantum leap in the amount and kinds of things that can be done within a human framework. That is, the development of the computer furnished opportunities for actions previously considered, but thought to be beyond the scope of human time, will, and energy.

Herein lies much of our story. When computers enter the complex area of politics and public bureaucracy, an "unlocking" effect can be observed. Old political and administrative dreams become realizable, and the protective limitations of a traditional information technology melt away. Administrative and political fears are created, as well as fantasies. How various actors respond to the new opportunities and liabilities of the computer in public bureaucracies is the substance of this book.

DEVELOPMENT OF COMPUTERS

In their essentials, computers have existed for thousands of years. The computer has two fundamental elements: a device for storing information, and a device or routine for performing operations on that information. In this sense the abacus is the first known digital computer, the slide rule the most widely used analog computer. Progress in computers is measured by advances in the techniques used to store and perform operations on information.

Until shortly before World War II, computer information storage and operations was accomplished by mechanical devices. The most sophisticated of these, invented by Herman Hollerith, was the punched card, which stores information and can be sorted mechanically. This device was used to tabulate the 1890 census.

The modern computer appears with the utilization of vacuum tubes, which came to replace mechanical devices for performing operations on stored information. The first electronic computing machines were introduced commercially in 1950. These machines could rapidly and quite efficiently perform a number of operations on electronically stored data as well as on punched cards.

By today's standards these first generation modern computers were unreliable, rather inflexible, and physically large and expensive. The flexibility of the early machines was severely limited because they could be programmed to perform only a few tasks. Second, limitations on their storage capacities meant that they had to rely on off-line facilities to store information such as decks of punched cards. Thus stored information could only be processed by a computer in a batch, or one file at a time. The kinds of computerized, on-line files now used by major airlines to book reservations were impossible with these early machines.

The development of transistors and magnetic memory-core storage devices introduced the second generation computer in the late 1950s. Hardware reliability increased while costs decreased. Magnetic core memories expanded by a factor of thousands the amount of information the computer itself could store. Magnetic drum and disk on–line storage devices made it possible to provide random access (as opposed to batch processing) to ever larger files of stored information.

Third generation computers began to appear in the early 1960s, extending the transistor revolution of the late 1950s through miniaturized and microminiaturized integrated circuits that increased reliability and once again decreased costs of basic computer elements. The new computers could store on-line (i.e., instantly available to users) very large information files with random access. To make this storage capacity available to users in different locations, remote access terminals connected by various telecommunications devices to a central computer were developed.

The potential of the third generation computers lay in their ability to create information networks connecting physically and heretofore socially distant users (frequently organizations or organizational subunits). During the 1960s these information networks came to be referred to as "information systems."

WHAT IS AN INFORMATION SYSTEM?

The growth of computerized information systems in all levels of American government has paralleled the phenomenal growth in the number of computers used in the larger society. In 1958 the number of installed computers in the United States was 1000; in 1959, 2000; and by 1966, more than 30,000. The federal government had two computers in 1950; by 1965 there were more than 2000, with 4000 predicted for 1970.[2] There are no readily available data on the use of computers by local governments. In California, however, from 1960 to 1965, the number of computers in state government increased from five to fifty-five; the number of counties using computers in California increased from twelve in 1958 to forty-eight in 1970.[3]

Almost any governmental application of computers is loosely referred to as an "information system" or "data bank," but usages differ in several aspects. For the purposes of distinguishing very broad types of applications, and to place our examination of four such applications in their proper context, we classify types of information systems according to the degree to which they transfer government information across organizational and political boundaries.[4]

The Electronic Clerk: Computerized Files

The first applications in business and government of computer technology in the 1950s and 1960s could be characterized as glorified office machines. The early applications were designed to automate simple, routine office tasks previously done manually within an organizational subunit (e.g., bureau or department). The tasks most susceptible to automation were accounting tasks—payroll, sales analysis, inventory, and general accounting.[5] In the federal government, the next most frequent use of computers was as a scientific and engineering tool to solve specific problems.[6] Examples of these early applications are found in the Internal Revenue Service, the California Department of Motor Vehicles License File, and the Chicago Police Department.[7]

A more sophisticated use of the "electronic clerk" type of application is the SPRINT system of the New York City Police Department.[8] SPRINT (Special Police Radio Inquiry Network) has automated certain functions of the police dispatcher, such as locating police cars, ranking calls in order of importance, describing the scene of the crime and its crime history, and recording the response of officers at the scene. Compressed and edited versions of daily dispatch activities are automatically sent to the Inspector of Operations, who ranks cars and precincts in order of response times and other criteria, and investigates cases of inadequate or total failure of police response.

Although the SPRINT system, and others like it in Oakland and San Francisco, have begun to automate the flow of information among various bureaus within agencies, such information is restricted to a single agency. For our purposes, it is classified as a sophisticated, single-agency, computerized file.

Integrated Systems: The Archival Data Bank

In the early 1960s computers had been developed that were large enough to link information collected by a variety of government agencies within a functional area (e.g., all agencies involved in housing, or all agencies involved in real estate or tax parcels) and usually within a single jurisdiction (e.g., city, county, or federal government). The information stored in these data banks was generally in the form of a one-time statistical survey, audit, or summary on people, places, or things within the jurisdiction. Converted into compatible machine-readable form, the surveys were submitted by a variety of agencies, usually stored within a single agency (e.g., the Auditor's Department or the Planning Department) and made available on request to other agencies within the jurisdiction.

The early integrated system data banks functioned primarily like automated libraries. Agencies in need of statistical information about people, places, or things within their jurisdiction, to comply with a federal order, to obtain federal funds, or to prepare annual reports, would turn to the archive data bank. In this sense the first data banks did not play a large role in the day-to-day affairs of the involved agencies and were limited in their use to very special purposes. Examples of such archive data banks are the Detroit Social Databank, the Washington, D.C., Real Property Databank, the Los Angeles Municipal Information System, the San Francisco Bay Area Transportation Study, the Tri-State (New York, Connecticut, and New Jersey) Transportation Commission Data Bank, and the Management Information System of the U.S. Office of Economic Opportunity.[9]

Integrated Systems: Centralized Administrative-Intelligence Systems

The development in the mid-1960s of third generation computers made possible a new kind of information system which we call a "centralized administrative-intelligence system"; others have used the terms "total unified information system"[10] and "total systems approach."[11] Certain political factors, discussed below, made these systems a reality.

Generally these systems were created by the executive branch of government—the city manager, county administrative officer, or governor—and typically they are based on a central computer service center that either is an independent agency directly responsible to the executive or is attached to another executive agency (e.g., the Auditor's Department, the state Department of Justice).

This second type of integrated information system served to transfer information about specific individuals, places (land parcels), or things (buildings), across organizational and political boundaries from its point of collection to other points in the government structure where such information was needed. In addition, these systems perform functions similar to those of the first type (computerized file systems) by providing participating agencies with computerized information storage and processing facilities.

We refer to these systems as "administrative-intelligence" systems to differentiate them from archival data banks. Administrative-intelligence systems collect, store, process, and transfer information about individuals *qua* individuals.[12] They are used to produce files about persons known to several agencies, and they have been used in compiling dossiers on individuals.[13] At the same time, we do not wish to conjure up images of Fouché's political intelligence files of the nineteenth century. Government agencies have always used information about individuals in the routine administration of social policies (e.g., welfare, education, health, and taxation). Thus we append the word "administrative" to descriptions of these systems to indicate their primary use as aids in processing routinely collected information about persons having contact with government agencies. What is new is the systems' ability to transfer information about a number of organizations and across various political levels, not the kind of information so transferred.

This second type of integrated system is typically based on a central computer service center that acts as a storage bank and exchange center. Line agencies (welfare, health, police agencies) are connected to this center by remote terminals and dedicated telephone lines through which information is placed into the data bank and from which information is taken out. These systems operate in "real time." That is, information is put into and taken out of the system almost instantaneously. For example, in one such system a welfare worker places the name of a prospective client into a terminal to search for the client's previous history of contacts with county government. A reply from the data bank requires about 30 seconds. In turn, decisions of the welfare worker vis-à-vis the client are recorded immediately in the central data bank and are available for use by other agencies (e.g., health, probation, or hospitals).[14]

By any contemporary standard, these systems are very large. Unlike the archive data bank, which stores a small amount of information about large populations or statistical groups, administrative-intelligence systems store a large amount of information about a great many individuals. One such system stores criminal information, including individual fingerprints, summary criminal histories, and other personal identifying information, about more than 6 million persons.[15] Unlike the archive data bank, which is restricted in use to a few specialists, the administrative-intelligence systems are used by hundreds, in some cases thousands, of government employees. Such breadth of utilization requires large-scale retraining programs and extensive efforts to "sell the system" to lower level supervisors and workers.

Examples of centralized administrative-intelligence systems are LOGIC (Local Government Information Center) System, in Santa Clara County, California; Management Information System, in Nassau County, New York; Municipal Data System, in Alexandria, Virginia; Los Angeles Municipal Information System-People File; the U.S. Department of Labor Regional Job Bank System; the Las Vegas, Nevada, Sheriff's SCOPE system; the FBI's National Crime Information Center; the National Driver Registration Service; the California Motor Vehicle Department AMIS (Automatic Management Information System); the U.S. Department of Transportation National Accident Injury Analysis Center; and the Defense Department's Central Index of Investigations at Fort Holabird, Maryland.[16] A list of such systems being planned or in the early operational stages would be enormous.[17]

The point of entry for this type of information system was local government, beginning in California in 1964 with the Alameda County People Information System; soon the innovation spread to other counties, cities, and states throughout the country. The federal government, generally the last to develop these systems, is currently assuming the task of coordinating local systems into state, regional, and ultimately national networks.[18] There are two reasons for this pattern of development. First many talked of "unified information systems" in the mid-1960s, but few knew how to build one, and local governments were chosen for experimental applications of the concept by computer and systems development firms. Second, the technology required to build state, regional, and federal systems did not exist a decade ago and only now is being developed.

The centralized administrative-intelligence information system raises a number of political issues and problems. It is frequently observed that these systems threaten to invade the privacy of individuals and to impair the confidentiality of professional relations between a client and government employees (e.g., social workers, nurses, probation officers.)[19] These threats are real. In one of our case studies an information system is used to produce a public list of all county employees receiving welfare payments and county medical services. However, these issues raised by information systems are discussed elsewhere by others and enter into our study only peripherally.

THE POLITICAL ECONOMY OF INFORMATION SYSTEMS

Here we want to determine how such information systems affect and are affected by interorganizational relationships and formal and informal political relationships between the executive branches of government and line agencies.

Obviously who gets what information about whom is a matter for contention among line agencies and politicians alike. Will the Probation Department have access to welfare clients' addresses? Who will decide what information is to be transferred among agencies and for what purposes? Who will control the data center where this information is stored? Who will establish the priorities of the data center? Will the system provide the governor's office with information about local police practices? Will the system lead to closer supervision of line agency budgets and daily decision making by the executive? Who will participate and on what basis, in the design and implementation of these systems?

How these and other questions were resolved in the process of building and operating four centralized administrative-intelligence systems is the subject of our study. As can be noted, these questions are hardly new; indeed, they are traditional questions involving the political relationships between executive branch decision makers in government and line agencies, and among line agencies themselves. They are political questions insofar as their resolution affects and is affected by the distribution of resources and authority within the governmental system.

SELECTION OF THE CASE STUDIES

When our study began in 1968 there were many plans for information systems; a few were being implemented, and even fewer had been operational for some time. As part of a larger study on the effects of information systems on government decision making, I reviewed the plans and system designs of approximately fifty information systems. I was particularly interested in centralized, administrative information systems, of which only a few examples could be found.

From the published plans and histories of information systems, ten were selected for closer review through site visits and interviewing. The sites were chosen on the basis of many criteria. First, from the published plans it appeared these ten were the most advanced systems in terms of design; that is, they conformed roughly to our model of a centralized intelligence information system. Second, each site had made itself very visible in journals, newspapers, and self-published documents, claiming to represent the future direction of government information systems. Third, in the computer journals and in documents published by computer firms servicing these systems, there appeared to be a consensus that these systems represented the most sophisticated uses of the computer. Fourth, initial interviewing of local government officials involved in the development information systems for local and state governments confirmed our impressions derived from the journals that the ten we had selected were considered by government officials to be the most advanced uses to date.

The ten sites selected for further exploration included two city systems in the western United States, four county systems also in the West, two state criminal justice systems—one in the West and the other in the East—and two state agency systems (a welfare department and a motor vehicles department in a western state).

Initial probing of these ten systems revealed that some would not be appropriate research sites. Four systems were finally selected for intensive study, on the following bases. These systems were operational and had been operational the longest. (Many of the systems that had been reported in the journals to be operational in fact were not.) The four systems selected were the most open to research in the sense that the directors were very willing to talk about their accomplishments. The systems chosen, moreover, provided a range of governmental levels from state, region, to county, for I felt that concentration on only state or county or city systems would bias the research by focusing on developments at one level of government and failing to consider developments at other levels.

The four cases selected for intensive study are one county system, one regional system, and two state information systems. The first case is a western county's Social Services Information System (SSIS). SSIS was established in the early 1960s to promote efficiency and coordination among the social service agencies of the county. It was the first attempt in the United States to build a centralized administrative-intelligence system for local government.

The second case study describes the Police Regional Information Systems (PRIS) of Western County. PRIS began in 1965 to coordinate wanted/warrant information flows among ninety-five regional police agencies. The first attempt to build a regional law enforcement information system in the United States, PRIS is the prototype for similar systems in surrounding counties of Western State and in the eastern United States.

Our third case is the Criminal Identification System (CIS) of Eastern State. This system began in 1965 to transfer fingerprints, summary criminal histories, and other criminal information among Eastern State's 3600 criminal justice agencies (e.g., police, district attorneys, and courts; probation, corrections, and parole agencies). CIS was the first state criminal justice information system in the United States.

Our last study describes the Criminal Information Network (CIN) of a western state, initiated in 1968 to perform functions similar to those of CIS. The differing political traditions of the two states, as well as the differing methods of organizing the technology, offer unique opportunities for comparison of the two systems.

The selection of these four cases, while reducing certain biases, introduces others. First, the systems are not typical of local government computerized information systems. Indeed, their sponsors correctly claim them to be among the most advanced and sophisticated local government systems in the United States. Of the 3000 counties in the United States, only one-half use computers of any kind; routine housekeeping (accounting, billing, and inventory) are the typical applications found in county systems. Here we are dealing with highly unusual local government programs.

We focus on these advanced systems because they may provide a view of computer utilization in local governments in the next decade. Although we examine closely only four case studies, the systems investigated were actively observed by city, county, and state governments from other areas of the country. We are studying prototypes of computer information systems.

THE CLINICAL APPROACH

Much research in the field of information technology and social change is accompanied by highly general, empirically unsupported statements. Still other research in this area is characterized by a premature statistical rigor, often based on assumptions hopelessly at odds with reality. Both kinds of research are reviewed and criticized in the following chapter.

The approach adopted here is a middle route between grand theoretical generalization and premature statistical rigor. Ours is a clinical exploratory study designed to generate descriptive hypotheses which, to be sure, apply only to the cases at hand. We stress the importance in all our case studies of the process of change, often ignored by fragmentary and undifferentiated statistical statements.

The sources relied on to gather information for the case studies include public documents, interviews recorded by the author on site visits over a period of two years, as well as personal documents supplied by the participants.

Given the sensitive nature of some of the information gathered during the course of this research, and the fact that the agencies described are still in operation, the author decided to disguise as best as possible the specific names, states, cities, and agencies involved in the study.

NOTES

1. Herman M. Goldstine, *The Computer from Pascal to Von Neumann,* Princeton, N.J.: Princeton University Press, 1972. Goldstine was one of the original developers of ENIAC at the University of Pennsylvania, between 1942 and 1945. His work is perhaps the most comprehensive and thorough history of the development of computers during this period.

2. John McLaughlin, *Information Technology and Survival of the Firm,* Homewood, Ill., Dow Jones-Irwin, 1966, pp. 24–26, and "Inventory of Automatic Data Processing Equipment in the Federal Government," U.S. Bureau of the Budget, Washington, D.C.: Government Printing Office, June 1965.

3. George L. Bergset and Robert Donati, "County Aspects of the State Information Study," Lockheed Missiles and Space Co., Sunnyvale, Calif.: Lockheed, Inc., 1965, pp. 2–3; "Survey of EDP Activities in State and Local Government, 1970," Intergovernmental Board on Electronic Data Processing, State of California, 1970 (mimeo). For a more comprehensive summary of computer activities in city government, see Clark D. Rogers and Claude D. Peters, "Directory of the Status of State and Local Systems," *AIP Survey of Automated Information Systems for Urban Planning: Part I,* Pittsburgh, Pa.: American Institute of Planners, 1967.

4. The typology presented draws heavily from that given by Michael Rose, *Computers, Managers, and Society,* Baltimore, Penguin, 1969, pp. 71–100. See also Alan F. Westin (ed.), *Information Technology in a Democracy,* Cambridge, Mass.: Harvard University Press, 1971. pp. 15–34, for a more detailed typology.

5. M. V. Higginson, *Managing with EDP,* New York: American Management Association, 1965, p. 38, cited in McLaughlin, *op. cit.,* p. 29.

6. McLaughlin, *op. cit.,* p. 31.

7. See "Use of Electronic Data Processing in the Federal Government," House of Representatives No. 858, Committee on Post Office and Civil Service, 88th Congress, 1st Session, 1963; R. E. Montijo, Jr., "California D.M.V. Goes on Police EDP System," *Datamation,* **13** (July 1967), pp. 52–53.

8. New York City Police Department, "SPRINT: Capability Design Specification," Police Department City of New York: 1970, s-02-sys-spec.

9. See Takuji Tamaru, "Prospects in Municipal Information Systems: The Example of Los Angeles," *Computers and Automation,* January 1968, pp. 15–18; Harold Black and Edward Shaw, "Detroit's Data Banks," *Datamation,* **13** (March 1967), pp. 25–27; *Manual for the Users of the District of Columbia Real Property Data Bank,* Executive Office, Government of the District of Columbia, November 1967; J. M. Kibbee and V. V. Almendinger, "The Bay Area Transportation Study Commission Information System: Data Description and Documentation," Santa Monica, Calif., Systems Development Corporation, December 1965; *Annual Report, 1967,* Tri-State Transportation Commission, New York City, October 1967; "Establishment of the OEO Planning-Programming-Budgeting System (PPBS)," U.S. Office of Economic Opportunity, Washington, D.C., 1966.

10. Edward Hearle and R. J. Mason, *A Data Processing System for State and Local Governments,* Englewood Cliffs, N.J.: Prentice-Hall, 1962.

11. Rose, *op. cit.,* Chapter 4.

12. For a discussion of the distinction between "intelligence" and "statistical" reporting systems in the context of the congressional debate over the National Data Center, see Edgar Dunn, "The Idea of a National Data Center and the Issue of Privacy," *The American Statistician*, 21 (February 1967), pp. 21–27.

13. For an example of the use of administrative-intelligence systems to produce dossiers on welfare clients, and the resulting protest from welfare workers, see the section Jurisdictions, Antonomy, and Professionalism in Chapter 7.

14. See Chapter 7 for an account of the Western County social services information system. The Santa Clara County, California, LOGIC system operates similarly.

15. See our account in Chapter 9 of a criminal identification in an eastern state.

16. See *The LOGIC Information System—Local Government Information Control*, Data Processing Center, General Services Agency, County of Santa Clara, California, August 1969; H. Blatt, "Organizing for Information in Nassau County," *Public Management*, October 1967, pp. 292–299; J. K. Parker, "Operating a City Databank," *Public Automation*, June 1965. For Los Angeles Information System-People File, see Tamaru, *op. cit.* For the Labor Department's Job Banks, see "More Job Banks," *Public Automation*, December 1969. See also "SCOPE Completes First Year of Fighting Crime in Nevada," *Computerworld*, December 11, 1968; "A National Crime Information Center," *FBI Law Enforcement Bulletin*, May 1966; *The National Driver Register Service*, Driver Licence Computer Organization, Washington, D.C. (no date); *An Automated Information System for the State of California Department of Motor Vehicles*, Transportation Agency, Department of Motor Vehicles, January 1966. See also "Traffic Safety—A National Data Center," *Systems Development Corporation Magazine*, 11 (May 1968).

17. See, for example, *Urban and Regional Information Systems: Support for Planning in Metropolitan Areas*, U.S. Department of Housing and Urban Development, Washington, D.C., 1968.

18. The Department of Housing and Urban Development began in 1969 to establish urban information systems in selected cities. See "Proposals for Municipal Information System Asked," *Datamation*, November 1969.

19. See Alan F. Westin, "Legal Safeguards to Insure Privacy in a Computer Society," *Communications of the Association for Computing Machinery*, 10 (September 1967), pp. 533–537; W. H. Ferry, "Must We Rewrite the Constitution to Control Technology?" *Saturday Review*, 51 (March 2, 1968), pp. 50–54; M. Gyarfas, "Social Science, Technology, and Social Work: A Case Worker's View," *Social Service Review*, 43, No. 3 (September 1969).

TWO

Computers: Hardware, Software, and Terminology

Although in simplest terms computers can be seen as devices for storing information and devices or routines that perform operations on the stored information, modern computers are in reality a complex organization of several distinct machines, devices, and sets of logical instructions.

COMPUTER HARDWARE

"Computer hardware" refers to the actual machines, the physical components of the computer. Hardware devices can be either mechanical or electronic. Four basic computer functions are performed by hardware; these are discussed next.

Input Units

Information must be stored before a computer can work with it, and several devices are commonly used to input information into the computer, and/or to store information the computer may need to perform its functions. Information can be stored and input to the computer by using mechanical devices such as punched cards or paper tapes. The more common storage unit is a magnetic tape or disk. A magnetic tape is typically used to store information when the computer will not require immediate access to the data. Such tapes are stored in tape libraries; when needed by the computer, they are placed onto tape drives that read the information into the main computer. Social surveys done by social scientists are typically stored on tape.

Disk storage is used when immediate access to information is required—in making airline reservations, for example, clerks need immediate access to the reservations file. Using disks, the information can be stored on-line for immediate access. Most of the systems examined in this book use disk storage as well as tape storage.

Computer Main Frames

The machine that actually processes the information given to it by input units is often referred to as the main frame. Information read into the main frame computer from input devices is stored in the computer's internal memory, which is typically composed of magnetic cores. A series of logical operations, given to the machine by programmers, is performed on the stored information.

Communications Units

It is increasingly common for computers to operate at great distances from computer users. A policeman in New York can now inquire of computers in Washington, D.C., California, and Michigan, whether a man he has arrested is wanted in the other areas. The development of telephone circuits that can connect computers, microwave data relay devices, and other communications media have made communication units a major element of most modern installations.

Display Units

The results of the computer's operations on the information it has stored are displayed on any of a number of units depending on the purpose of the installation. Typewriters, teleprinters, cathode ray display panels, and graph plotters are among the display units typically employed. In several cases examined by us, computers print out pictures on facsimile devices to represent criminal histories of known offenders.

There are five major producers of computer main frame units in the United States: International Business Machines, Control Data Corporation, Burroughs Corporation, Univac, and National Cash Register. There are several hundred producers of input, communications, and display devices—the so-called peripheral equipment. Compatibility of peripheral equipment with computer main frames was a problem in the early development of computers, but this has largely been solved through the establishment of common standards and through market pressures.

COMPUTER SOFTWARE: PROGRAMS

Computer programs are sets of coded instructions that direct the computer to perform a logical or mathematical operation on a piece of stored information. Computer software refers to the complex of programs used by a computer installation to input/store, process, communicate, and display information. That is, most computer installations employ a variety of programs to accomplish their varied tasks. First let us consider the more general functions of programs.

The basic function of a computer program is to instruct the machine to perform some mathematical operation on a quantity stored in location x and to transfer the resulting information to another point, location y, in the computer memory. Thus a program is composed of orders or commands involving a location and an operation, and it becomes necessary to determine how mathematical quantities and operations can be economically stored in electronic devices.

Very early in the development of electronic computers, principally through the work of von Neumann, it was decided that numbers and operations could most economically be expressed on electronic devices in binary digit form. Vacuum tubes, transistors, and other electronic switches are in one of two physical states: on or off, positive or negative, and so forth. Since in the late 1940s vacuum tubes could operate at speeds of 10^{-6} sec, it was recognized that a series of such tubes would be able to store and process binary digits very rapidly. Each operation (e.g., addition, multiplication) can be assigned a binary number, each location in the computer memory can be assigned a binary number, and each quantity stored can be translated from decimal to binary. Thus the first computer programs were composed of a series of statements, all in binary form, which the computer read and performed sequentially.

Although vacuum tubes can work faster with binary numbers than with decimal numbers, man cannot. The decimal number system requires ten digits to represent numbers, the binary system only two digits, 0 and 1. Thus 100 in the decimal system is represented as

$$100 = 1 \times 10^2 + 0 \times 10^1 + 0$$

In the binary system it is

$$100 = 1 \times 2^6 + 1 \times 2^5 + 0 \times 2^4 + 0 \times 2^3 + 1 \times 2^2 + 0 \times 2^1 + 0$$
$$= 1100100$$

The process of translating numbers in decimal into binary is cumbersome for people. The first programmers, we can conclude, led a dreary life.

The life and speed of programmers picked up considerably in the early 1950s with the appearance of automatic programming. Automatic programs let the machine do the translating from decimal to binary, from ordinary mathematical language to binary form commands. FORTRAN (*for*mula *tran*slation program) the earliest of these automatic programs, was designed primarily for use by scientists in translating their mathematical statements and logical commands automatically into machine-readable or binary form. Later a commercial automatic program was developed: COBOL could automatically convert the commands associated with typical business procedures such as inventory control, ordering, payroll, and budgets into machine-readable form. In recent years programs designed especially for social scientists (e.g., Statistical Package for the Social Sciences—SPSS) and other specialists have been developed.

There have been enormous advances in the development of hardware—both peripheral and main frame—which can be expressed in terms of speed of processing; but perhaps the most important developments have occurred in software. After all, the principal function of computers is to store, process, and display information, with appropriate speed and in a manner understandable to ultimate users. Regardless of how fast the computer itself could work, the comprehensibility requirement could not have been met without software development.

The development of FORTRAN, COBOL, SPSS, and other programs has meant that increasingly the natural language we all use and are accustomed to can be automatically read into a machine, and vice versa. Several persons who are informed about computer developments suggested during this study that the major advances of the future will lie in better software and a better fit between the specific needs of people for information and computer capacity. The articulation of demand and capacity is a major focus of our study.

GLOSSARY OF SOME COMPUTER TERMS

BATCH PROCESSING:　processing of a number of separate computer jobs in the same machine run; also an off-line job where information is processed in a batch, stored, and retrieved later

CORE:　the internal memory of a computer

DEBUG:　removal of mistakes from programs and program modifications

DISK:　a device for storing information by magnetic recording

FAX:　a facsimile transmission device used to communicate images or records between computer and ultimate user

INTERFACE:　the point of articulation between two systems (e.g., the interface between input and main frame computers)

MACHINE LANGUAGE:　information recorded in a form understandable to the main frame computer

MAGNETIC MEMORY CORE:　a device used to store information in the main frame computer; it is composed of a magnetic material that can assume two states of magnetism

MAGNETIC DRUM:　a storage device composed of a magnetized metal drum spinning in a supercooled liquid; the drum preceded the use of magnetic disk devices

MAGNETIC TAPE:　a tape similar to home recording tapes used to store information, generally off-line

ON-LINE:　a system that receives input data directly from point of origin, typically regarding a transaction (e.g., a judge passes a sentence, which is immediately recorded by an on-line system)

PERIPHERAL EQUIPMENT:　hardware devices that serve and are controlled by the main computer (e.g., input card readers, disk and tape drives, FAX machines, and other display units)

RANDOM ACCESS:　describing memory devices that can retrieve bits of information in nonsequential order, thus reducing the amount of time required for the computer to obtain the correct or desired information

REAL TIME:　describing a computer system that is on-line (receives data directly from an initial transaction) and outputs information directly back to its source, to influence that transaction (e.g., a policeman inquires of a remote computer if a suspect stopped in his car is wanted elsewhere). Usually a real-time computer can respond in seconds.

RESPONSE TIME: the time required for a computer system to respond to user requests

TIME-SHARING COMPUTERS: computer systems designed to service a number of users; the computer allocates sufficient time to each user and processes requests so fast that the user might perceive the computer to be dedicated solely to him, although several clients are being serviced.

CHAPTER

THREE

Bureaucratic Change and Technological Innovation: A Review

The literature of technological innovation, bureaucratic change, and their interrelationship is both vast and confused. This reflects the disparate backgrounds of researchers—ranging from sociologists, to industrial psychologists, to operations researchers—and the lack of common organizational theory as well as the absence of common schemata for classifying technology, technological change, and bureaucratic change. Compounding the pluralistic ignorance of researchers in this area is their tendency to select very different types of organizations (blue collar vs. white collar, public vs. private, large vs. small, etc.) as research sites. Different theories, assumptions, technologies, and research sites produce different and unrelated results.

Despite the incoherence of much of this literature, it is nevertheless germane to our work as a means of generating hypotheses for further examination, as well as providing the reader with some comparative perspective on our assumptions and findings.

TECHNOLOGY AND ORGANIZATIONAL STRUCTURE

The study of organizational structure has two intellectual roots. The one rises from the work of Max Weber, whose study of public bureaucracies in Germany led him to emphasize the social character of bureaucracies as structures of statuses organized hierarchically, with a rationally planned division of labor based on specialization and articulated through a set of rules:

> The following may thus be said to be the fundamental categories of rational legal authority:
>
> (1) a continuous organization of official functions bound by rules
>
> (2) A specified sphere of competence . . . marked off as part of a systematic division of labor.
> . . . Bureaucratic administration means fundamentally the exercise of control on the basis of knowledge.[1]

A second intellectual root of sociological thought about organizational structure is due to Karl Marx, whose study of industrial organization in England suggested to him the significance of the technological imperatives of modern organization which derive from modern technology and machines:

> In handicrafts and manufacture, the workman makes use of a tool, in the factory, the machine makes use of him. There the movements of the instrument of labour proceed from him, here it is the movements of the machine that he must follow. In manufacture the workmen are parts of a living mechanism. In the factory we have a lifeless mechanism independent of the workman, who becomes its mere living appendage.[2]

The Weberian emphasis on the universal social characteristics of bureaucracy long dominated sociological research. The result was that technological variations among bureaucracies and industrial organizations, and their behavioral and attitudinal consequences, were by and large ignored. However, in the last fifteen years a growing body of literature has reintroduced the importance of technology for organizational structure.

The best known work concerned with the impact of technology on industrial structure is that of Joan Woodward and the Tavistock School in England.[3] Woodward, analyzing approximately 100 industrial firms in South Essex, found systematic relationships between various kinds of "sociotechnical systems" and organizational structure. Conceiving of technical systems as small batch production (such as apparel), large batch production (automobiles), or process production (chemicals), Woodward discovered that in small batch and process production firms, supervisors had lower spans of control (number of workers supervised), work groups were smaller and more informal, communications tended to be more horizontal among equals, and more consultative, and there were fewer formal, vertical commands.

Using a distinction developed by Burns,[4] Woodward characterized the batch and process production industries' administrative styles as "organic" rather than "mechanistic." In batch and process forms, she observed "flexible organization with a high degree of delegation both of authority and responsibility for decision making, and with permissive and participative management, was characteristic. . . ."[5] In addition, Woodward found a relationship between organizational success (as measured by profits and firm growth), technology and structure:

> The five successful unit production firms had organizational characteristics in common, so had the five large batch and mass production firms, and the six process production firms. It was found that . . . the organizational characteristics of the successful firms in each production category tended to cluster around the medians for that category as a whole . . . Not only was the system of production an important variable in the determination of organizational structure, but also that one particular form of organization was most appropriate to each system of production.[6]

Although based on a small sample of firms in one country, the findings of Woodward suggest the plausibility of positing links between technology and organizational structure. Apparently these links are such that technology defines a range of constraints and opportunities within which the social structure of an organization must be built. Moreover, although technology is not determinative of organizational structure, some structures are more suitable than others to a given technology as measured by firm success. Thus it is implied that the greater the technological sophistication of a firm's basic production process, and the greater the skills required of its workers, the more appropriate is an "organic" style of management in which authority rests on competence and not formal office, supervision in the work group is more informal and participative, and work groups have greater autonomy from central supervision and rules.

Research on the attitudinal and behavioral consequences of various industrial production technologies is complicated because early research focused almost entirely on mass production firms as representative of the most "advanced" industrial techniques.[7] More recently scholars have begun to consider intra- and interindustry variations in technology as a source of attitudinal differences.[8] Best known of these works is Blauner's *Alienation and Freedom*.[9]

Beginning with the proposition that the "most important single factor that gives an industry a distinctive character is its technology," Blauner distinguishes four principal kinds of industrial technology: craft (such as printing), machine tending (textiles), assembly line (automobile), and continuous process (chemicals). These technologies, although not determinative of social organization in the factory, imply certain functional requisites for their effective use, which in turn imply certain kinds of organizational structure (e.g., hierarchy, division of labor, and specialization). The interaction of technology and organizational structure produces characteristic patterns of alienation.

Blauner's chief finding is that assembly line and machine tending technologies produce a "deskillization" in the labor force, loss of worker control, and heightened perceptions of meaninglessness, powerlessness, and work estrangement.[10] Craft and continuous process technologies, as well as highly automated mass production techniques, allow for greater worker control and higher skills, thus lower alienation.[11]

TECHNOLOGICAL INNOVATION AND BUREAUCRATIC CHANGE

Implicit in much of the research on technology and organizational structure is the idea that any significant change in the technology of an organization is necessarily accompanied by changes in organizational structure. However, few longitudinal studies have been performed on the consequences of technological change for worker attitudes or bureaucratic structure. No published studies have examined the consequences of various ways of implementing a single technological innovation in comparable settings. Instead the results of implementing a single technological innovation in a single setting are typically examined.

Longitudinal case studies by Faunce (1968), Walker (1957), Woodward (1965), and Seashore and Bowers (1970) support the notion that the introduction of more sophisticated technological devices in blue collar jobs results in more autonomous and smaller work groups, greater required skills, and less personal supervision.[12] Worker attitudes were initially hostile to technological change: Walker found that nonautomated jobs in the mill he studied were respected at first but after three years became resented as mentally easier but physically more taxing.[13] Because these studies were conducted in a single location, the methods used to implement the technological change were not considered to be a variable. Thus whatever structural and attitudinal consequences were produced cannot with certainty be ascribed to the technology itself.

The structural and attitudinal consequences of technological innovation in white-collar jobs primarily involve the impact of electronic data processing equipment (what we have referred to as "electronic clerk" applications). The evidence here is even less systematic than for blue collar organizations. Faunce suggests that computers lead to increases in the number of semiskilled office workers who replace skilled office workers.[14] Mueller also found that office automation brought about a greater centralization of decision making as well as a decline in the number of skilled and supervisory jobs.[15]

The attitudinal consequences of white collar automation are decidedly less optimistic than for blue collar automation. In part this discrepancy may reflect the initial pessimistic reception of computers as popularized in the public media.[16] Mann and William's five-year study of office automation indicated that job security was at first a principal cause of concern to white collar workers, but it was lessened through management retraining programs and later declined even further as workers became familiar with the machinery.[17] Satisfaction with enlarged jobs, level of responsibility, and new skills increased, although job satisfaction as a whole did not change.[18] Somewhat contrary to the conclusions of Mann and Williams is the research of Ida Hoos (1961), who found that computers ultimately reduce the required skills, autonomy, and job content so severely that workers' satisfaction in the long run decreases after the initial retraining period.[19]

More recent research by Meyer on a large number of accounting agencies suggests that office automation leads to more levels of hierarchy, increases in the span of control of first-line supervisors, and decreases in control spans for higher executives.[20] Increased hierarchy is related to the need for greater horizontal communication among technical and administrative experts. In support of Meyer's findings, Blau et al. discovered that computerization of accounting offices leads to more professionalization and fewer low skill jobs than in nonautomated offices.[21]

SUMMARY: TECHNOLOGY AND ORGANIZATIONAL STRUCTURE

A number of general findings that emerge from the literature should clarify how our study relates to and yet diverges from previous work.

Organizations differ in terms of such social criteria as goals, environment, and history, which have both structural and attitudinal consequences; but the technology utilized by an organization is a significant and independent determinant of both structure and related attitudes.[22] Recent research rejects the early "technological determinant" views of Ogburn.[23] Yet Blauner and Woodward clearly imply that technologies per se possess certain functional requisites for successful utilization which must be served by a given social structure and supported by appropriate attitudes. Organizations, for various ad hoc reasons, may ignore these technological imperatives, but they do so at the risk of being unsuccessful. In this sense it is possible to talk of "sociotechnical" systems.

Both the static and longitudinal studies of technological change suggest that automation enhances worker responsibility and discretion and provides autonomy from close supervision. This tendency seems to be less certain in white collar automation studies, but much would depend on the nature of preautomation jobs and the scope of technological innovation.

Although automation is initially unsettling to workers and is perceived by them as threatening, in time it produces favorable attitudes. This finding follows quite logically from the above-mentioned changes in work due to automation, but it is also true that worker attitudes toward automation depend to a large extent on the manner in which management introduces and implements the new technology.[24] In advanced technology organizations, where change is commonplace, workers seem to be more accustomed and amenable to technological change.[25]

METHODOLOGICAL AND SUBSTANTIVE ASSUMPTIONS: A CRITIQUE

Without exception, the previous literature on the interaction of technology and social organization emphasizes the "impact" of technology on organizations. Ignored in these works are the initial conditions, the social and political options, and the choices that affect the social organization of the technology. As Meyer points out, the human relations research on attitudes toward automation assumes that the impact of technology on the worker, the work process, and the authority structure within the organization is unmediated by the formal organizational structure itself.[26] But the blade cuts both ways. Meyer and Blau et al., the most recent large survey studies in the "structuralist" school, simply do not consider either the history of the organizations they study or the values and interests impinging on the decisions pertaining to the innovations they examine.[27]

The methods utilized by both the "human relations" school (most often single case studies) and the "structuralist" school (most recently surveys of hundreds of organizations) are not suited to capturing important features of technological change. For instance, large surveys are incapable of gathering in-depth information from leaders and participants in technological change; nor can they take into account the history of the organization or its peculiar environmental constraints. Single case studies, which can and do often pay attention to these factors, lack any comparative perspective from which judgments can be made about the impact of these social features of an organization on the use of the new technology.

The choice of research site also imparts a bias to the findings of single case studies. Most of the technological innovation studies involve private industrial enterprises, not public bureaucracies. We discuss the unique features of public bureaucracies later, noting here that private industries operate under the pressure of profits. Technological innovations they adopt are likely to be reasonably well tested and often are copied from other successful prototype users. This is especially true in the case of electronic data processing, where one or two national firms provide the technical and organizational advice needed by users of the new technology. This means that applications of new technology in a hundred or a thousand firms or agencies are not statistically independent. Whatever impact they have on organizational structure is just as likely to be an artificial result of accepting a national computer firm's advice as a result of the technology per se.'

The methodological constraints of previous research have theoretical implications also. When methods attenuate or eliminate the operation of interesting social variables that influence the social organization of a new technology, one is much more likely to ascribe whatever structural or attitudinal changes occur to the technology itself.

THE PRESENT STUDY: ASSUMPTIONS AND METHODS

The general assumption of the present study is that technological innovation is a social and in some respects a political process that occurs in organizations. Of course organizations have unique histories and are subject to the constraints imposed by specific environmental pressures; they also pursue collective and individual goals. These three factors can combine to produce the need and desire for organizational change in specific directions. New technologies can facilitate organizational change. In the presence of new technologies, history, environmental pressures, and goals combine to produce various strategies for bringing about change. When implemented, these strategies result in a determinate social organization of the new technology. This determinate social organization of the technology generates specific kinds of structural and attitudinal consequences. Figure 1 represents schematically the basic causal reasoning used in our work.

Figure 1. Causal diagram of technological change in organizations.

Our schematization implies that technologies do not "impact" on organizations like two ships colliding at sea. Instead, technological innovations are filtered through an organization's traditions, constraints, and resources. Moreover, organizations are populated by men who make decisions about innovations within the context of their own organizations. The burden of our work is to show how various actors in public bureaucracies interpreted their histories, the pressures operating on them, and their goals, to create what others call "sociotechnical" systems.

Research Location

In locating our study within public bureaucracies—state and local governments in the United States—we set definite conditions on our research. Not governed by the profit motive or by pressure, public bureaucracies have greater flexibility in designing and financing technological innovations of very large scope. Subject to political scrutiny, public bureaucracies are more likely than private firms to publicize their innovations, both as a means of seeking public monies and to encourage citizens in the belief that government is meeting contemporary challenges with modern technology. As we see later, high technology confers status on its users. As employers of Civil Service personnel, however, public bureaucracies are more vulnerable than other organizations to criticism and resistance from within.

The public and political character of the bureaucracies we study make their innovations more open to scholarly observation, but it also tends to make their innovations more controversial than in private firms. The very advanced character of the innovations we investigate enhances the probability of failure. Since things seldom work as they are supposed to, innovation (and the expenditure of public money) can become controversial.

The Technology

Previous studies of white collar automation have focused entirely on automation of office and clerical tasks. This kind of innovation was associated with the use of first generation computers in the late 1950s and early 1960s.

This is the first systematic study of large-scale civilian use of third generation computers in integrated information systems. As pointed out in Chapter 1, these machines have the capacity to link together the communication and information storage facilities of hundreds of heretofore relatively isolated offices, bureaus, and agencies. As we see later on, the potential consequences for the kinds of relationships that bind these agencies together are highly significant. The importance of third generation computers studied here lies not in their impact on office and clerical workers, but rather in their *potential* to more closely integrate and centralize decision making in public bureaucracies. We emphasize "potential" because whether computers have this effect depends on various social and political circumstances.

The historical entrance point of this new technology of integrated information systems is typically a unit of local government (state, county, or city), not a single agency or office. Because of their expense, and because of their information capacity, efficient use of the machines requires that entire governmental units purchase and utilize them. Our analytical unit of reference is this unit of government—in some cases a state; in others, a county. Often we are interested only in a subunit of the larger entity—a state criminal justice bureaucracy, for example, or a county social service bureaucracy that may include many separate agencies and bureaus. In any event, when we refer to "a public bureaucracy" we do not mean a single agency or department but the complex of agencies that administers public policy.

Methods

We utilize a clinical comparative method to study the relationship of technology and bureaucratic change. Thus we can examine closely the impact of organizational history, external pressures, and goals on the development of strategies of change. A comparison of these strategies of change will allow us to say something systematic about how technology is shaped by social forces, and with what effect. Together these methods are appropriate to the exploratory study of a new technology. We hope that they will help us to avoid the pitfalls of previous work, to produce descriptive hypotheses for further research, and to create a "sense of understanding" about an important social phenomenon.[28]

SUMMARY

Our current knowledge concerning the relationships between technology and organizational structure is meager. Very plausible arguments and some research support the notion that various kinds of industrial technologies are loosely correlated with certain organizational structures and attitudinal behaviors. This line of thought has given rise to the idea of a "sociotechnical system." The pattern of causation implied by this concept and its use is one in which inherent technological requisites impose specific structural and attitudinal consequences. Moreover, change in the technical subsystem of an organization is seen as "impacting" on the organizational subsystem. Thus the principal research question in the reviewed literature is, "What is the impact of technological change on society? Attempting to determine the "impact" of technologly on organizations and society, we have suggested, represents an ill-defined research problem.

The assessment of the social consequences of a technology must be viewed within the context of a particular social and economic structure. Quite clearly, the social effects of a given technology will vary as the circumstances of its control, design, and purpose vary. By and large, previous research has ignored this aspect of the reciprocal relations between society and technology.[29]

In the next chapter we discuss how the general social and political context of the 1960s shaped and broadly defined the use of integrated information systems in public bureaucracies.

NOTES

1.   Max Weber, *The Theory of Social and Economic Organization* (Talcott Parsons trans., New York: Free Press, 1966) pp. 330–339.

2.   Karl Marx, *Capital,* New York: Modern Library ed., 1966, pp. 461–462.

3.   Joan Woodward, *Industrial Organization: Theory and Pratcice,* Oxford: Oxford University Press, 1965.

4. Tom Burns and G. M. Stalker, *The Management of Innovation,* London: Tavistock, 1961, pp. 119–125.

5. Woodward, *op. cit.,* p. 64.

6. Woodward, *op. cit.,* pp. 69–71.

7. See, for instance, Gladys L. Palmer, "Attitudes Toward Work in an Industrial Community," *American Journal of Sociology,* **70** (1957), pp. 17–26.

8. See Charles R. Walker, *Modern Technology and Civilization,* New York: McGraw-Hill, 1962; also Clark Kerr and Abraham Siegel, 'The Interindustry Propensity to Strike—An International Comparison," in Robert Dubin and Arthur Ross (eds.), *Industrial Conflict,* New York: McGraw Hill, 1954, pp. 189–212; Charles R. Walker, *Steeltown,* New York: Harper & Row, 1950; Charles R. Walker and Robert Guest, *Man on the Assembly Line,* Cambridge, Mass.: Harvard University Press, 1952. These works, even though based on the study of single industries, nevertheless emphasize intraplant differences in job tasks as well as the interindustry variations in job tasks (Kerr and Siegel).

9. Robert Blauner, *Alienation and Freedom,* Chicago: University of Chicago Press, 1964.

10. *Ibid.,* p. 168.

11. See also for confirming evidence of Blauner's findings: F. C. Mann and L. R. Hoffmann, *Automation and the Worker,* New York: Holt, 1960); C. R. Walker, *Toward the Automatic Factory,* New Haven, Conn.: Yale University Press, 1957; A. N. Turner and P. R. Lawrence, *Industrial Jobs and the Worker,* Cambridge, Mass.: Harvard University Press, 1965.

12. W A. Faunce, "Automation in the Automobile Industry," *American Sociological Review,* **23** (1958), pp. 401–407; Walker, 1957, *op. cit.;* Woodward, *op. cit.;* and S. E. Seashore and D. G. Bowers, "Durability of Organizational Change," *American Psychologist,* **25** (1970), pp. 227–233.

13. Walker, 1957, *op. cit.,* pp. 73–100.

14. Faunce, *op. cit.*

15. E. Mueller, *Automation in an Expanding Economy,* Ann Arbor, Mich.: Institute for Social Research, 1969.

16. See, for example, Gilbert Burck, "Management Will Never Be the Same Again," and "Will the Computer Outwit Man?" in *Fortune Magazine,* August, September, and October 1964. Burck argues that computers will lead to the demise of middle management. A more realistic rejoinder to Burck followed. See Tom Alexander, "Computers Can't Solve Everything," *Fortune Magazine,* October 1969.

17. See Floyd L. Mann and Lawrence K. Williams, "Observations on the Dynamics of Change to Electronic Data Processing Equipment," *Administrative Science Quarterly,* **5** (1960), pp. 217–256.

18. See also Thomas L. Whisler and George P. Schultz, "Automation and the Management Process," *Annals,* **340** (March 1962), pp. 81–89. And Jack Seigman and Bernard Karsh, "Some Organizational Correlates of White-Collar Automation," *Sociological Inquiry,* **32** (1962), pp. 108–116.

19. Ida R. Hoos, *Automation in the Office,* Washington, D.C.: Public Affairs Press, p. 196. For another analysis of the impact of technological change on job requirements, see James R. Bright, "Does Automation Raise Skill Requirements?" *Harvard Business Review,* **36,** No. 4 (July–August, 1958), pp. 85–89.

20. Marshall W. Meyer, "Automation and Bureaucratic Structure," *American Journal of Sociology*, **74**, No. 3 (1968), pp. 256–264.

21. Peter M. Blau, W. V. Hydebran, and R. E. Stauffer, "The Structure of Small Bureaucracies," *American Sociological Review*, **31** (1966), pp. 179–191.

22. For works emphasizing these determinants of organizational structure, see Amitai Etzioni, *Complex Organizations*, New York: Holt, Rinehart, & Winston, 1961; P. R. Lawrence and J. W. Lorsch, *Organization and Environment*, Cambridge, Mass.: Harvard University Press, 1967; and Alfred D. Chandler, Jr., *Strategy and Structures*, Cambridge, Mass.: M.I.T. Press, 1962.

23. W. F. Ogburn, in F. R. Allen, H. Hart, D. C. Miller, and W. F. Ogburn (eds.), *Technology and Social Change*, New York: Appleton-Century-Crofts, 1957.

24. Mann and Hoffman, 1960, *op. cit.*; Bright, *op. cit.*, 1958.

25. James C. Taylor, *Technology and Planned Organizational Change* Ann Arbor, Mich.: Institute for Social Research, 1971.

26. Meyer, *op. cit.*, p. 257.

27. Meyer, *op. cit.*; and Blau et al., *op. cit.*

28. Paul Reynolds, *A Primer in Theory Construction*, Indianapolis, Ind.: Bobbs-Merrill, 1971, p. 7.

29. A truly comparative (e.g., cross-national) study of organizational structure and attitudes has not been written. How broad cultural and societal differences affect the utilization and organization of given technologies is not known. For a classic comparative study of organizational ideologies see Reinhard Bendix, *Work and Authority in Industry*, New York: Harper & Row, 1963; the many European experiments in various kinds of worker participation and decision making are relevant here, but they too have yet to be analyzed by American sociologists. For an excellent review of that literature, see Paul Blumberg, *Industrial Democracy—The Sociology of Participation*, New York: Schocken, 1969.

CHAPTER

FOUR

The Context of Bureaucratic Reform in the 1960s

It is essential that we place the reform projects described by the case studies in the appropriate historical and political contexts. For, as we argue throughout, the use of computerized information systems by public bureaucracies is an extension of ongoing political trends and programs with deep roots in American political tradition.

Historians and political scientists have shown that American politics since the Civil War can be characterized in part as a struggle between two competing political ethos, each with a distinctive social base, each expressing the practical economic and political situations of two groups: the native-born American urban middle class and the newly arrived European immigrants.[1] Richard Hofstadter, in his classic analysis of American politics of the late nineteenth and early twentieth centuries, describes these different systems of political thought thus:

> One, founded upon the indigenous Yankee–Protestant political traditions, and upon middle class life, assumed and demanded the constant disinterested activity of the citizen in public life, argued that political life ought to be run . . . in accordance with general principles and abstract laws apart from and superior to the personal needs, and expressed a common feeling that government should be in good part an effort to moralize the lives of individuals while economic life should be intimately related to the stimulation and development of

individual character. The other system, founded upon the
European backgrounds of the immigrants, upon their unfamil-
iarity with independent political action, their familiarity with
hierarchy and authority, and upon the urgent needs that so
often grew out of their migration, took for granted that the
political life of the individual would arise out of family needs,
interpreted political and civic relations chiefly in terms of
personal obligations, and placed strong personal loyalties
above allegiance to abstract codes of laws or morals.[2]

It is not difficult to understand that the rush of immigrants of different
religions, class backgrounds, and nationalities (at a rate exceeding one million per year toward the end of the nineteenth century), their growth to
more than one-seventh of the population, and their new majority status in
all but a few of the large eastern and midwestern cities, caused unease
among native Americans—city men of property especially. But particularly
galling to the native Yankee–Protestants of this period was the political
strength acquired by the new groups as they organized tightly knit political
machines.

Not two generations before, the same Yankee–Protestants (then small
farmers and cross-road merchants) had wrested political control from the
Federalist aristocrats by extending universal suffrage, establishing home
rule in the cities, and reducing the appointive powers of governors and
mayors. In New York State, for instance, after successive Constitutional
Conventions of 1821, 1826, and 1846, the governor's Council of Appointment was stripped of its 15,000 discretionary positions, and subsequently
most of these offices from district judge to fire chief became elective.[3]

Under the guise of Jeffersonian and Jacksonian agrarian populism, which
regarded the citizenry as autarchic yeoman, state politics changed from a
caucus of landed notables to congeries of small local groups formed on the
basis of local organizing of votes and under the direction of local leaders,
generally the sheriff or the mayor.[4] With the demise of the Federalists, state
and local government, both civilian and military, changed from a playground for the wealthy and educated, and holding public office became
somewhat akin to having a legitimate occupation that was not yet something to which one aspired in the Yankee-Protestant tradition, but rather
a task to which one was called by a sense of civic duty and the desire for
the admiration of one's neighbors.[5]

Under the banner of such Populist slogans of the 1820s as "Keep the
Power with the People," coined by a rebellious young aristocrat of New
York, Peter R. Livingston, suffrage was extended to the smaller holders,

landless farm workers, mill town laborers, and fishermen living in what were still quite homogeneous, small communities.[6] Public office became the domain of popularly elected citizens, informed by the view that any citizen "was qualified to decide any matter of public importance."[7] It appeared that special qualifications for office, voting by a limited electorate, and other paraphernalia used by the wealthy to dominate the early republic had been eliminated from American politics by the 1840s.

However, the waves of immigration beginning in the 1850s with the Irish to the high tide of 1907 posed a dilemma to the Yankee–Protestant middle class. On the one hand they were committed to the principles of universal suffrage and government literally by the people. At the same time, as Boss Tweed illustrated perhaps too well, the mechanisms of universal suffrage could be used to elect the wrong people for the wrong reasons.[8]

The functions of the urban political machines of the post-Civil War period have been well described by others, both for the society at large and for special groups.[9] Briefly, the machine was a utilitarian organization that delivered services—mainly material, but also personal—to clients, in return for money or votes that maintained the machine.[10] The services of the machine were of particular use to two groups in the society: big business and immigrants. In return for promises of his vote and loyalty, the newly arrived immigrant received quick naturalization, a job, housing, access to authority, and protection from the police and courts. In short, all the things a newcomer needs to begin life in a foreign country. Business, especially those requiring long-term capital expenditures, such as railroads, utilities, and real estate, received in return for their monetary contributions franchises, building permits, and rights-of-way. The political machine provided support and security for the industrial expansion that characterized the latter half of the nineteenth century.

The growth of the political machines under the umbrella of universal suffrage became a favored target of those politically dispossessed by the machine: not the expanding industrialists and financiers, to be sure, but largely the city dwellers whose wealth over time had become honorable through disassociation from its origins, and a much larger group of lawyers, merchants, engineers, and other descendants of the Yankee–Protestants. Labeled derisively at first as "Mugwumps," literally those who stuck their noses in other people's business, these groups formed the basis of the Progressive movement, which bears directly on our subject.[11]

To the Progressives of the late nineteenth century, universal suffrage and elective public office may have helped make government more responsive to the people in an earlier time; but under the circumstances of mass immigration, they did not make directly for financial purity, efficiency, public morality, or administrative ability. Harking back to Federalist philosophies, the Progressives believed that governance ought to be a moral science conducted in accord with universal principles and directed toward the achievement of "the public interest," which preempted any consideration of personal gain or competing private interests.

But the Progressives developed different, non-Federalist political heroes and proposed different solutions to the problems of a democracy. Renouncing the proposition that any citizen was qualified to make any decision of public importance, the Progressives just as clearly rejected landed wealth as a criterion of an enlightened government. Instead, education and technical expertise, and the lawyers, engineers, and accountants who possessed them, became, respectively, the Progressives' cultural ideals and political heroes.[12]

Although extension of suffrage to illiterate, propertyless immigrants threatened the maintenance of the democracy, it was obvious that the antidote was not the limitation of suffrage. Many Progressives supported campaigns to limit immigration, but in general, they turned to mass education, citizens' research committees, muckraking, and other forms of public education to increase the people's capacity to judge politicians and to expose corruption.[13]

Armed with these proposals, countless Progressive organizations sprung up in the larger eastern and midwestern cities: New York's Vigilance League, Detroit's Citizens' League, the League of Women Voters, Chicago's Civic Federation, and the Boston Municipal Research Bureau. Despite the large number of loosely connected organizations, they had in common a number of specific goals and programs expressed by their largest and most powerful national organization, the National Municipal League, formed in 1894.

Broadly defined, the goals of the Progressives were to eliminate corruption and inefficiency in government, and to make government more democratic by abolishing political machines, thus taking away the ability of professional politicians to organize votes. These goals were translated into a number of specific programs. Means of curbing the power of the professional politicians included the adoption of petitions, initiatives, and referenda, and the use of the recall. Short ballots, research bureaus, and citizens' associations, it was hoped, would lead the citizen to perform his civic functions more judiciously. Nonpartisan, at-large elections in cities and counties were designed both to separate local issues from state and federal politics, and to reduce the influence of ethnic groups concentrated in certain neighborhoods.[14]

Finally, the adoption of the council–manager form of city government, the county administrative officer plan, and the return of appointive and budgetary powers to state governors were urged by the Progressives to centralize authority and responsibility along the lines of the "big business" model.

Without ever winning a national election, and with only a handful of local elections to their credit, the Progressives nevertheless succeeded in having the major elements of their program adopted by local and state governments, thereby altering the structure of government.

Like most movements in American history, progressivism presents a mixed picture of success through failure. Like the Populists of the 1890s, the Progressives could not make the transition from movement to party, when in 1916 Theodore Roosevelt failed to defeat Wilson under the banner of an independent party. Sharing with the agrarian populists a distrust of big business and monopolies, the Progressives were instrumental in the enactment of some of the first legislation regulating private enterprise—the Interstate Commerce Act (1887), the Sherman Anti-Trust Act (1890), the Pure Food and Drug Act (1906), and another consumer bill, the Meat Inspection Act (1907).[15] Perhaps more important, at least symbolically, was the prosecution of the Northern Securities Company in 1902 by that Progressive hero, Republican Theodore Roosevelt. Along with his intervention in the railroad mergers of Morgan in 1904, this action was designed to establish "the principle that government was supreme over the great corporations."[16]

But as an independent party, the Progressives failed in 1916. As with other third parties in America, the stronger they became, the more the two major parties adopted their political platforms and rhetoric. It was primarily in the local governments—states and cities—that the Progressives had their most important impact.

Aside from the fear of business trusts and organized labor on the national scene, it was in the cities that the Progressives faced their popular enemy: the political machine. In turn, the large cities of the eastern United States and in the Midwest were the most hostile toward progressivism. To the new immigrants the Progressive reformers were a mysterious lot. Nothing could be more irrelevant to the newcomers than concern for the rule of abstract laws, universally applied, for the sake of lofty moral ends—public decency, individual integrity, and so on. Nothing was so strange as the vigorous campaigns for temperance in drink.

Although organized in hostile surroundings, and rarely attaining the complete adoption of their platform, the Progressives have been remarkably successful in at least two respects: nonpartisanship and the council–manager plan of city government. According to one authority, 61% of American cities having more than 5000 population are nonpartisan.[17] Regional adoption of the plan is also illustrative (see Table 1).[18]

Table 1 Regions Ranked by Proportion of Non-partisan Cities, 1960

Regions	Number of cities over 25,000	Percentage nonpartisan
Plains	49	98.0
West	68	95.6
Mountain	12	83.3
South	96	75.0
Border	34	73.5
New England	71	62.0
Great Lakes	101	54.5
Middle Atlantic	97	23.7

The council–manager form of city government has also received wide-spread acceptance and in general is adopted along with nonpartisanship (Table 2).[19]

Table 2 Council–Manager Cities Distributed by Population Groups, 1961

Population group	Total number cities in group	Cities with council—manager plan	
		Number	Percent
5,000–10,000	1292	360	27.9
10,000–25,000	1033	393	38.2
25,000–50,000	406	207	51.0
50,000–100,000	192	95	49.5
100,000–250,000	80	39	48.8
Over 500,000	21	4	19.0

Tables 1 and 2 illustrate one feature of the Progressive movement; namely, that their reforms have been most heavily adopted in the newer cities of the West, Midwest, and Mountain states, and in the middle-sized cities. In the older cities of the East and Midwest, where machine politi-cians were firmly entrenched, their plans have been less frequently accepted. Indeed as others have recorded, where such plans have been accepted, the machines have been able to use them for their own ends.[20]

The Progressive movement began to have an impact on state and county governments somewhat later than in the cities but for all intents and purposes was really coterminous with developments in the city. In his senatorial campaign of 1908, Robert La Follette, although a Populist by inspiration, adopted many of the Progressive reforms—the open primary, recall, and referendum.[21] In New York State Alfred E. Smith established in 1918 a long tradition of progressive, reform-minded governors who inherited his Democratic organization—men such as Franklin D. Roosevelt and Herbert H. Lehman.[22]

Following the lead of Smith, Roosevelt and Lehman recentralized administrative authority and political power that previously had been abdicated to the cities in the populist reforms of the early nineteenth century. Reforms begun in New York included central control of the state budget by the governor, establishing state commissions to review city government, and initiation of state departments of welfare, education, and highways controlled by the governor; other states, such as Michigan, Pennsylvania, and California, followed suit in this period of progressivism.[23]

State reforms also had an impact on the counties. Perhaps the most prevalent Progressive reform in county government, besides at-large elections and referenda, is the county administrative Officer (CAO) plan. First appearing in the programs of the National Managers in 1911, the CAO plan is a direct relative of the city manager plan in which a strong central executive assumes responsibility for all administrative matters in the county and informally plays a large policy-making role.[24] The CAO plan has made notable progress in "suburban" counties. In California, between 1950 and 1960, the number of counties having a CAO grew from seven to twenty-three, or about one-half of the counties in the state.[25]

ARTICLES OF FAITH: RATIONAL GOVERNMENT AND THE STRONG EXECUTIVE

Two themes unite the myriad Progressive reform groups and pervade their plans for electoral and governmental reform: first, that the practice of government should be characterized by the rational administration of public resources; and second, that this can be accomplished only through a centralized, strong, and professional executive.

The goal of the reformers was ultimately a more perfect union of democracy and efficiency in which the public interest would be served and decided on by expert technicians and protected by elected officials. City, county, and even state government did not entail the delicate balancing of interests but revolved instead about the pursuit for the most rational and efficient means to attain an end. As explained by one early Progressive:

> My fundamental contention is that the city is a corporation; that as a city it has nothing whatever to do with general political interests. . . . The questions in a city are not political questions. They have reference to the laying out of streets. . . . The work of a city being the creation and control of the city property, it should logically be managed as a piece of property by those who have created it. . . .[26]

The divisions facing local government were to be solved by engineers, lawyers, and professional administrators who alone possessed the requisite skills. Even the sometimes populistic rhetoric of the Progressives (e.g., the education campaigns and public research bureaus designed to expose corruption) were inspired by the belief that once the public became aware of the rationally selected "public interest" solution, it would support the technicians' decisions.

Rational government was in turn possible only by placing administrative authority in the hands of a single executive. In large part the Progressive movement's emphasis on a strong executive is a reaction to the Populist reforms of the nineteenth century, and their consequences. That is, during the earlier period governors, county supervisors, and city mayors had been stripped of powers of appointment, and control, over government agencies. The Progressives believed that the election of agency directors, and their budgetary independence from executives, led directly to corruption, incompetence, and competition among agencies.[27] One of the largely unrecognized functions of political machines was to bring these feuding and independent agencies under the guidance of one man, the boss, who by virtue of his political power—not legal authority—could forge policies and "get things done."[28]

The Progressive answer to the machine boss was the central executive— either elected, as in the case of governors, or appointed on the basis of qualifications, like city and county managers. Possessing legal authority, this individual could arrive at a coherent, rational policy and yet be responsive to the people:

> Democracy is preserved in the popular election of a small council. . . . Efficiency is achievable by the employment of a manager professionally trained for the technical job of administration. The danger of bureaucracy irresponsible and

> unresponsive to the will of the community is met by giving
> the council complete control of the managers' tenure of
> office.[29]

Wherever the reformers succeeded, their selection of people who were predominantly engineers as city and county managers, and professional administrators with advanced degrees in public administration, social work, public health, criminology, and even police science, illustrated their commitment to the values of rationality and efficiency.[30]

"URBAN CRISIS": RATIONAL GOVERNMENT IN THE 1960s

Beginning in the 1960s and extending to the present, the United States has been experiencing what observers call an urban crisis. For our purposes it is relatively unimportant whether this condition is construed as an objective phenomenon related to a diminishing supply of urban housing, a lack of urban transportation, a rise in selected rates of crime, an increase in drug addiction, a rise in welfare rolls, a decreasing urban tax base, growing numbers of secondary school dropouts, poverty, and riots, or as a subjective phenomenon related to changes in racial, political, and social consciousness, a sort of mass mental paroxysm.[31] The point is that a large number of people have perceived a problem of governance and politics and have proferred solutions accordingly.

At least two fundamentally different perspectives emerged in the search for a solution to the "urban crisis": one emphasized that the problem and its solution were political, the other suggesting that regardless of the problem's origins, the solution was to be found in more rational decision making. Both sought to solve certain generic problems facing the social reformer in the United States, whom one student of this period has described as follows:

> He [a reformer] must recruit a coalition of power sufficient for
> his purpose; he must respect the democratic tradition which
> expects every citizen, not merely to be represented, but to
> play an autonomous part in the determination of his own
> affairs; and his policies must be demonstrably rational.[32]

Political Reformers

Those who perceived the "urban problem" as a political one, supported programs that were radically democratic first, politically viable and scientifically rational second. Their solutions followed quite naturally from their analysis, which began with the observation that local, state, and federal governments were unresponsive to the largely unarticulated needs of the urban poor—especially racial minority groups. Unlike the impoverished immigrants of the nineteenth and twentieth centuries, the urban poor of the 1960s failed to organize community-based political machines, thus lacked the political power necessary to gain access to the economy.[33] Given the change in the economy since 1900, and the near-monopoly over low-skilled public service jobs held by other ethnic minorities in urban areas, the contemporary urban poor faced both political and economic barriers to advancement. For urban blacks, racial barriers were yet another obstacle, but one that was thought to flow from the basic economic and political problems. Moreover, the lack of political organization and economic opportunities in the urban areas had led to a "culture of poverty," in which the urban poor accommodated to the realities of their situation by lowering their expectations for socioeconomic advancement and political participation.[34] Crime, juvenile delinquency, drug addiction, and welfare became accepted avenues of survival, serving to maintain the political and economic impotence of the urban poor.[35]

The solution advocated by the politically oriented reformers was colored by other observations on American politics. The proposal to enact federal legislation establishing grants-in-aid to the individual states, on the model of the Works Progress Administration, was not politically viable. Key congressional committees were controlled in the early 1960s by conservative, one-party-jurisdiction legislators who had little interest in urban problems.[36] The Federal Housing Administration begun in 1949 illustrated only too well how federal grants funneled through state political parties to the cities could be used to benefit the urban rich instead of the urban poor.[37] In turn, state and local governments, parties, and bureaucracies could not be expected to move on their own initiative to aid the urban poor, both for lack of funds and lack of concern. Indeed, local agencies and governments were considered to be part of the problem, not of the solution.

The solution proferred by the political reformers was a very large dose of "radical democracy" supported by federal monies in an innovative manner. Beginning in 1959 with the Ford Foundation's "Grey Area Projects," later funded by Executive Order through the President's Committee on Juvenile Delinquency and Youth and extended, after significant alterations in Congress, through the Office of Economic Opportunity in 1964, the community action project (CAP) emerged as the vehicle for reform.[38]

The CAP projects of the period were politically radical in that they attempted to involve and organize the urban poor themselves to participate in local community projects. The aim was twofold: first, it was argued that political and social involvement in community projects would have a therapeutic effect on the "culture of poverty," raising the self-confidence of the urban poor, providing legitimate avenues and opportunities for advancement and survival (thus decreasing recourse to illegitimate means), and supplying a forum in which new political roles and skills could be learned and tested.[39]

Second, and more directly, the CAP projects were intended to act as a platform from which the urban poor, and their existing community groups, could exert pressure on local bureaucracies and government to be more responsive to their needs. Much like the political machines of an earlier period, the community action projects were seen by their sponsors as a mechanism for articulating the needs of the urban poor and including them in the economy and politics of the larger society.[40]

From the very beginning the CAP projects came under attack from local bureaucracies and politicians. The projects were funded directly from federal district offices, or foundations in some cases, which circumvented the traditional political structure of states and localities. The prevailing political powers in local government received nothing from the projects. Susceptible to and dependent on changes in federal funding, bitterly opposed by local politicians, the CAP projects, with few exceptions, failed to "develop a coalition of power" sufficient to their purposes.[41] In the absence of the necessary coalition, the projects were often devalued into projects with little or no political or economic impact (e.g., training in job etiquette instead of job skills, employing neighborhood youths for meaningless summer jobs).[42] Not infrequently, such projects collapsed under the weight of political in-fighting among various factions.[43] Many projects that did survive through accommodations with local political structures are now being dismantled for lack of federal funds.[44]

Administrative Reformers: Better Decisions Through Technology

While the political reformers became impaled on the thorns of political opposition and federal cutbacks, the inheritors of the progressive "rational government" tradition were devising their own solutions to the urban crisis. The solutions due to this second perspective, if not especially respective of "democratic traditions" and certainly not experiments in radical democracy, emphasized instead rationality and political viability.

The administrative reformers' solutions to the urban crisis sprung from the belief that the crisis was attributable to the failure of organizational, not political skills. It was suggested that government in the 1950s had attempted to be responsive to urban needs as evidenced by federal aid to housing, welfare, transportation (highways), unemployment insurance, and Social Security. That these programs did not satisfy the needs of the urban poor and of racial minorities was due primarily to strategies of social intervention that were poorly conceived, inadequate to the need, ineffective, and inefficient, hence costly. The failure of the Federal Housing Act of 1949, amended in 1954, to create residential housing (as opposed to business construction) in urban areas resulted from the inability of the federal government to evaluate the program and to redesign it if necessary to achieve its stated goals.[45] The Highway Act of 1955, along with the Housing Act and FHA program, spawned the growth of middle-class suburbs; and when the middle class abandoned the "core" cities, the tax base of city governments decreased, encouraging racial segregation. Yet these conditions—largely unintended results of a number of poorly coordinated federal programs—could have been avoided with adequate studies; certainly redesign of the programs would have followed adequate evaluation.[46]

The key to many of these failures at social intervention lay in the inability of federal and local governments to collect, store, and process information with adequate speed and in sufficient volume to provide feedback on the consequences of its acts. An aide to President Lyndon B. Johnson lamented that:

> We know how many children get a piece of paper that says they graduated from elementary schools but we don't know what a first grade education is. If a President asks the Defense Department how fast and how efficiently can you transport so many troops from A to a variety of countries around the world he would get an answer of extreme sophistication with a wealth of detail on all contingencies, close costs estimates for every possible variation, and calculation of expected political effects. . . .
> The disturbing truth is that the basis of recommendations by an American cabinet officer on whether to begin, eliminate, or expand vast social programs more nearly resembles the intuitive judgment of a benevolent tribal chief in remote Africa than the elaborate sophisticated data with which the Secretary of Defense supports a major new weapons system.[47]

Not only at the federal level but also in the cities, counties, and states, and frequently much earlier, local officials and politicians who administered national programs were decrying the lack of adequate information and the resultant failure of public policy. In Alameda County, California, a Welfare Citizens' Committee reported to the County Grand Jury in 1961 as follows:

> Philosophically, the purpose of the Aid to Families with Dependent Children (AFDC) is to maintain and strengthen family life—help towards the attainment of self-support and personal independence consistent with maintenance of continuing parental care.
>
> Ironically enough, the administration of the program, in many instances, not only defeats its purpose but actually appears to create the very conditions it would seek to resolve. The local administration of the program is encumbered by
>
> the duplication of services by the various departments and by a distinct lack of communication among them in relation to mutual cases. Thus it is not unusual to find the Welfare, Health, Probation and Institutions Deparments servicing the same family . . . each setting up its own forms, rendering its own or some service common to other departments and maintaining its own exclusive files.
>
> In seeking facts which will permit an analysis of the problems and an evaluation of the programs, we find reliable statistics are conspicuous by their absence. It appears the stock answers to many pertinent questions which are the basis of administrative decisions, are based upon the conjecture or an outdated, insufficient sampling in areas which may or may not be compatible with local conditions.[48]

A study in New York State in 1962 of the state's 3600 criminal justice agencies (police, district attorneys, courts, probation, correction, and parole agencies) attributed low apprehension rates, lengthy court proceedings, and rising crime rates to the inability of the local agencies to communicate with one another.[49] A 1964 study by police agencies in the San Francisco Bay Area concluded that local jurisdictions were losing $5 to $7 million annually because of traffic scofflaws; in addition, since the police agencies had no efficient means of transferring warrant/wanted information among themselves, rates of criminal apprehension were declining.[50]

The "information crisis" perceived by the administrative reformers in the early 1960s had at least two elements. First, in many cases the information required to formulate, evaluate, or implement more efficiently certain public policies existed in the repositories of local, state, or federal agencies but did not circulate among decision makers at the various levels

who required it to make "rational" decisions.[51] Second, it was often found
that the right kind of information was simply not collected. As one student
of planning in the Department of Health, Education, and Welfare
commented:

> Those who picture Washington as one mass of files and com-
> puters containing more information than they would like
> will be comforted by the experiences of program-planners
> in attempting to evaluate ongoing programs. Whatever the
> files and computers do contain, there is precious little in them
> about how many and whom the programs are reaching and
> whether they are doing what they are supposed to do. If the
> purpose of an adult education program is to teach people
> how to read and write, the Office of Education might reason-
> ably be expected to know how many people thereby actually
> learned how to read and write, but it does not. The higher
> education study was delayed because there simply was too
> little information about who was receiving federal scholar-
> ships, or what happened to all those who had been receiving
> National Defense Education Act loans since 1958. Did they
> finish college? Did it affect their subsequent careers? No
> answers. The Public Health Service might be expected to know
> whether its various health services are in fact making people
> healthier, but it does not.[52]

The sources of the so-called information crisis, and indirectly, the crisis
in public policy, lay in the organizational structure of American government—that is, fragmentation of power among thousands of small political
jurisdictions, decentralization of authority within these jurisdictions, and
"localistic" attitudes of politicians and bureaucrats, which encouraged
them not to cooperate with one another or with other jurisdictions. These
organizational factors, it was thought, impeded the flow of information
within government and inhibited rational decision making:

> Although the units of local government are distinct organiza-
> tional entities, it should be remembered that many of them
> overlap in territorial jurisdiction. Cities are within Counties,
> and districts of all types overlap cities, counties, and one
> another. This patchwork of overlapping geographic respon-
> sibilities is a major characteristic of local government. . . .
>
> State and local governments conventionally organize data
> around their functional uses, such as police data, welfare
> data, and agricultural data. This practice has created many

parallel data systems, each limited to the requirements of the function it serves. The following are some of the results:

(a) there is extensive duplicate collection and storage information items. . . . Each agency uses the information for a different purpose, even though the information itself is essentially the same.
(b) Information collected by one function is often unknown to other functions which could use it if they were aware of its availability and if it were in a form usable to them. . . .
(c) Because of jurisdictional or procedural problems, information items are not efficiently shared among functions and agencies. . . .
(d) Often, data that would be useful to a department are not collected at all, even though another department could easily gather these data in the course of its regular operations if it knew of the need.

These problems have resulted from the fact that each state and local government function typically has developed its own information system to fit its particular needs alone. No one has taken a comprehensive view of all the data available in one form or another within state and local governments and suggested how these data can be organized to make them more usable by all functions that need them. The advance of EDP equipment, with its increasing capability to store and process enormous quantities of data, enables such a fresh and comprehensive analysis to be made.[53]

The problem posed by the urban crisis in the eyes of the "rational government" group was one of pulling together these pieces of authority and coordinating decisions at various levels of government.

Fresh from the defeats of regional and metropolitan government plans in the 1950s, the rational government groups eschewed further engagements in political contests designed to strengthen the executive branch of local government and to unify them.[54] In any event, a new technology of computers obviated the need for further political reform and presented the potential for developing a "Total Unified Information System" that would answer the need for "feedback" between decision makers and social reality:

In essence the Unified Information System provides an information center to store and process data that are gathered and used by state and local governments within a particular state. The system is designed primarily to enable environmental data to be efficiently organized into records about persons and about properties.

These data would be gathered in the regular operations of government agencies and transmitted to the information center via a communication channel, often conventional telephone networks. Similarly, agencies could obtain from the center either raw or processed data.

The system does not require the collection of any new data and is entirely independent of the purposes or procedures for which the data are used. It simply provides for a technological facility to file these data and to process them according to the instructions of participating agencies.

Therefore it does not alter the present relationship between any citizen and the government or those between government agencies.[55]

The notion of a "Total Unified Information System" for state and local governments preceded by five years the proposal for the creation of a national data center sponsored by the federal Office of the Budget in 1967.[56] Both proposals embody the same idea: namely, that the answer to many of the nation's social problems lay in the consolidation of existing government records, full circulation of government information from point of collection to point of need by a decision maker, and the bringing to bear of this mother-lode of data on the critical issues of the day.

In theory, the integration of government records involved no changes in political jurisdiction, authority, or funding, thus appeared to be politically viable.[57] Moreover, the use of computers as the mechanism for transferring government information conferred to computer projects an aura of rationality (if not also prestige) that had been denied those advocating radical democratic reforms.

The New Prince in Theory and Practice: Ideologues

Emboldened by the growing sophistication of computer machines and their applications in the late 1960s, one social scientist announced the dawning of a new age, the "post-industrial society," in which the role of the politician as a broker among interest groups would change to that of a technical decision maker:

The combination of these two elements (the influence of foreign policy and the "future orientation" of society) brings into play the increasing role of technical decision-making. The shaping of conscious policy, be it foreign policy, defense, or economics, calls to the fore the men with the skills necessary to outline the constraints ahead, to work out in detail the management and policy procedures, and to assess the consequences of choices. The revolutions in military technology (the introduction of nuclear power, the replacement of manned aircraft by missiles) were initiated by scientists. The development of systems analysis and cost-effectiveness techniques, which have revolutionized both the strategy process as well as the management structure of the Pentagon, was brought about by mathematicians and economists. The management of the national economy . . . increasingly becomes technical decisions.

But the most important political consequence of all this is the passing of effective power, in almost all political systems, from the legislative and parliamentary bodies to the executive, and the reemergence of what Bertrand de Jouvenal has called, in his elegant fashion, the Principiate.[58]

While the philosophers of rational government were casting about for characters capable of assuming the Principiate, the more traditional local Princes had already stolen some of the new magic. If the wine and its fragrance were not new, at least the bottle and its label were novel.

The first attempts at building unified information systems were sponsored in large part, as we describe at length later, by city managers, county administrative officers, reform governors, and professional local government agency managers—inheritors and supporters of Progressive reforms begun 60 years previous. Practical men of politics, they were less interested in ushering in a new age than in exercising greater control over social service budgets (e.g., for welfare, "modernization" of police forces, establishment of state standards and control over local criminal justice agencies, and reduction of the costs of local administration). Gordon F. Milliman, the director of the Los Angeles city government computer information system, explained the practical considerations that motivate the local Princes:

The increased mobility of the population, the rising rate of crime, the growth in welfare and health programs, and the sheer growth of population, all these factors meant that going into the 1960s county government just couldn't keep up with demands being made upon it to administer people, and property.

County supervisors are not interested in fancy plans for Total

Unified Information Systems, or Management Information
Systems. They don't exist now and they probably never will.
They want to know how to keep budgets and taxes down,
they want to know what's happening in their countries. The
Auditors want tax parcel automation, the CAO's want better
budgeting, more central control over departments, the clerk
wants automatic vote tabulation, even the dog catcher wants
automatic licensing.[59]

For these more mundane pursuits rooted in the Progressive tradition
(e.g., centralizing executive authority, increasing budgetary control over
agencies, establishing state standards, and "professionalizing" the police),
the new technology of computers proved to be an excellent tool, and in
some cases a guise for reforming state and local bureaucracies. The remainder of our study is concerned with such practical applications of computers in selected local governments, with the social and political conditions that precede them, the political process of their construction, and
their consequences for the local governments and agencies.

SUMMARY

The traditional American values of rationality and centralization are the
broad themes that united computer firms, public officials, and ideologues
of the new post-Industrial, computer age. These values have their roots in
the Progressive political tradition, and they were espoused most often in
the 1960s by precisely those public officials who inherited the fruits of
progressivism: reform governors, county administrative officers, city managers, and professional public administrators. But in the 1950s and 1960s
the capacity of these administrative reformers to attain their goal of politically integrated, urban metropolitan government was spent. The public was
thinking of more pressing issues—first tax reform, later, urban riots.

The arrival of third generation computers—more exactly, the hard selling by computer firms—offered new hope for administrative reformers and
was almost immediately extolled by them. The new computers promised to
more closely integrate (read centralize) the disparate elements of federal,
state, and local bureaucracies. They promised—at least the manufacturers
promised—better decision making, thereby better governance, through high
technology.

Last, and most important, although clothed in the values of Progressive
reform, the computerized information systems did not require a test of
those values in the electoral process. Here the bureaucratic reforms we

describe depart sharply from their precursors in the progressive tradition.

When an embarrassingly large number of citizens were seeking out those other American values—justice and equality—few threatened politicians or public administrators remained untempted by the virtues of a new technology that imposed few or no political costs but initiated its users into the new "Principiate."

These broad social and political factors shaped the design and goals of computerized information systems in the mid-1960s, but the specific circumstances surrounding the design and control of these systems varied. In the next two chapters we examine systematically how specific strategies of innovation and patterns of control over the technology produced determinate social outcomes in the four cases investigated.

NOTES

1. See Richard Hofstadter, *The Age of Reform,* New York: Vintage, 1963. See also Hofstadter's *The American Political Tradition,* New York: Vintage, 1960, especially Chapters 7–9.

2. Hofstadter, *The Age of Reform, op. cit.,* p. 9.

3. Dixon Ryan Fox, "New York Becomes a Democracy," in Alexander C. Flick (ed), *History of the State of New York,* Vol. 6, New York: Columbia University Press, 1934, p. 25.

4. *Ibid.,* pp. 30–68.

5. Hofstadter, *The Age of Reform, op. cit.,* pp. 204–205.

6. Fox, *op. cit.*

7. Edward C. Banfield and James Q. Wilson, *City Politics,* New York: Random House, 1963, p. 23.

8. Edward Platt Turner, "Post-War Problems and Political Reformers," in Flick, *op. cit.,* Vol. 7, pp. 137–168. For a graphic display of dedicated muckracking of William Marcy Tweed, see "How New York is Governed—Frauds of the Tammany Democrats," *New York Times* Supplement, 1871.

9. Robert K. Merton, *Social Theory and Social Structure,* New York: Free Press, 1957, pp. 71–81. See also Banfield and Wilson, *op. cit.,* Chapter 9, and Hofstadter, *The Age of Reform, op. cit.,* pp. 182–185.

10. The concept of the political machine as an apolitical utilitarian organization based largely on material inducements is that of Banfield and Wilson, *op. cit.,* Chapter 9.

11. Lorin Peterson, *The Day of the Mugwump,* New York: Random House, 1961.

12. Peterson, *op. cit.,* Chapter 1. See also Banfield and Wilson, *op. cit.,* Chapter 11.

13. See the account of the Mugwumps' attempt to limit immigration in Barbara M. Solomon's *Ancestors and Immigrants,* Cambridge, Mass.: Harvard University Press, 1956.

14. See James Q. Wilson, "Politics and Reform in American Cities," in Ivan Hinderaker (ed.), *American Government Annual, 1962–1963,* New York: Holt, Rinehart, Winston, 1962.

15. See Hofstadter, *The Age of Reform, op. cit.,* pp. 118–119.

16. *Ibid.,* p. 238.

17. Banfield and Wilson, *op. cit.,* p. 151.

18. Table 1 from *ibid.,* p. 155.

19. Table 2 from *ibid.,* p. 169.

20. *Ibid.,* pp. 148–150.

21. Hofstadter, *The Age of Reform, op. cit.,* pp. 269–271.

22. Finla G. Crawford, "Recent Political Developments," in Flick, *op. cit.,* Vol. 7, pp. 243–279.

23. Crawford, *op. cit.;* for developments in other states, see also Jack L. Walker, "The Diffusion of Innovations Among the American States," in *American Political Science Review,* September 1969, pp. 880–899; and Eugene C. Lee, *The Politics of Nonpartisanship,* Berkeley: University of California Press, 1960.

24. See National Municipal League, *The County Manager Plan,* New York: National Municipal League, 1945. See also John C. Bollens, *American County Government,* Beverley Hills, Calif.: Sage, 1969.

25. John C. Bollens, "Administrative Integration in California Counties," in *Public Administration Review,* **11** (1951), pp. 26–34; and Bollens, *American County Government, op. cit.*

26. Andrew D. White, first president of Cornell University, in *The Forum,* 1890, cited in Banfield and Wilson, *op. cit.,* p. 153.

27. Turner, *op. cit.*

28. Banfield and Wilson, *op. cit.,* Chapter 8, distinguish between the centralization of political influence common to political machines and centralization of administrative authority common to strong mayor or council–manager governments.

29. International City Managers' Association, "Recent Council Manager Developments," cited in Banfield and Wilson, *op. cit.,* p. 172.

30. Harold Stone, Don K. Price, and Kathryn Stone, *City Manager Government in the United States,* Chicago: Public Administration Service, 1940.

31. There is evidence to indicate that objective social conditions were worsening in the cities during the latter half of the 1950s, especially for racial minortiy groups. See Herbert J. Gans, "The Failure of Urban Renewal," in Herbert J. Gans (ed.), *People and Plans,* New York: Basic Books, 1968, pp. 260–278; and Martin Anderson, *The Federal Bulldozer,* Cambridge, Mass.: M.I.T. Press, 1964. For evidence of declining relative income for blacks, see also Herman T. Miller, "Is the Income Gap Closed? 'No, '" *New York Times Magazine Section* (November 11, 1962); and Allan Batchelder, "Decline in the Relation of Negro Men," *Quarterly Journal of Economics,* **68** (August 1964). For a similar "objective condition" perspective, see Mitchell Gordon, *Sick Cities,* Baltimore, Md.: Penguin, 1965.

For the view that the "urban crisis," especailly urban riots, was largely a function of changes in social and political consciousness, see Gary T. Marx, *Protest and Prejudice,* New York: Harper & Row, 1969.

For a theoretical discussion of the definition and nature of social problems, see Robert K. Merton, "Social Problems and Sociological Theory," in Robert K. Merton and Robert A. Nisbet (eds.), *Contemporary Social Problems,* New York: Harcourt Brace Jovanovich, 1966, pp. 775–823.

32. Peter Marris and Martin Rein, *Dilemmas of Social Reform,* New York: Atherton, 1967, p. 7.

33. Nathan Glazer and Daniel P. Moynihan, *Beyond the Melting Pot,* 2nd ed., Cambridge, Mass.: M.I.T. Press, 1970.

34. Charles A. Valentine, *The Culture of Poverty—A Critique and Counter Proposals,* Chicago: University of Chicago Press, 1968.

35. Richard Cloward and Lloyd Ohlin, *Delinquency and Opportunity: A Theory of Delinquent Gangs,* New York: Free Press, 1960. The theory of delinquent gangs presented by Cloward and Ohlin became the theoretical and political underpinning of the Mobilization for Youth program in the Lower East Side of New York in 1960. See Marris and Rein, *op. cit.,* pp. 19–20.

36. Marris and Rein, *op. cit.,* pp. 7–8; and James MacGregor Burns, *The Deadlock of Democracy: Four Party Politics in America,* Englewood Cliffs, N.J.: Prentice Hall, 1963.

37. Anderson, *op. cit.*

38. For an account of the early "Grey Area Projects" of the Ford Foundation, see Marris and Rein, *op. cit.,* pp. 14–20. See also Executive Order 10940, May 11, 1961, and Public Law 87-274, The Juvenile Delinquency and Youth Offenses Control Act of 1961.

39. Valentine, *op. cit.*

40. Marris and Rein, *op. cit.,* Chapter 2.

41. See Daniel P. Moynihan, *Maximum Feasible Misunderstanding,* New York: Free Press, 1969. And also Marris and Rein, *op. cit.,* Chapter 6.

42. Marris and Rein, *op. cit.,* Chapters 6 and 7.

43. Melvin Herman and Michael Munk, *Decision Making in Poverty Programs: Case Studies from Youth Work Agencies,* New York: Columbia University Press, 1968, pp. 1–41.

44. Marris and Rein, *op. cit.,* Chapter 9.

45. Ithiel de Sola Pool, Stuart McIntosh, and David Griffel, "On the Design of Computer-Based Information Systems," paper issued by the Massachusetts Institute of Technology, Cambridge, Mass., 1968. See also Robert L. Chartrand, "Congress Seeks a Systems Approach," *Datamation,* **14** (May 1968), pp. 46–49.

46. See, for example, Simon Ramo, *Cure for Chaos,* New York: McKay, 1969, and T.R.W. Systems Group, *Systems Technology in the Service of Society,* a brochure published by T.R.W. Inc., 1969, and reprinted in Alan F. Westin (ed.), *Information Technology in a Democracy,* Cambridge, Mass.: Harvard University Press, 1971, pp. 126–129. Mr. Ramo is a founder of Thompson–Ramo–Wooldridge Inc., a California-based systems development firm.

47. Joseph Califano, former aide to President Johnson, in testimony given before a Senate Labor Subcommittee. Cited by Tom Wicker, *New York Times,* December 25, 1969.

48. Welfare Citizens' Committee Report, *Alameda County Grand Jury Final Report, 1961,* Alameda County Grand Jury, Alameda, Calif.: 1961, p. 41.

49. See CIS case study.

50. "Bay Area Law Enforcement Information Control Study Committee Report," Oakland Police Department in cooperation with IBM, Oakland, Calif., 1965.

51. Edward Hearle and R. J. Mason, *A Data Processing System for State and Local Government,* Englewood Cliffs, N.J.: Prentice-Hall, 1962, pp. 49–55.

52. Elizabeth B. Drew, "HEW Grapples with PPBS," *Public Interest* (1967), p. 11.

53. Hearle and Mason, *op. cit.,* pp. 22; 29–30. See also Ramo, *op. cit.*

54. A federal commission found that between 1950 and 1961 proposals for significant change in local government structure were introduced in only eighteen of the nation's 212 metropolitan areas and were approved in only eight. See the U.S. Advisory Commission on Intergovernmental Relations, *Factors Affecting Voter Reactions to Governmental Reorganization in Metropolitan Areas,* Washington, D.C.: Government Printing Office, May, 1962. See also Melvin R. Levin, *Community and Regional Planning,* New York: Praeger, 1969. For "successful" metropolitan reorganizations, see Edward Sofen, *The Miami Metropolitan Experiment,* Bloomington: Indiana University Press, 1963. See also Henry J. Schmandt, *The Milwaukee Metropolitan Study Commission,* Bloomington: Indiana University Press, 1965.

55. Hearle and Mason, *op. cit.,* pp. 50–51.

56. See Carl Kaysen, "Data Banks and Dossiers," *Public Interest,* Spring 1967, and also "Hearings Before the Subcommittee on Administrative Practice and Procedure of the Committee of the Judiciary, U.S. Senate, 90th Congress, 1st Session, 1967.

57. See Hearle and Mason, *op. cit.,* p. 51, who argue that use of computerized information systems in local government would not alter political relationships within the government. For a speculative view, see Anthony Downs, "A Realistic Look at the Final Payoffs from Urban Data Systems," *Public Administration Review,* **27** (September 1967), pp. 204–209.

58. Daniel Bell, "Notes on the Post-Industrial Society," *Public Interest,* 1967, p. 107.

FIVE

Bureaucratic Innovation and Bureaucratic Reform

TWO KINDS OF BUREAUCRATIC CHANGE

In an era in which almost anything new is heralded as significant, it is important that we clearly distinguish the bureaucratic reforms examined here from the far more common event of bureaucratic innovation.

The stereotype of bureaucratic pathology is one in which the faithful bureaucrat narrowly pursues the means of administration—rules and regulations—only to displace the intended goals of administration—the delivery of a service or product.[1] Ritualized overconformity to procedure, according to the stereotype, leads to a trained incapacity to act appropriately under conditions of change. The common practice of armies preparing for future wars using procedures developed in the last successful war is just one example of this type of bureaucratic pathology.

Close observation of bureaucracies has altered our picture of how bureaucrats react to change. Blau found, for instance, that welfare workers developed informal strategies to cope with situations not envisaged by the formal rules.[2] Gouldner showed how rules and regulations respond to the self-interests of those who govern and are governed. Managers and workers can ignore rules to accomplish certain ends or to adjust to change, but they need not and do not follow rules blindly.[3] Others have gathered an impressive array of evidence to indicate not only that bureaucrats can adapt to change but that bureaucracies themselves are in a constant state of change due to the adoption of new goals,[4] the succession of leaders,[5] and perceived environmental pressure for change.[6]

Indeed, even a casual observer of public bureaucracies in the 1960s soon would have learned that bureaucratic innovation can be fun and profitable. Schrag comments on the Boston public school system:

> Boston is not immune to change or innovation. . . . The system is now fairly littered with demonstration projects and experiments, head starts, pre-schools, enrichments, compensatory programs, second chances, reading laboratories, summer reviews, pilot schools, team teaching trials, and a whole host of other departures. . . .
>
> But so far, the system's long list of changes . . . has had almost no effect on educational substance for most of the children most of the time. . . . The innovations tend to remain well encapsulated, like droplets of oil on still water.[7]

Whether the bureaucratic innovations described by Schrag and familiar to us all from the hoopla atmosphere of the 1960s were induced by environmental pressure, the enticement of federal grants, or the exuberance of young school teachers, they represent the kind of bureaucratic change that is normal. It is normal precisely because these kinds of change present little or no threat to ongoing bureaucratic routines, little or no challenge to existing structures of authority. They are indeed "encapsulated." We call this kind of change "bureaucratic innovation."

Bureaucratic reforms differ from innovations in that they lead to a rearrangement of the basic authority structure of an organization. Bureaucratic reforms occur when there is a redistribution of control over critical organizational resources. An inherent feature of bureaucratic reform is the loss of control by some persons or units of the organization over the resources that count most: formal authority, money, and information. Bureaucratic reforms in public bureaucracies do not necessarily result in any change whatsoever in the kinds of product they deliver to the public, any more than massive reforms undergone by General Motors or a Sears Roebuck led to a change in their basic corporate outputs.[8] Historically, the sources of reform in American public bureaucracies have varied from political movements such as the early Progressive reforms to new legislation such as the Tennessee Valley Authority described by Selznick.[9] In the cases we examine bureaucratic reform is made possible by a new technology that leads to the redistribution of control over a critical resource—information. This in turn has implications for the exercise of authority within public bureaucracy. To understand this process fully, we should examine briefly the role of information in the bureaucratic process.

INFORMATION AS A CRITICAL ORGANIZATIONAL RESOURCE

The role of information as a personal resource in organizations has been discussed by sociologists in previous works, but the role of information as an organizational resource vis-à-vis an organization's environment is less well understood.[10] Here we wish to describe four critical functions that information fulfills for government agencies, and to suggest some of the problems that may arise when a government agency loses control over critical information processes.

1. Perhaps the most obvious use of information by a government agency is the maintenance of its reputation with clients, the public, and its own employees. The sensitive activities of many government agencies, such as those concerned with welfare, health, and education, demand that agency clients be protected from public exposure and that in interactions with the agency, a client may expect fair and impartial treatment. In turn, public support for many governmental activities of low visibility will depend on the ability of the agencies to inhibit the release of derogatory information, to expedite the spread of favorable information, and otherwise to inform the public of the services performed. Public employment agencies frequently advertise their services, for instance.

Finally, the ability of an organization to control the information it generates itself is important for maintaining employee loyalty. Government agencies, as much as other formal organizations, depend on a certain degree of loyalty from their own employees, and this loyalty can be destroyed if employee–client interactions, or employees themselves, become the object of public scrutiny. By protecting its personnel from unwarranted investigation by other organizations and the public, a government agency allows the employees to bend rules, to interact more freely among themselves, and to establish control over the pace of their work. When government agencies have been unable to provide this protection, employees have responded with low morale, low organizational loyalty, and even hostility toward the agency.[11]

2. A second critical function of information for government agencies is that of preserving autonomy. By closely controlling the release of agency information to political executives and legislatures, the government agency

preserves for itself a degree of freedom from close supervision and a large measure of discretion in performing its duties. If a government agency is forced to continually furnish information about its work and employees to outside officials or the public, it has more difficulty in playing an independent role in the formation of public policy. The idea of the specialized governmi nt agency with separate powers and authority is threatened whenever that agency loses a significant amount of control over its information processes. As Wildavsky points out in his analysis of the budgetary process in public bureaucracies, the technological incapacity of elected officials to process information generated by agencies they formally control preserves for the agencies a great deal of discretion in attaining their legitimate ends.[12]

3. A third critical function performed by information in government agencies, as well as in other organizations, is self-evaluative. Wilensky suggests that internally generated information about its own activities is a vital resource used by an organization to evaluate the success of its activities and the performance of its employees, and to plan for the future.[13] Loss of control over internal information processes threatens effective self-evaluation, and more importantly weakens the position of forces in an organization actively seeking to change the institution from within. When an organization loses control over its internal information, self-evaluation tends to be displaced by defensive reactions. Niederhoffer asserts, for instance, that public investigations of police departments result in a weakening of internal reform forces and give rise to conservative forces attempting to defend the organization from outside interference.[14]

4. A fourth important use of information for a government agency and for other organizations is the preservation of public ignorance concerning the informal accommodations an agency may have to make with its environment. It is well recognized that all organizations, to survive, must occasionally engage in activities that violate their announced ideals. Full public knowledge and scrutiny of such informal accommodations to the environment may threaten the viability of the organization. Therefore, organizations and government agencies try to restrict access to information bearing on the discrepant behavior.[15] To accommodate the interests of certain faculty members, for instance, universities, may be forced to accept military research contracts; to increase income, universities may engage in real estate speculation. Although such activities may be functional for preserving the quality of the faculty and the growth of the university budget, in recent years their public disclosure and subsequent investigation has

created a problem of legitimacy for the university, both with its own students and with the faculty and the public.

SUMMARY

Information about itself or its clients is a vital organizational resource in the daily life of a public bureauracy, and control over this kind of information is an important boundary-maintaining device. Changes in the technological capacity to process, store, and transfer information can in turn imply rather basic changes in the boundaries of organizations. The unique feature of the computer-inspired bureaucratic reforms we examine is precisely that a new technology has emerged which can transport information across organizational boundaries.

NOTES

1. Robert K. Merton, *Social Theory and Social Structure,* New York: Free Press, 1968, p. 253.

2. Peter M. Blau, *Dynamics of Bureaucracy,* Chicago: University of Chicago Press, 1955, pp. 201–219.

3. Alvin Gouldner, *Patterns of Industrial Democracy,* New York: Free Press, 1954.

4. David L. Sills, *The Volunteers,* New York: Free Press, 1957, pp. 253–270.

5. Richard H. McLeery, *Policy Change in Prison Management,* East Lansing: Michigan State University, 1957.

6. Alfred D. Chandler, Jr., *Strategy and Structure,* Cambridge, Mass.: M.I.T. Press, 1962.

7. Peter Schrag, *Village School Downtown,* Boston: Beacon, 1967, pp. 71–72.

8. Chandler, *op. cit.*

9. Philip Selznick, *TVA and the Grass Roots,* Berkeley: University of California Press, 1949.

10. See, for example, Peter M. Blau, *The Dynamics of Bureaucracy,* Chicago: University of Chicago Press, 1963).

11. Harold L. Wilensky, *Organizational Intelligence,* New York: Basic Books, 1967, Chapter 6.

12. Aaron Wildavsky, *The Politics of the Budgetary Process,* Boston: Little, Brown, 1964.

13. Wilensky, *op. cit.,* Chapter 6.

14. Arthur Niederhoffer, *Behind the Shield,* Garden City, N.Y.: Anchor, 1969, Chapter 6.

15. Wilbert Moore and Melvin Tumin, "Some Social Functions of Ignorance," *American Sociological Review,* **14** (1949).

SIX

Toward a Morphology of Bureaucratic Reform

In this chapter we compare some of the salient social features of the case studies prior to exploring each case in depth. Comparison leads to the development of a typology of bureaucratic reform useful in further analysis of our cases. For purposes of brevity, we must introduce the following acronyms to refer to our cases.

SSIS: Social Service Information System of Western County
PRIS: Police Regional Information System of Western County
CIS: Criminal Information System of Eastern State
CIN: Criminal Information Network of Western State

The centralized information systems we investigate pool together information taken from a number of government agencies, and this, perhaps, is their most outstanding feature. Moreover, the process inherently leads to the shift of control over vital organizational information from the participating organizations to the centralized information data bank. Given the importance of information to government agencies, we are interested in two consequences of its redistribution through information systems: the level of resistance to participation in the systems, and the degree to which centralization of authority and power results from the creation of these systems.

DEPENDENT VARIABLES: RESISTANCE AND CENTRALIZATION

Previous writers have suggested that government agencies will resist participation in centralized information systems because they recognize that such participation will lead to a decline in their power over traditional spheres of activity. Anthony Downs says, for instance:

> Most city officials are acutely aware of this potential power shift. Each operating department naturally wants to retain as much power as possible over its own behavior and its traditional sphere of activity. Its members are especially anxious to prevent "outsiders" from having detailed knowledge about every aspect of the department's operations. Hence nearly every department with operations susceptible to computerized management will at least initially fight for its own computer and data system controlled by its own members.[1]

Two of our case studies tend to support Downs's hypothesis. In the SSIS and CIS reform projects, resistance by the user agencies to participation in the information systems was very high. In the PRIS and CIN reform projects, however, resistance was either low or nonexistent.

Our first task in the case studies is to suggest some of the factors that account for different levels of resistance by user agencies to participation in information systems. Second, we explore the sources of agency resistance. Downs suggests two factors that lead to agency resistance: the loss of power per se, and the potential for "outsiders" to have knowledge of agency activities. Other possible sources of resistance may be the rejection of the entire technology—a sort of Luddite reaction to the use of computers. Another possible source of resistance is the perception by agency managers and personnel that the technology serves values and goals that are not considered to be legitimate.

Our second dependent variable involves the substantive political effects of information systems in local governments. Without exception, each information system we investigate accepts as its goal greater efficiency and coordination of decision making among diverse agencies of local government. As Aaron Wildavsky has remarked, the pursuit of efficiency in government can have political consequences:

> Yet the economizer, he who values efficiency most dearly, may discover that the most efficient means for accomplishing his ends cannot be secured without altering the machinery

for making social decisions. In this case, he not only alters means and ends . . . simultaneously, but makes them dependent on changes in political relationships. While he claims no special interest in, or expertise concerning, the ways in which decisions are made outside the market place, the economizer pursues efficiency where it leads him: to the heart of the political system. Let us call this "total efficiency."[2]

And Downs says that the pursuit of efficiency through the use of information systems will be viewed favorably by central executives as a means of increasing the power and influence of their office:

At the other extreme, city planners and budgetary officials will both eventually espouse centralized data systems. They will view such systems at least in part as means of gaining control over information channels vital to all operating departments—and thereby capturing some of the latter's power.[3]

The hypothesis suggested by Wildavsky and Downs—namely, that information systems will lead to more centralized local governments—is supported in two of our case studies. The SSIS system of a western county has resulted in an increase in the control of county budgetary officials and political executives over social service agencies in the county, especially welfare. The CIS system in an eastern state provides another example of political and budgetary executive authorities at the state level gaining in capacity to regulate and control line agencies through the use of an information system.

Two of our cases do not support the centralization hypothesis. In the CIN case the building of a central information system does not alter the traditional relationship between state executive authorities and local police agencies; in addition, the local user agencies derive significant resource benefits from participating in CIN. In the PRIS case study a centralized information system involving the police agencies of a region is supportive of highly decentralized police agency administration.

Our second principal task in the case studies is to explore some of the factors that account for the differential impact of centralized information systems on the local governments investigated. Specifically, we must look for different strategies used to organize these systems, determining who initiated them and who participated in their design and implementation.

THE INDEPENDENT VARIABLES

In investigating the four case studies, I first became aware of the existence of different levels of resistance and centralization in the cases. Looking systematically for factors that might account for these differences led me in two directions. The first involved a search of the sociological literature for apt analogies to the kind of social process I was observing. Since no sociologist had studied formal information systems, however, there was no directly relevant literature. Once interesting analogies had been found, further research and analysis of the case materials was required to discover whether the analogies produced a better understanding of the cases.

In an exploratory study such as this, the process of theorizing is never far removed from the actual observing and probing. Often the two occur simultaneously, with ideas suggesting themselves from the materials at hand and new observations being undertaken to confirm or disprove an idea.

That the building of centralized information systems is analogous to the process of social integration seemed to be a promising observation. The cases are similar in that each information system takes important information from separate line agencies of government and places it in a common repository. Information collected by a welfare agency becomes almost instantly available to a health or probation agency in the same county. An arrest warrant issued by one small police agency in a rural area becomes available immediately to a big city agency hundreds of miles away. Briefly, the information systems in each case were creating new interaction networks among traditionally isolated and separate agencies, and they were significantly speeding up the process of interaction.

To accomplish this higher level of interaction through the use of information systems, agreements had to be reached or imposed on traditionally autonomous agencies concerning the information transferred, the rules governing its use, and the format of storage. Information systems presupposed new areas of collaboration among separate agencies and implied that each agency lost some control over its internal information to a centralized data bank. To record official transactions with a client in a welfare agency, for instance, necessitated the following of a specific format of information collection that could be read by the central computers. In turn, this meant that other agencies in the system could have access to this information.

The level of interaction among social units, the spheres of activity in which they collaborate, and the extent to which they are subject to a common authority is referred to by sociologists as the level of social integration characterizing social units.[4] Thus we can fruitfully observe that centralized information systems are attempts to increase the level of social integration among selected agencies of local government. Centralized information systems imply an increase in the number of activities in which local agencies collaborate, an increase in the speed and frequency of their formal interacttion, and some loss of control over a critical resource—information.

Although an increase in the level of integration characterizing local agencies of government is one of the common denominators of our four cases, there are large differences among the systems in terms of the initial characteristics of the agencies they are attempting to integrate. In two cases the user agencies performed very similar kinds of activities and shared a common set of values and ideologies. Thus in the PRIS and CIN case studies the information system integrates police agencies: PRIS at the regional level and CIN at the state level. Moreover, in both cases the user agencies had traditionally cooperated with one another formally as well as informally, and resistance to the information system was very low.

In two other cases, SSIS and CIS, opposite initial conditions obtained: the agencies were very different in terms of activities and values, and historically they were hostile to suggestions that they cooperate with one another. In these cases resistance to sharing information under the aegis of a centralized data bank was very high.

The first independent variable that appeared to explain some of the variance in the dependent variable "resistance" was composed of the initial conditions of the user agencies. A search of the literature on social integration yielded three indicators of initial conditions: homogeneity, interdependence, and internal integration. These indicators are discussed below, and the cases are compared to reveal how favorable were the initial conditions of the user agencies to higher levels of integration.

A second independent variable emerged from observations of the cases concerned with the differing strategies used to initiate and legitimate the information systems to the user agencies. In two of our cases, the CIN and PRIS systems, the user agencies played a large role in designing, implementing, and administering the information system; here resistance was low, and the systems did not appear to increase administrative centralization. When participation of the user agencies was low or nonexistent, as in the CIS and SSIS cases, resistance was comparatively high, and the systems appeared to be supportive of a high degree of administrative centralization.

Here the sociological literature on mechanisms of political and administrative reform proved to be very useful for conceptualizing the different patterns of reform that characterize our case studies. The patterns of reform are discussed below, and each case is compared with the others in terms of the concrete mechanisms used to build and legitimate the respective systems.

THE CONCEPTUAL FRAMEWORK

The conceptual framework arrived at to discuss and compare the case studies can be represented by Figure 2.

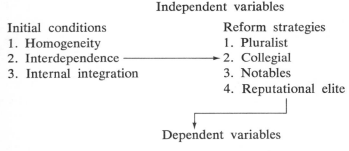

Independent variables

Initial conditions
1. Homogeneity
2. Interdependence
3. Internal integration

Reform strategies
1. Pluralist
2. Collegial
3. Notables
4. Reputational elite

Dependent variables

1. Resistance to information system
2. Degree of centralization

Figure 2. Schematization of conceptual framework.

We next discuss the independent variables at greater length, introducing findings from other sociological studies to illustrate and clarify the variables.

CONDITIONS OF INITIATION

The literature points to three significant factors determining the conduciveness, or alternatively, resistance, of social units in a system to efforts to increase the levels of integration of the system. These factors are homogeneity, interdependence, and internal integration; respectively, they describe the prereform characteristics of the aggregate of units, their relationship to one another, and the characteristics of the individual units themselves. These factors, we emphasize, are in no sense necessary or sufficient conditions for higher levels of social integration. Instead, they are influential in determining the level of resistance to higher levels of integration.

An Aggregate Characteristic: Homogeneity

The extent to which social units are similar is often cited as an important determinant of the level of integration those units can attain. Thus it is suggested that the more homogeneous are small groups, communities, and nations, the more interaction occurs within these groups, and the more likely each one is to be highly integrated.[5] In turn, it has been shown that interaction within groups is age and rank graded, occurring predominantly within status subgroups and less frequently across status lines.[6]

The formation of monopolies within national boundaries, and international cartels, also suggests that homogeneity is related to the level of integration obtained among economic units sharing products and markets.[7]

On the other hand, there are significant exceptions to the hypothesis that similarity is conducive to high levels of integration. Complementary heterogeneity may also become the basis for high levels of integration.[8] Vertical integration in certain industries (e.g., the steel or petroleum industries and in the British Commonwealth provides examples of economic integration under conditions of low homogeneity.[9] Certain nation-states such as the United States or Canada do not seem to require a high degree of cultural or racial homogeneity to maintain relatively high levels of political integration. Some political movements rest on homogeneous subgroups in the population, but the civil rights movement in the United States and most nationalist movements in Third World countries have been shown to rely on a very heterogeneous racial and class base of support.[10]

However, in the exceptions frequently cited to gainsay the homogeneity hypothesis, it is nevertheless true that the social units of these systems are homogeneous with respect to some dimensions, heterogeneous with respect to others. The British Commonwealth countries, although economically heterogeneous, share many political and cultural traditions—New Zealand, Canada, and Australia, in particular, even if these are remnants of the colonial period. Vertically integrated industries are heterogeneous with respect to the operations they perform to produce an output, but homogeneous with respect to a final product; for example, vertically integrated steel industries combine a number of different organizations to produce a single output.

Thus in each case the particular dimension of homogeneity must be specified and its relevance to integration ascertained. Furthermore, under some social conditions, the relevant dimensions of homogeneity may change. In periods of war or civil disturbance, class and racial differences may lose relevance as determinants of the level of social integration.[11]

Under conditions of low homogeneity, moreover, there are political and social mechanisms that operate to preserve a necessary amount of system integration. Within seemingly heterogeneous nation-states, class, ethnic, and racial segregation act as mechanisms of social distance to diminish the social recognition of heterogeneity and to reduce intergroup conflict, thus preserving a minimal amount of political and social integration. What appears to be a "melting pot" is in fact an intricate, interwoven set of relatively homogeneous communities, as others have shown in descriptions of communities in the United States.[12] It has also been pointed out that cross-cutting cleavages reduce the effects of low homogeneity as measured on one dimension (e.g., race) by increasing homogeneity on another dimension (e.g., occupation).[13]

Thus although homogeneity may be an important factor in determining the level of integration in a social system, there appear to be social and political mechanisms for overcoming the effects of low homogeneity. For example, Gerlach in his study of political movements found that the diffuse ideology and cellular organization of the civil rights movement allowed persons and groups from very diverse social backgrounds to participate in a single movement.[14] Mechanisms of social distance, such as age/rank graded interaction, segregation, cross-cutting cleavages, and highly decentralized and cellular organization, are the kinds of mechanisms that should be looked for in attempting to explain relatively high levels of integration under conditions of low homogeneity. (In addition, the degree of interdependence that characterizes the units of a system may mitigate the effects of low homogeneity, as discussed below.)

Yet even with these considerations, we expect high homogeneity to be conducive to higher levels of integration in a social system, and when homogeneity is lacking, we expect to find either low integration and instability in the system, or the social and political mechanisms that effectively overcome the consequences of low homogeneity. Specifically, we are concerned in our study with three dimensions of homogeneity: (a) the extent to which units occupy similar positions in a division of labor, thus are homogeneous with regard to the tasks they perform; (b) the extent to which units occupy similar positions in a hierarchy of power and prestige; and (c) the similarity of status recruitment and role requirements among social units.

Homogeneity with regard to tasks, rank in a hierarchy of prestige and power, and personnel status–role requirements have been found by others to be important determinants of system integration.[15] We hypothesize that *ceteris paribus,* the more organizations are homogeneous with respect to tasks—the production of similar products or services—the more likely they share similar environmental and internal problems, the more likely it is that they will interact with each other in dealing with shared problems, and the more likely they are to pursue collective solutions to those problems.[16]

The more homogeneous organizations are with respect to rank in a hierarchy of prestige and power, the less competition and hostility there will be among them, and the more likely they are to support collective endeavors.[17] Finally, we hypothesize that the more homogeneous organizations are with respect to personnel status–role requirements, the more likely is agreement among them regarding shared problems and proposed collective solutions.[18]

We consider these to be independent dimensions of homogeneity. Our case studies reveal the degrees of homogeneity in the participating social units in terms of an overall ranking on these three dimensions. One of our cases, the PRIS system, is highly homogeneous; the SSIS system is medium-high, the CIN system medium, and CIS very low. Our data are not exacting enough to give each system a specific score, and in some instances homogeneity must be inferred indirectly (e.g., the difference in prestige between police agencies and courts being inferred from occupational prestige rankings). Nevertheless, as the text later indicates, we believe that our cases can be given relative rankings of homogeneity and that our hypothesis can be explored at some length.

Interdependence: A Prereform System Characteristic

The need for regularized communication among social units increases as a function of their interdependence.[19] "Interdependence" refers here to the extent to which the activities of one social unit affect the activities of others. That social units are interdependent qualifies them as members of a system but tells us nothing of the levels of integration in that system (e.g., the quantity and nature of social bonds among the units).

Thompson identifies three kinds of interdependence among social units.[20] Social units may exist under conditions of "pooled" interdependence, in which failure of one unit jeopardizes the entire system (e.g., in an electrical distribution network). In addition, social units may be sequentially interdependent, like workers in automobile assembly plants; or they may be reciprocally interdependent—that is, the input of one social unit is the output of one or several other social units (and vice versa), as occurs in telephone conversations.[21] Economists also refer to sectoral interdependence in input–output matrices and to market interdependence, where a few large firms in an industry share a finite market for their products.[22]

Interdependence among social units presents the units with uncertainties inasmuch as the activity of one is dependent on the activity of another. Uncertainty has been found to be psychologically and sociologically dysfunctional for the stability and in some cases the preservation of social units.[23] For this reason it is suggested that social units attempt to reduce uncertainty through a variety of formal and informal social mechanisms that act to coordinate unit activities and to increase the level of integration of the system.[24]

It has been found that workers who are interdependent develop informal norms to regulate the flow of work among themselves.[25] Similarly, increases in trade among nations have led to the development of formal economic unions.[26] The structure of formal organizations from this perspective can be seen as an attempt to coordinate the flow of work among interdependent units: departmentalization—the grouping together of highly interdependent units, standardization—the use of formal rules to guide and coordinate activities, and hierarchy—the use of authority to regulate the activities of interdependent units.[27]

Here we hypothesize that high and increasing levels of interdependence among social units are conducive to higher levels of social integration among those units, and supportive of efforts attempting to increase integration.

Moreover, efforts to increase the level of integration among units of low interdependence will be less likely to succeed and will be less stable than they would be if interdependence were high. Under the latter conditions of low interdependence, it will not be in the interest of individual social units to devote resources to increases in the level of system integration, since the returns from such investment will not measurably affect their own performance.

In the systems we investigate it is possible to attach relative rankings of interdependence based on available documents of unit exchanges and the statements of individuals within the units. We can characterize our systems according to their preform interdependence as follows:

High	1.	PRIS system
	2.	SSIS system
	3.	CIN system
Low	4.	CIS system

Homogeneity and Interdependence: A Tradeoff

There is some evidence that under conditions of high interdependence, the level of homogeneity of the interdependent units may become less important, especially if measures are taken to maintain social distance among heterogeneous units. The segregation of production from research units in certain organizations, and their articulation through limited channels of communication, is an example of high levels of integration being maintained among interdependent but heterogeneous social units.[28] Racial cleavages in combat groups decline in importance as interdependence, created in the battlefield situation, increases—a finding paralleled in other small group research.[29]

Therefore, we hypothesize a tradeoff between homogeneity and interdependence in relation to integration of a social system. If both qualities are high in a system, increases in integration would be supported. If both are low, further integration would be most difficult. If of opposite sign, one low and the other high, the effects should tend to cancel out.

Internal Integration: Unit Characteristics

The level of internal integration of social units may impede their inclusion into larger social entities or cause resistance to attempts to strengthen social bonds between units in an existing system. Thus civil wars in emerging nations, such as Nigeria, are attributed in large part to the resistance of prenationalist ethnic subgroups possessing very high levels of internal social, economic, and political integration.[30] Religious subgroups in colonial countries have generally been the first to oppose integration into colonial regimes, but they have also been the most resistant to nationalist movements.[31] Regional, religious, cultural, and economic subunit loyalties in India have prevented that nation-state from achieving a fully integrated market system, with the result that food grains are hoarded in surplus regions.[32] Regional loyalties in China, as late as the Cultural Revolution of 1966, have traditionally hindered political integration there.[33]

Although very high levels of unit integration may impede or even prevent integration into larger social systems, it has also been shown that maintenance of a certain level of subunit integration is functional for the integration of those subunits into larger systems. Village and regional loyalties of urban workers in industrializing African nations are considered to be a stabilizing factor in periods of transition from agrarian to industrial society; such loyalties are important in providing a flexible labor force to the cities, inhibiting the development of urban–rural cleavages, and in preserving traditional kinship structures.[34] In the United States the maintenance of political, economic, and cultural integration among immigrant ethnic groups has been identified as a factor contributing to their successful integration into the society.[35] The failure of blacks to achieve a similar "ethnic" pattern in America is attributed by others at least partly to their relatively low levels of political integration (e.g., the inability of blacks to successfully mobilize their populations behind community-based political machines). Lower levels of internal social and cultural integration have also been cited.[36] (It is recognized, however, that other factors, such as changes in the structure of the economy, the pervasiveness of racial prejudice in the United States, and the interpenetration of white and black cultures over 300 years have contributed to the low levels of social integration in the black communities.)

Thus it is by no means easy to ascertain the degree of internal unit integration of units into larger entities. However, evidence from other investigations appears to indicate that very high or very low levels of internal unit integration are the least conducive to integrating efforts. Under conditions of very low internal integration, unit elites lack the political support, economic resources, loyalty of their own members, and hence lack the bargaining power required for integration of their respective units into a larger system under favorable terms. The higher the level of internal unit integration, the more favorable the terms for inclusion into a larger system become. This effect may operate to the point at which individual units either control the integrating effort or demand more than the larger system can supply; further integration is then impossible, or force is required to reduce unit integration. This situation will prevail when individual units are of very high internal integration.

For these reasons we hypothesize that under conditions of high internal unit integration, resistance to system integrating efforts will be very high, and/or the terms under which such units are included into larger systems will be very favorable (i.e., highly integrated units will disproportionately control and direct the integration effort, therefore receiving a disproportionate share of the benefits of integration). Furthermore, we suggest that if resistance remains high, and if the demands of highly integrated units are very high, the integrating effort will cease or force will be resorted to.

Similarly, under conditions of low internal unit integration, resistance to system integrating efforts will be low, but the terms of the units inclusion in the system will be highly unfavorable with respect to the distribution of power and benefits within the system. Systems integrated under these conditions, we suggest, will be less stable, although they may "survive"; and they will produce alienation among members of the individual units (or at least fail to produce commitment to the larger system).

In local American systems of government, which constitute the unit and the larger system referents, respectively, in our case studies, the levels of internal integration of agencies of local and state governments differ markedly. How we measure or describe the levels of integration in a social unit depends on the unit being described and kinds of integration—social, political, economic, cultural—that we want to describe. Some units possess all these kinds of integration, such as political communities; others, such as unions with strong political and social integration but relatively weak economic and cultural integration, have only a few. Each of the systems we investigate can be described and ranked in relation to others along three dimensions of integration—political, cultural, and social. Specifically, we describe the internal integration of the social units in these systems according to: (a) the extent to which unit elites possess the resources to control unit members and to defend them from external review, (b) the extent to which the social unit is the predominant focus of members' occupational and political identification, and (c) the extent to which individuals interact predominantly with members of the same social unit.

The specific historical and political factors that explain how and why these differences among government agencies emerged are discussed in the case studies. Here we merely note that they exist and that they have consequences for integrative efforts, such as information systems. Compare, for instance, the different levels of internal integration characterizing local police agencies as opposed to local welfare agencies. The police agencies are semimilitary social units with correspondingly close supervision of members, as well as internal judicial–disciplinary mechanisms separate from civil law mechanisms.[37] Local agencies, with few exceptions, have prevented civilian review of their members' activities.[38] The local agency is the principal source of members' occupational (as opposed to professional) identity; esprit de corps is generally high relative to other agencies of government, and the agency is also a source of political attitudes for individual members. Interactions of members with one another is high both on and off the job.

Welfare agencies are markedly different. Members' work is less closely supervised and is subject more to the application of impersonal rules, while at the same time these agencies are frequent and popular targets of public investigation and criticism.[40] Professional caseworkers do not identify with the agency as much as with their profession;[41] in many instances, the welfare agency becomes a source of occupational frustration for caseworkers.[42] Other workers in the welfare agencies—clerical workers, largely—do not exhibit high levels of occupational or professional identification any more than clerical workers in insurance firms.[43] Interaction among members is confined mainly to the job, with few extra curricular interactions.

The foregoing brief description is indicative of the various levels of integration seen in local agencies of government. We believe that these levels of integration—whatever their historical origins—will have consequences for the resistance of these units to integrative efforts, such as information systems, and for the nature of their participation in information systems.

Within broad categories of levels of internal integration, we may rank the systems we study according to their respective degrees of internal integration:

High	1.	CIS
	2.	CIN
Medium	3.	PRIS
Low	4.	SSIS

THE CASES COMPARED ON INITIAL CONDITIONS AND RESISTANCE

The initial conditions of the four cases differ, as indicated in Table 3.

Table 3   Initial Conditions and Resistance

Cases ranked by resistance level[a]	Homogeneity	Interdependence	Internal integration
CIS	Low	Low	High
SSIS	Low	Medium	Low
CIN	Medium-High	Medium	Medium-High
PRIS	High	High	Medium-High

[a] From a high to a low resistance level.

As suggested in our discussion of the dependent variables, initial conditions appear to be directly related to the dependent variable resistance. We tentatively ranked the cases by level of resistance to the information system, with the CIS and SSIS systems creating the greatest resistance, followed by the CIN and PRIS systems, in which resistance was comparatively low.

From the preceding discussion of initial conditions and the table just presented, it can be seen that the systems encompassing agencies with characteristics favorable to higher levels of integration produced less resistance to information systems. Clearly the PRIS and CIN systems possess high to medium levels of homogeneity, interdependence, and internal integration; and we suggested that these qualities were conducive to higher levels of integration. The SSIS and CIS systems, in contrast, possessed low to medium levels of homogeneity and interdependence, which we predicted would lead to high levels of resistance to integration efforts. On the internal integration dimension, the SSIS system is very low, and CIS very high. Other studies have shown that neither condition is conducive to higher levels of integration.

STRATEGIES OF REFORM: THE SECOND
INDEPENDENT VARIABLE

Initial observation of the case studies pointed to the possibility that there were large differences among them in terms of who initiated the information system, who participated in its design and implementation, and who controlled the system in its day-to-day operation. Subsequently, differences in the kinds of strategy used to initiate and operate the systems seemed to explain some of the variance in the dependent variables, resistance and centralization.

A review of some of the literature concerned with political and administrative reforms was helpful in conceptualizing and in some cases directing observations of the case studies. Next we discuss the different types of reform process characterizing the cases, and we illustrate briefly the importance of this variable for explaining different levels of resistance and centralization reported in the cases.

The Process of Reform: Requisites of Initiation

Bureaucratic reform projects are never carried out by individual social units—although they are frequently initiated by individual units. The principal reason for this is the scarcity of resources necessary to the attainment of the projects' objectives. That is, a reform project, as much as if not more than any existing organizational structure, is dependent on the money, political influence, social prestige, and expertise of other social units, the degree of such dependence varying with the circumstances.[44] The initial conditions discussed tell us much about the social milieu in which a reform project operates and are suggestive of the ease with which the reform project can mobilize constituent resources, but they tell us nothing of the concrete social mechanisms used to initiate a reform project. Even if the initial conditions are extremely favorable, reform projects may not begin; or conditions may be very hostile, and yet a successful reform project will result. The explanation to this seemingly paradoxical situation lies not with further study of "background" factors, but with an examination of the mechanisms utilized by a reform project both to initiate and to maintain itself as a viable social entity.

Specifically, we suggest that the natural history of reform projects may be fruitfully considered in two stages, which are distinguished from each other by the kinds of mechanisms observed and by their functions for the reform project.

In the first stage—the initiation stage—reform projects encounter two generic problems in the process of securing the support of other social units: (a) they must have a minimal consensus on the goals or ends of the reform among participating social units, and (b) they must obtain the expertise necessary to carry out the reform (e.g., project leaders and a trained staff possessing the social skills and specialized knowledge appropriate to the reform). The mechanisms designed in response to these two problems correspond to the goal attainment and adaptation structures that Parsons identifies as necessary to an ongoing social unit.[45] Weber in turn suggested that a consensus on ends and technical expertise are the general conditions of a legitimate, legal-rational social order considered as a state of affairs.[46] Here we do not wish to differentiate reform projects according to whether they possess legitimacy or with respect to the structures necessary to their maintenance as stable, ongoing social entities. Rather, we wish to explore the process of legitimation, the process of initiating a stable social order. That is, we are interested in the kinds of activity engaged in to produce a state of legitimacy, or alternatively, to initiate a reform project.

In the second stage reform projects encounter a different set of problems which can be called problems of maintenance. To execute the goals decided on in the first stage, the project must come to exercise control over constituent units; as a consequence, it may encounter stiff resistance to the implementation of reform. In addition, the reform project must attempt to maintain the commitment of members of the project, largely because its maintenance and execution rely on constituents, and it must develop mechanisms in response to this problem (e.g., newsletters, seminars, training groups).

Although we argue that all bureaucratic reform projects face these two problems—generally referred to as problems of adaptation and problems of maintenance—there are a variety of specific social structures (i.e., concrete mechanisms) capable of solving them. The structure chosen depends on the initial conditions described earlier, the social character of those who initiate the reform, and the relative power of the constituents.

The Social Character of Initiators: Elites

A basic distinction is to be made with regard to the social origins of the units initiating reforms. When the body initiating a reform is a member unit of the system to be reformed, we refer to an *internal elite*. When the initiator is a member of another system, we refer to an *external elite*.[47] For instance, if the governor of a state or his staff begins a reform of local police practices, we would label it an externally initiated reform even though, as in the CIS case here, the external elite is, loosely speaking, a member of the same governmental system (i.e., state government) as the reform constituents. If the governor initiated a reform in his own executive branch, we would refer to an internally initiated reform.

Our general definition of "elite" is as follows: a social unit possessing a disproportionate amount of resources and effective means, with the result that it can disproportionately affect the behavior of other social units. Elites have been distinguished from nonelites in terms of the amount of interaction they initiate and the extent to which they allocate resources to guiding social processes.[48] We argue here that these behavioral features of elites are a product of their possession of disproportionate resources and effective means (identitive, utilitarian, and/or coercive resources) relative to other social units.

With special regard to reform projects, we make two more distinctions. When one constituent of a reform project exercises a disproportionate influence over the reform, we identify the condition as a high level of *elitism*—a reference to the distribution of power within the reform. Second, when a reform project is controlled and operated by units that devote all their energy and resources to the operation and maintenance of the reform project, we refer to those units as a *system elite*. As we shall see, not all reform projects are maintained by system elites. Some are guided by temporary coalitions of external and internal elites, others by a coalition of internal elites.[49]

The determination of who initiates a reform project—internal or external elite groups—is consequential for understanding the mechanisms of reform adopted. External elites are less likely than internal elites to possess the initial legitimacy and the requisite technical expertise appropriate to the reform. As members of systems not participated in by the constituents, external elites are less likely to share the goals of constituent members. In turn, lacking expertise necessary to the reform, external elites are more likely to "import" expertise from outside than to recruit it from constituent units of the reform. The importation of expertise (e.g., the hiring of a consultant firm) is a method of attaining expertise rapidly, but it carries the risk that the expertise generated will be inappropriate to the task.[50]

Mechanisms of Adaptation and Maintenance: A Morphology of Reforms

Bureaucratic reform projects can be distinguished from one another according to the mechanisms of adaptation and maintenance they employ. We suggest that there are two types of adaptive mechanisms—cooptation, and recruitment of system elites—and that both are designed to produce an initial consensus on the ends of reform and to recruit sufficient expertise to initiate the project. Selznick describes "informal cooptation" as " a mechanism of comprehensive adjustment, permitting a formal organization to enhance its chances for survival by accommodating itself to existing centers of interest and power," and he distinguishes this mechanism from "formal cooptation" in which groups are selected by the reform project to "share the responsibilities for or the administrative burdens of power, rather than power itself."[51]

We see with Selznick that cooptation is one social device for adapting the goals of a reform project to the social realities of the environment. Cooptation refers to the general process whereby the constituents of a reform project are brought into the leadership of the reform, to share power and/or to share the burdens of administration.

But our data and materials provide an example of another kind of adaptive mechanism. We refer to this kind of mechanism as "recruitment of a system elite." Whereas cooptation is designed to create a coalition of external and internal elites, or the impression thereof, recruitment of a system elite involves the creation of a formal organizational entity directed solely by a system elite (e.g., full-time members of the reform project whose central interest is the maintenance of the project).[52]

The recruitment of a system elite can also be distinguished in terms of its content. Content is formal when members are selected to the system elite to share the burdens of power and administration, generally after the central questions of goals and methods of reforms have been decided. Content is informal when members are selected to accommodate local centers of opposition and power, in some cases to abdicate control over the reform to these locally powerful groups.

The two kinds of adaptive mechanisms and their two different contents, formal versus informal, serve to demarcate four strategies of reform we found useful in describing our case studies (Table 4).

Table 4   Models of Bureaucratic Reform

Content of adaptive mechanism	Adaptive mechanism	
	Cooptation	System elite
Formal	Notables model	Reputational elite
Informal	Pluralist model	Collegial elite

We briefly describe each of the four types of reform project, suggesting how each of the cases fits into this framework.

The Pluralist Model of Reform. The Pluralist model of reform adheres closely to the kind of cooptation described by Selznick as "informal." Here groups with the capacity to completely scuttle a reform project or to seriously impair its implementation are brought into a coalition with external initiating elites. Representatives of these powerful groups are selected by the groups themselves, and they are expected to protect their groups' interests when reform policies are being made.

Generally, such reforms are less elitist than other models. That is, no single group or social unit dominates the reform; instead, a number of social units are found to be relatively equal in power, although in different areas. Diverse special interest groups are capable of protecting their own interests without endangering the interests of other groups. Thus in the example of the TVA described by Selznick, both the land grant colleges and the county farm agents in the region are capable of benefiting materially from the project without coming into serious conflicts.[53]

In the Pluralist model, the criterion for including significant interest groups in the reform is the power of those groups to prevent the reform from taking place or to impair its progress. This power has two characteristics. First, influential special interest groups, which may include other agencies of government, can often resist governmental efforts through political lobbying at the federal, state, or local levels, thus preventing the reform project from receiving the resources necessary for initiation. Second, these included groups typically possess the expertise required to implement the reform. In the TVA, the expertise needed to design irrigation projects, dams, hydroelectric plants, and soil conservation programs, was "possessed" in a sense by local interest groups. The TVA might have "imported" such expertise—for example, by hiring consultant firms or by training its own experts to guide its policies. However, both these alternatives would have been very time consuming and probably would have generated expertise inappropriate to the region. For instance, the Community Action Projects discussed in Chapter 4 were criticized for generating solutions to nonexistent problems.[54] The structural basis for this phenomenon is, we suggest, the failure to incorporate existing pools of local knowledge and expertise into the CAP projects. It is exhibited more clearly in our study of the CIS project in Chapter 9.

In our studies, the case that most closely approximates the Pluralist model is the Criminal Information Network (CIN) of Western State. CIN, described in Chapter 10, was initiated by an executive agency of state government to establish a statewide information exchange. Four local regions had already built area criminal information systems, thus acquiring the expertise and equipment called for by the CIN project. In addition, the regional systems were supported by their respective county and city governments, local police agencies, and the state Association of Peace Officers (a powerful local police lobby). Accommodation to these centers of regional power and expertise was thus a necessity for the CIN project, as described in detail in Chapter 10.

The Pluralist model of reform, although accommodating to constituent interests, implies at the same time a reduction in the influence and control of external elites over the substance and direction of reform. As concessions to powerful constituent interests are consummated, the reform project loses some of its capacity to induce social change among constituent units. Frequently, the reform project becomes merely a resource conduit that functions to maintain rather than change constituent unit behavior.[55]

Thus the Pluralist model bears the risk that reform will suffer what Tennessee Williams called the "catastrophe of success." External initiating elites, sensitive precisely to this possibility, often choose another model of reform to prevent the dilution of reform goals.[56]

Finally, the success the Pluralist model obtains is a function of its capacity to offer material benefits to powerful constituent groups. When this is not possible—because it would dilute the reform goals, because initiating elites lack the resources to deliver such benefits, or because of hostility and competition among constituent groups that share organizational domains—the Pluralist model is not appropriate. The use of adaptive mechanisms such as the Pluralist model is contingent on the initial conditions observed in the constituent units.

We suggest that the Pluralist model is feasible when the constituent units are heterogeneous, when they exist under conditions of facilitative interdependence (as opposed to competitive interdependence), and when the constituent units possess moderate to high levels of internal integration. By dividing the reform into specialized and insulated packages, each producing benefits for special interest groups, the Pluralist model is capable of tolerating diversity. Under conditions of facilitative interdependence, or in some cases very low interdependence of any kind, the constituent units are less likely to engage in competition with one another for the benefits of reform, and more likely to support coexistence under a single umbrella of reform. Last, when the constituent units possess very little internal integration, the Pluralist model simply should not be resorted to, since under these conditions the units are of very low power, and there is no reason for negotiating with powerless constituents. Under conditions of very high internal integration, the constituent units may decide not to negotiate with the reform project; indeed, this occurs frequently during local reform attempts to bring national health agencies into local health coordinating exchanges.

Thus the Pluralist model is not a panacea for reform projects but is very much dependent on the initial conditions of the constituent units. When initiating elites are willing to tolerate diversity, the dilution of reform goals, and the loss of some external elite control over the project, however, the model would appear to be appropriate.

The Collegial Model. The Collegial model of reform is present whenever external initiating elites, or in some cases a group of internal initiating elites, successfully encourage a number of groups to form a coalition to develop their own reform with little or no participation by external elites. Certain Community Action Projects are typical of this model of reform. Federal "seed" money establishes a local coalition of agencies or groups that subsequently plan and initiate a reform project. External elites participate only to the extent of providing initial planning resources; ultimately, it is expected that the local reform will develop independent sources of income.[57]

The Collegial model is typically the least elitist—no single unit dominates the reform, and all units have equal capacity to veto or propose items of the reform. The mechanism utilized most frequently in the initiation of a Collegial reform is the advisory committee, where all constituents are represented by persons chosen by the constituent groups. (Thus it differs from similar committees in the Reputational Elite and Notables models of reform discussed below). The advisory committee in this model has two functions: (*a*) to produce a consensus among participants on the goals and methods of the reform, and (*b*) to train and recruit the expertise from constituent units required to implement the reform.

Once the reform project has produced an initial consensus among participants and a program has been adopted for implementation, the advisory committee is reduced in size and is renamed a "policy committee." That is, the day-to-day administration of the project and the subsequent planning are carried out by a permanent system elite composed of members from the constituent groups. Here the Collegial model distinguishes itself from other models of reform in that the system elite—the unit that controls the implementation of the reform—is typically organized by periodic rotation of the leaders from constituent groups. The constituent groups "loan" one of their members to the reform project for a year. Such an arrangement differs from the Pluralist model, in which constituent representatives serve occasionally on policy committees but have no administrative responsibilities, and from the Reputational Elite model, discussed below, in which selected notables become full-time members of the reform project.

Only the Collegial model functions to minimize the likelihood of the reform taking on a life of its own, independent of the constituent organizations. The periodic rotation of the reform's system elite preserves the multiple role affiliations of the elite members and serves to make them more responsive to constituent interests.

External elites in the Collegial model exert very little control (even less than in the Pluralist model) over the substance of the reform; indeed, they tend to withdraw from the reform after it is initiated, playing only a supportive role. As a result, the only changes brought about by the Collegial model of reform are those considered by constituent groups to be in their interest. The very structure of the Collegial model ensures that the reform is self-serving to its constituents. Like the Pluralist model, however, the Collegial types of reform tends to produce more stable projects and a higher consensus among participants.

In our studies the reform most closely adhering to the Collegial model is the Police Regional Information System (PRIS). Initiated by a small group of local police agencies, and supported by city–county political elites, PRIS has developed into a regional reform involving more than ninety police agencies. Each constituent contributes members to the leadership of the project on a rotating basis, and each receives a number of material benefits from participation—higher warrant service rates and increased auto theft arrests, not to mention favorable public relations.

The Collegial model is uniquely suited to certain initial conditions of the participant units. We suggest that the Collegial model be used when constituent units of the reform are highly homogeneous, when they exist under conditions of high facilitative interdependence, and when constituent units possess a high degree of internal integration. The structure and recruitment of the reform's system elite allow individual constituents to maintain a high internal integration within their units and prevents the reform from incurring costs for its members. The higher the levels of facilitative and reciprocal interdependence among constituent units (e.g., the more appropriate actions by one unit facilitate the task of another, and vice versa), the more likely will be their voluntary cooperation in common endeavors aimed at coordinating that interdependence for mutual benefit. High degrees of homogeneity of task, personnel, and rank are conducive to creating areas of mutual benefit among constituent groups, tending also to diminish levels of competition among those units.

Besides resting on unique initial conditions, the use of the Collegial model depends on the toleration of external elites—who either initiate or support the Collegial reform—for the kinds of reform produced by Collegial models. The Collegial model is analogous to self-regulation by industries and professional groups, whose history suggests that self-regulation can lead to self-enhancement at the expense of other groups in the society. Insofar as external elites are incapable—through lack of sufficient power or lack of expertise—of directing and implementing reforms of some groups in the society, and insofar as external elites find the Collegial reforms tolerable, the Collegial model appears to be appropriate and is frequently used.[58] As we argue below, the recent history of reform among local police agencies closely adheres to the conditions named.

The Notables Model of Reform.   The Notables model is a transitory phenomenon. Either it is used to support rather short-lived reform efforts or it serves as a transition to some other model, typically the Reputational Elite model discussed below.[59]

The Notables model begins when an external initiating elite selects certain highly visible individuals from the groups to be reformed. The claim is made that this body of notables is in some sense representative of interests involved in the reform. In fact, since the selection of notables is made by external elites, usually before the constituents of the reform have the time to produce a consensus among themselves through discussion and debate, the body of notables largely reflects the initiating elite's opinion of who would be most "useful" to the reform effort.

The criterion for selection to the body of notables, which generally takes the form of an advisory committee, is "usefulness" to the reform, which means (a) familiarity with the operations and "politics" of the constituents, (b) influence within the constituent groups, and (c) a favorable disposition toward the reform.

Once selected, the body of coopted notables serves a number of vital functions for the reform project. First, the notables provide the reform with an aura of legitimacy and presumed consensus among constituents when in fact neither exists. This is especially important when the reform will depend on the support of third parties (e.g., state legislatures and federal departments that can allocate grants). The constituents themselves may well recognize that the project lacks their support, but distant third parties are less likely to know. Second, the body of notables serves to sensitize the initiating elites to the location and nature of opposition to the reform, and to suggest ways in which the reform can either pacify that opposition (e.g., through changes in the reform plan) or neutralize it. The announcement of the reform plan, like the selection of the notables itself, acts as a "trial balloon" that brings the opposition into the open. Third, the body of notables is selected by external elites not to represent the interests of their constituency but, rather, to "use their influence" within their constituency to generate support for the reform.[60]

None of the foregoing is meant to imply duplicity on the part of the external initiating elites or the coopted notables. Both groups may believe that the reform is in the interests of the constituents, who will support it once it has been presented and explained in the appropriate manner. On the other hand, it is also thought generally that if the decision is left to the constituents, narrow political considerations, even outright irrationality, will prevent any reform from occurring. Thus the concern and need for a well-orchestrated and carefully prepared campaign to obtain the support of constituents and third parties.

The Notables model is characterized by a high degree of elitism. External initiating elites decide on the nature of the reform, involving the constituents later, and then only to consider problems of implementation and minor alterations. Constituents in this model are involved, in Selznick's words, to share the burdens and responsibilities of power, and not power itself.[61]

In part this explains the short duration of the Notables model in practice, as well as its relative instability. First, the reforms begun through the use of this model are closely identified with the external initiating elites, and in fact generally remain in their complete control. Opposition to the reform uses this fact to attack not only the substance of the reform (i.e., the desirability of its goals) but also its political structure. The reform effort, whatever its merits, can thus be perceived and criticized as external interference in the affairs of the constituents.[62]

The requisites of long-term reform projects constitute a second reason for the short duration of reforms of the Notables model. A long-term reform project is under pressure to stabilize its procedures and leadership. A relatively permanent organization, plus full-time bureaucrats and a professional staff, are required to operate the reform. These requirements of maintenance cannot be fulfilled by part-time, coopted notables who retain membership in their constituencies. For these reasons, we suggest, the Notables model is of limited effectiveness in long-term efforts or is predominantly used in reforms that have short-term goals and consequently do not face problems of maintenance.

As noted previously, the Notables model is typically utilized by external elites when the social milieu is thought to be hostile to the proposed reform. In terms of our paradigm, the Notables model is suited to conditions of low homogeneity, low or competitive interdependence, and high internal unit integration. By selecting notables favorably disposed to its cause, and by minimizing direct participation of constituents while maximizing access to them, those employing the Notables model can reduce and fragment opposition to the reform, making real concessions to constituents only when absolutely necessary. The Notables model is not especially successful in obtaining resources and expertise from its own constituents, having to be satisfied with their acquiescence at best; third parties, however, frequently can be induced to provide these requisites. In our investigation the eastern state's Criminal Identification System (CIS) closely adhered in its initial stages to the Notables model—with near disastrous results. Lacking the support of constituents and often importing expertise and knowledge from outside the community of reform, reform efforts utilizing the Notables model are less stable and produce lower levels of commitment to the reform than either the Pluralist or the Collegial model.

The Reputational Elite Model of Reform. Our fourth model of reform, the Reputational Elite model, is similar in many respects to the Notables model. However, persons selected to the reputational elite lose formal membership in their original constituency and become full-time members of the reform project. The reputational elite is thus a system elite recruited from constituent groups. It frequently develops out of a Notables model with the selection of notables to a permanent commission, civil association, project, or in some cases a new agency of government, which then carries out the reform decided on by the external elites. Floyd Hunter, for example, describes the use of a Reputational Elite model of reform in a southern city in which new projects were initiated by "power leaders" but carried out by committees and commissions composed of less powerful but well-known notables selected from involved constituencies.[63]

A Reputational Elite model is especially appropriate when the initiating elite does not wish to be identified with reform and/or when such identification could inhibit the maintenance of the reform. In addition, the Reputational Elite model is used when a permanent or long-term effort is required, such as a community redevelopment board, a community action project, or a new agency of government designed to deliver a new service. In these and other cases, full-time leaders are recruited by initiating elites.

The basis of selection of the reputational elite is quite similar to that of the Notables model; besides personal competence, it emphasizes a favorable disposition toward the reform, intimate familiarity with constituents in the reform, and above all, influence and a good reputation among the constituents.

The principal function of the reputational elite in the early stages of a reform is not to represent constituent interests but to influence participating constituents to accept the reform and to create an aura of legitimacy that can be used to persuade third parties, as well as constituents, to support the reform. In long-term projects requiring some support from constituents in the form of resources and expertise, the hiring into the leadership of the reform of well-known and respected personnel from the nonelite constituents is expected to console the constituents in the feeling that "one of their own" is representing their interests. Typically, the leadership positions in the Reputational Elite model are filled by members from the most resistant constituents, and they are expected to "turn off" any revolts or organized opposition that might crop up among these resistant constituents.[64]

The theoretical basis of both the Reputational Elite and Notables models, which rely on selection of high-status, respected members from constituent groups, is suggested in certain studies of small groups. Specifically, it has been found that high-status members of groups deviate more from group norms than low-status members (where member ranking is either by self-perception or peer ranking), and high-status members are more successful than low-status members in defining the group situation.[65]

After the very early stages of initiation, the external initiating elites withdraw from active participation in the reform project. These external groups continue to exercise influence on the reform, however, largely through their selection of the reform's leadership. Once external elites withdraw, the reform is expected to be self-maintaining.

As with the Notables model, the Reputational Elite model is resorted to when the social milieu is not amenable to the reform. The Reputational Elite model is used under conditions of low homogeneity, competitive interdependence, and/or high internal unit integration. The selection of a system elite from the most hostile but important constituents tends to defuse their opposition and to render them accessible to the reform. Real concessions made to powerful constituents seem to lessen their opposition to cooperating with other constituents, toward whom they feel hostile and competitive.

The reforms that utilize a Reputational Elite model produce low levels of commitment among constituents—acquiescence being the typical accommodation of constituents—and they are less stable than either Pluralist or Collegial reforms. Although offering the promise of great change, sometimes even radical change, Reputational Elite reforms more often than not lack the support of constituents necessary to produce these changes. This is well illustrated in two of our case studies (SSIS and CIS) which ultimately rely on a Reputational Elite model.

ELITES, POWER, AND REFORM PROJECTS: MAINTENANCE OF REFORMS

The conditions under which a reform is initiated, and its methods of adapting to those conditions, largely determine the methods used by the reform project to maintain itself over time. The two problems of maintenance faced by a reform project, aside from the need for continual adaptation to its environment, are increasing its control over constituent units and maintaining among the constituents a sufficient degree of commitment to the reform.

Reforms can be distinguished in terms of the kinds of power they rely on to maintain themselves. "Power" refers here to the capacity of one social unit to cause other social units to act in a manner desired by the former, and it rests on a stratified distribution of resources among social units. In turn, we distinguish three kinds of power: coercive, utilitarian, and identitive power, each one contingent on the possession of appropriate resources.[66] Thus coercive power involves the use or threatened use of force and relies on the possession by one social unit of superior means of violence. Utilitarian power entails the use of money to induce others to act in a desired manner and rests on a stratified distribution of economic resources. Last, identitive power involves the use of social status or prestige to control the actions of others.

Whether the exercise of power is thought to be legitimate by the units acted on is problematic in each case. The use of any kind of power can be distinguished according to whether it serves to induce or to compel others to act. The use of any kind of power as a negative sanction (e.g., physical destruction of another unit) is referred to as *compulsion*. The use of any kind of power as a positive sanction (e.g., physical protection of another social unit, increased economic support or enhancement of that unit's prestige) is referred to as *inducement*.[67]

Others have argued persuasively that the kind of power exercised to maintain a social unit is related to the nature of commitments that members develop toward that social unit. We suggest, however, that such a relationship depends on whether power is used to compel or induce members to act in a certain way. Thus it is frequently said that exerting coercive power on a social unit tends to produce alienative involvement among members to that unit.[68] But superior force can be used to protect as well as to compel; and when used to protect, coercive force acts as an inducement. Coercive force applied as an inducement is not inherently alienating. Thus one important basis of Japanese–American cooperation since 1945 has been the use of American strategic power to protect Japan, which in turn induces Japan to act in concert with the United States in military and other matters.

Our Notables and Reputational Elite models of reform, although they initially use power to induce other units to act appropriately, soon come to rely on the use of *power to compel* participating units to exhibit the desired behavior. Both models rely less on constituent resources and more on resources supplied by third parties. Failing to obtain the voluntary compliance of constituents to the program of reform, thus seeing the maintenance of the project and the attainment of its goals threatened, the elites have recourse to various kinds of compulsion.[69]

The CIS case study illustrates the use of compulsion to maintain a reform project. Initiated by Republican party officials on the governor's staff, CIS received planning resources from the state legislature. During the planning stage it became clear that many constituents of the reform would not voluntarily participate or lend their resources to the reform. Resources to implement the reform were obtained, again from the legislature. When constituent agencies to the reform continued and increased resistance to the project, the legislature was once more relied on—this time to compel constituents to participate in the reform. The consequences of the use of a Reputational Elite model and the use of power to compel constituents to act appropriately are discussed in Chapter 9.

The Pluralist and Collegial models of reform rely typically on *power as an inducement* to maintain themselves (i.e., to control the behavior of constituents). The Collegial and Pluralist models are used under conditions favorable to reform, when initial consensus regarding the reform itself is likely to be high. Whereas initially the Pluralist model relies more than the Collegial on external resources, actual implementation of the project is dependent on constituent compliance. This compliance is obtained by including constituents in the reform project at a very early stage, but it is maintained and increased through positive inducements. Collegial reforms tend to rely almost exclusively on positive inducements to constituents to maintain high levels of compliance with the reform project.[70]

A good example of a Pluralist reform model is provided by the history of the Office of Economic Opportunity (OEO), which was initiated by a group of advisors close to Presidents Kennedy and Johnson. The OEO planners quickly realized that poverty had no constituency: those it utimately hoped to benefit were the least powerful groups in the country. The only hope for congressional support of OEO lay in including the departments of Labor and Health, Education, and Welfare in the reform project at a very early stage. Once funded, OEO programs in education, employ-

ment, and job training depended for implementation on the compliance of
Labor and HEW. This compliance was forthcoming as long as OEO could
supply the funding for these new programs. In return, the constituents of
OEO provided its principal base of congressional support.[71]

For an example of reliance on inducements to control and increase the
commitment of constituents in a Collegial reform project, see Chapter 8.

THE CASES COMPARED BY POLITICAL REFORM PROCESS

The differences in process and mechanisms of political reform utilized by
our four vases can be illustrated by Table 5.

Table 5   Models of Bureaucratic Reform

Content of adaptive mechanism	Adaptive mechanisms	
	Cooptation	System elite
Formal	Notables model: CIS	Reputational elite: SSIS
Infromal	Pluralist model: CIN	Collegial elite: PRIS

THE BUREAUCRATIC REFORM PROCESS AND THE
DEPENDENT VARIABLES

In our case studies the information systems that utilized methods of reform
characteristic of the Notables and Reputational Elite models tended to
produce high levels of resistance from user agencies and to be supportive
of greater administrative centralization. In the CIS and SSIS case studies,
the user agencies were allowed only minimal participation, largely to share
in the burdens of administering the systems. Both these cases are examples
of central executives gaining control over significant resources at the expense of the participating line agencies, ultimately coming to utilize these
resources to exert greater authority and closer supervision over these
agencies.

In the CIN and PRIS case studies, which utilize methods of reform similar to those of the Pluralist and Collegial models, user agencies were
granted a large role in the design and implementation of the information
system. Resistance to the information was either low or nonexistent, as in

the PRIS case. Moreover, neither system resulted in significant redistribution of control over information resources; thus neither system is supportive of levels of administrative centralization higher than those which existed before. In one case, PRIS, the user police agencies control the information system entirely. As a result, the system functions to maintain the traditional police monopoly over critical information.

THE ROLE OF A CONCEPTUAL FRAMEWORK

The conceptual framework just discussed, which represents an attempt to learn how initial conditions and types of reform strategy influence the levels of resistance and centralization observed in the cases, is not itself proved by the case studies. Instead, the framework is intended to serve as a guide to the cases, as one way of looking at the empirical materials. I found this framework fruitful for answering the central question, What are the social and political factors that intervene between a new technology and its social consequences?

The utility of a conceptual framework is measured by its capacity to guide the student to an understanding of the subject matter. At the same time it blinds him to aspects of reality that are not considered by the framework. This becomes all the more troublesome in exploratory studies of new areas of intellectual concern, where neither convenient guideposts from previous studies nor accurate measurement methods are available to afford the student any notion of "information loss."

Thus a political scientist may suggest that our conceptual framework is inadequate for comparing the very diverse local governments we examine, and the historian may argue that our cases focus on entirely different areas of government activity, each with a distinctive social history, which together make comparison dangerous.

Perhaps, then, it is appropriate to remind the reader that each of the local governments we describe is a highly complex entity, subject to its own unique past, and guided by men of diverse views and interests.

We have attempted to account for the diversities that characterize the case studies, and to limit comparative statements to a low level of analysis. Consequently, since we are comparing differences in orders of magnitude, not measures along some interval scale, the concepts and their measures may appear to be rather vague.

The utility of a conceptual framework is ultimately judged in terms of additional studies of the subject conducted from diverse intellectual perspectives. Hopefully, future studies will attempt to verify some of the hypotheses suggested here, in addition to providing alternative frameworks for viewing the subject.

NOTES

1.   Anthony Downs, "A Realistic Look at the Final Payoffs from Urban Data Systems," *Public Administration Review*, **27** (September 1967), pp. 204–209.

2.   Aaron Wildavsky, "The Political Economy of Efficiency," *Public Interest*, No. 8 (Summer 1967), pp. 30–48.

3.   Downs, *op. cit.*

4.   George C. Homans, *The Human Group*, New York: Harcourt Brace Jovanovich, 1950, p. 369.

5.   See, for example, Homans, *op. cit.*, Chapters 5 and 6. For a discussion of homogeneity and its bearing on metropolitan, as well as national communities, see Philip E. Jacobs and James Toscano (eds.), *The Integration of Political Communities*, Philadelphia: Lippincott, 1964, pp. 1–46. See also Karl Deutsch, *Nationalism and Social Communication*, Cambridge, Mass.: M.I.T. Press, 1953, pp. 72–80.

6.   Homans, *op. cit.*, Chapter 8; diffusion studies typically find interaction within groups occurring predominantly among homogeneous subsets, which provide a network through which innovations filter. See James B. Coleman, Elihu Katz, and Herbert Menzel, *Medical Innovation: A Diffusion Study*, Indianapolis, Ind.: Bobbs-Merrill, 1966.

7.   John Kenneth Galbraith, *American Capitalism: The Concept of Counter Vailing Power*, Boston: Houghton Mifflin, 1956. Markets characterized by a low degree of product differentiation, such as the basic metals and chemicals industries, are subject to high levels of concentration and oligopolistic cooperation among major producers. See Joan Robinson, *Economics of Imperfect Competition*, 2nd ed., London: Macmillan, 1969.

8.   This is the kind of heterogeneity that John Locke (and later, of course, Emile Durkheim), saw as characteristic of modern societies under conditions of national, unrestricted markets; it was thought that this quality would weave modern societies together. Each man would become dependent on others, and nations on other nations, as specialization proceeded; presumably men and nations alike would take account of their dependence on others and conduct themselves accordingly. Although men emerged from the yoke of tradition, they also created intricate webs of interdependence. See John Locke, *Two Treatises on Government*, edited by Peter Laslett, 2nd ed., Cambridge: Cambridge Press, 1961, "On Property," Chapter 5; Emile Durkheim, *The Division of Labor in Society*, New York: Free Press, 1960, pp. 256–282.

9.   See Harry Townsend, *Scale, Innovation, Merger and Monopoly*, New York: Oxford University Press, 1968. See also Amitai Etzioni, *Political Unification*, New York: Holt, Rinehart, & Winston, 1965, for a discussion of political unifications under conditions of heterogeneity.

10.   See Luther Gerlach, *People, Power, Change: Movements of Social Transformation*, Indianapolis, Ind.: Bobbs-Merrill, 1970, pp. 79–97. See also Rupert Emerson, *From Empire to Nation*, Cambridge, Mass.: Harvard University Press, 1961.

11. Murdoch found that under conditions of threat to a system of interaction, high-power and low-power participants developed contractual norms to preserve the interaction more readily than under other conditions. See Peter H. Murdock, "The Development of Contractual Norms in the Interdependent Dyad with Power Differentiation," *Dissertation Abstracts,* **27** (1966), (1-A), p. 253. To account for divergent findings with regard to homogeneity and group cohesiveness, Blau and Scott suggest that the salience of homogeneous factors varies and depends on the relevance of those factors to task completion problems. See Peter M. Blau and W. Richard Scott, *Formal Organizations,* San Francisco: Chandler, 1962, p. 109. Experimentally changing the salience of group memberships has been shown to affect attitudinal responses. See W. W. Charters, Jr., and Theodore M. Newcomb, "Some Attitudinal Effects of Experimentally Increased Salience of a Membership Group," in Eleanor E. Maccoby, Theodore M. Newcomb, and Eugene L. Hartley (eds.), *Readings in Social Psychology,* 3rd ed., New York: Holt, Rinehart, & Winston, 1958, pp. 276–280.

12. Nathan Glazer and Daniel P. Moynihan, *Beyond the Melting Pot,* 2nd ed., Cambridge, Mass.: M.I.T. Press, 1970.

13. See Bernard Berelson, Paul Lazarsfeld, and William McPhee, *Voting,* Chicago: University of Chicago Press, 1954. For the effect of cross-cutting pressures on political integration, see Karl Deutsch, "Transaction Flows as Indicators of Political Cohesion," in Jacob and Toscano, *op. cit.,* Chapter 3. Deutsch argues that cross-cutting pressures reduce support for integration efforts but prevent conflict among diverse groups participating in an integration effort. Harold Cruse, as well as other commentators on the politics of minority groups, condemns middle-class black intellectuals for making accommodations with whites in the hope of receiving rewards through participation in the larger American society. If this is an accurate assessment of black politics, it would tend to support the notion that cross-cutting pressures reduce conflict among heterogeneous groups. See Harold Cruse, "Revolutionary Nationalism and the Afro-American," *Studies on the Left,* **2,** No. 3 (1962).

14. Gerlach, *op. cit.,* Chapters 3 and 6.

15. See, for example, two excellent articles on interorganizational coordination and exchange, Eugene Litwak and Lydia F. Hylton, "Interorganizational Analysis: A Hypothesis on Coordinating Agencies," *Administrative Science Quarterly,* **6** (1962), pp. 395–415; and Sol Levine and Paul E. White, "Exchange as a Conceptual Framework for the Study of Interorganizational Relationships," *Administrative Science Quarterly,* **5** (1960), pp. 583–601. Both articles show how organizations sharing a common domain—performing similar tasks—are likely to develop exchange relationships partly because such organizations share certain organizational problems (i.e., where and how to obtain clients) and because they possess common values, such as health goals.

16. Under some conditions, organizations performing similar tasks may be characterized by "competitive interdependence" (e.g., a zero-sum condition). But even here competition is frequently avoided by specialization (e.g., the specialization of volunteer health agencies by or through informal agreements—contracts—dividing up the shared domain, as is common in oligopolistic industries). For a distinction between facilitative interdependence and competitive interdependence, see Edwin J. Thomas, "Effects of Facilitative Role Interdependence on Group Functioning," *Human Relations,* **19** (1957), pp. 347–366.

17. Levine and White, *op. cit.,* found that large national social service organizations possessing large assets could avoid interorganizational exchanges with less powerful local agencies and could continue to compete with those agencies, whereas the less powerful agencies were forced to enter into contractual relationships to preserve their own stability. See also the small group research of Murdoch, *op. cit.,* who discovered that under conditions of gross inequality, the more powerful members were more likely to be aggressive toward the less powerful, and less likely to reach contractual understandings.

18. It may appear that organizations that share tasks also must share similar status-role requirements of organizational members. This may sound logical, but investigation reveals that it is not factual. Within a single county, the many organizations that share the task of delivering health services to the community may be widely divergent with respect to the types of personnel they employ (Litwak and Hylton, *op. cit.*). Specialization enters to create diversity of status-role requirements. Even among organizations assigned precisely the same task but performing it in different jurisdictions (e.g., rural vs. urban judicial districts, or state police and county sheriffs), specialization can induce wide discrepancies in the status-role requirements. Thus homogeneity of status-role requirements must be considered to be independent from task homogeneity.

19. Durkheim, *op. cit.,* pp. 256–257.

20. James D. Thompson, *Organizations in Action,* New York: McGraw-Hill, 1967, p. 56.

21. *Ibid.,* pp. 57–65.

22. Galbraith, *op. cit.,* Chapter 1.

23. James G. March and Herbert A. Simon, *Organizations,* New York: Wiley, 1958, pp. 164–165. See also Tom Burns and G. M. Stalker, *The Management of Innovation,* London: Tavistock, 1961.

24. Thompson, *op. cit.,* pp. 34–35, outlines a number of interorganizational strategies for dealing with uncertainties arising from shared organizational environments. He specifies contracting, coopting, and coalescing strategies that arrange negotiated environments (i.e., stable environments).

25. Homans, *op. cit.,* Chapter 5.

26. Etzioni, *op. cit.,* Chapter 7.

27. Thompson, *op. cit.,* pp. 57–65.

28. See Joan Woodward, *Industrial Organization: Theory and Practice,* London: Oxford University Press, 1965, pp. 137–142. Woodward discusses the arrangements made in firms employing various technologies for the articulation of research and production staffs. In most cases failure to insulate the two functions resulted in a "confusion of roles" and hostility among the groups.

29. See Samuel A. Stouffer et al., *The American Soldier,* Vol. 1, Princeton, N.J.: Princeton University Press, 1949, pp. 586–595. See also Murdoch, *op. cit.*

30. Eme O. Awa, *Federal Government in Nigeria: A Study in Federalism,* Berkeley: University of California Press, 1964.

31. See Fred R. von der Mehden, *Religion and Nationalism in Southeast Asia,* Madison: University of Wisconsin Press, 1963.

32. George Rosen, *Democracy and Social Change in India,* Berkeley: University of California Press, 1966.

33. Franz Shurman, "The Attack of the Cultural Revolution on Ideology and Organization, Berkeley: University of California, Center for Chinese Studies, 1967 (mimeo).

34. See M. Banton, "Adaptation and Integration in the Social System of Temne Immigrants in Freetown," and J. Van Velsen, "Labour Migration as a Positive Factor in the Continuity of Tonga Tribal Society," in Immanuel Wallerstein (ed.), *Social Change: The Colonial Situation,* New York: Wiley, 1966, pp. 158–167, 402–420.

35. Glazer and Moynihan, *op. cit.,* pp. vii–xci.

36. *Ibid.,* and also Harold Cruse, *Rebellion or Revolution,* New York: Morrow, 1969, Chapters 7–9.

37. See the excellent description of the police "working personality" in Jerome Skolnick, *Justice Without Trial,* New York: Wiley, 1967, Chapter 8.

38. *Harvard Law Review,* "The Administration of Complaints by Civilians Against the Police," **77** (January 1964), pp. 499–519.

39. Skolnick, *op. cit.,* p. 61, also Chapters 3 and 8. Chapter 8 of this volume provides additional discussion.

40. See Harold Wilensky and Charles N. Lebeaux, *Industrial Society and Social Welfare,* New York: Free Press, 1968, pp. 265–273.

41. A. D. Green, "The Professional Social Worker in the Bureaucracy," *Social Service Review,* **40,** No. 1 (1967), pp. 71–83.

42. For an account of the conflict between professional and bureaucratic staffs in welfare agencies, see Blau and Scott, *op. cit.,* p. 174.

43. For a description of the related attitudes of clerical workers in a large public bureaucracy, see Michael Crozier, *The Bureaucratic Phenomenon,* Chicago: University of Chicago Press, 1964, Chapters 1 and 2.

44. See, for example, the description of building a housing project in a metropolitan area by William L. C. Wheaton, "Integration at the Urban Level Political Influence and the Decision Process," in Jacob and Toscano, *op. cit.,* p. 130.

45. Talcott Parsons, *The Social System,* New York: Free Press, 1951.

46. Max Weber, *The Theory of Social and Economic Organization,* A. M. Henderson and Talcott Parsons (transls.), New York: Free Press, 1947, pp. 324–345.

47. The distinction between internal and external elites is made by Etzioni to distinguish between initiators of political unification efforts. See *Political Unification, op. cit.,* pp. 45–47.

48. See Homans, *op. ct.,* pp. 148–149, and Etzioni, *op. cit.,* p. 45.

49. For instance, the European Economic Community, considered as a reform effort, is said to possess a strong system elite, whereas other regional political unions have weak system elites and are guided largely by a coalition of internal elites. See Etzioni, *op. cit.,* Chapters 6 and 7.

50. Our study of Eastern State's CIS system (Chapter 9) reveals some of the consequences of importing expertise into a reform project.

51. Philip Selznick, *TVA and the Grass Roots,* Berkeley: University of California Press, 1949, p. 219.

52. For an excellent discussion of how a system elite develops interests separate and apart from those of the initiators of reform and the constituents of the reform, see Etzioni, *op. cit.,* Chapter 7, which describes the policies of the European Economic Community leadership group.

53. Selznick, *op. cit.,* Chapters 3 and 4.

54. See, for example, Daniel P. Moynihan, *Maximum Feasible Misunderstanding,* New York: Free Press, 1969, Chapter 8.

55. See, for example, Selznick, *op. cit.,* pp. 184–213, for a description of relations between the TVA and regional agriculturalists with regard to land use policy.

56. See, for example, Moynihan's account of the planning of the antipoverty programs and the decision to avoid involving local governments in the programs. Moynihan, *op. cit.,* Chapter 5.

57. See, for example, the Community Progress Incorporated, New Haven, Conn., and Action for Boston Community Development, as described by Peter Marris and Martin Rein, *Dilemmas of Social Reform,* New York: Atherton, 1967, pp. 25–27.

58. Insofar as Collegial reforms are not in the interest of external elites, however, they withdraw support and seek to dismantle such reforms. See Marris and Rein, *op. cit.,* pp. 152–153, for a description of the defeat by a mayor of a community action project. Also, see Moynihan, *op. cit.,* Chapter 6, for a description of a mayor's attempts to gain greater control over the Mobilization for Youth project in lower Manhattan after its activities had become a political liability.

59. In his study of community power, Hunter describes the use of a Notables model of reform to support a regional city plan of development. See Floyd Hunter, *Community Power Structure,* Chapel Hill: University of North Carolina Press, 1953, Chapter 8.

60. See Selznick, *op. cit.,* pp. 220–226.

61. *Ibid.,* p. 219.

62. This process of resisting reform through criticism of its political structure is elucidated in Chapter 9.

63. Hunter, *op. cit.,* pp. 215–227.

64. See, for example, the advice of Saul Alinsky to community organizers to incorporate into the reform project influential leaders of resistant groups for their ability to bring others like them along. Saul Alinsky, *Reveille for Radicals,* Chicago: University of Chicago Press, 1946, Chapter 3.

65. See Norma D. Feshbach, "Nonconformity to Experimentally Induced Group Norms of High Status Versus Low Status Members," *Journal of Personality and Social Psychology,* **6,** No. 1 (1967), pp. 55–63.

66. The typology of power is that found in Amitai Etzioni, *Complex Organizations,* New York: Holt, Rinehart, & Winston, 1961, Chapters 1 and 2.

67. Small group research on interpersonal bargaining and exchange distinguishes between power used as a threat detrimental to others and power used as an inducement. See Morton Deutsch and Robert M. Krauss, "Studies in Interpersonal Bargaining," *Journal of Conflict Resolution,* **6** No. 1 (1962), pp. 52–76. See also Richard Longabaugh, "A Category System for Coding Interpersonal Behavior as Social Exchange," *Sociometry,* **26** (1963), pp. 319–344.

68. Etzioni, *op. cit.,* Chapter 2. Political Unification, op. cit.

69. Both the Notables and the Reputational Elite models tend to be elitist, characterized by one or a small number of powerful members, usually the initiating group. Research in small groups has indicated that under conditions of unequal bargaining power, the use of threats and aggression by the more powerful increases when favorable responses from the less powerful are not forthcoming. The use of threat and aggression, in turn, has been found to reduce the probability of reaching agreements among members. See W. Smith, "Power Structure and Authoritarianism in the Use of Power in the Triad," *Journal of Personality,* **35** No. 1 (1967), pp. 65–89; and Harvey A. Hornstein, "The Effects of Different Magnitudes of Threat upon Interpersonal Bargaining," *Dissertation Abstracts,* **26** No. 8 (1966), pp. 4852–4853.

70. Equal threat potentials (i.e., low elitism) tend to reduce use of threat and aggression as tactics and to increase the probability of agreement among partners. See Hornstein, *op. cit.,* p. 4852. The Collegial and Pluralist models are both generally of low elitism.

71. For a brief sketch of the history of OEO, see Moynihan, *Maximum Feasible Misunderstanding, op. cit.,* Chapters 5–7.

PART **TWO**

CHAPTER

SEVEN

Total Efficiency in Western County

A brief history of the intensive application of computer technology in Western County government begins with the county auditor, a politically powerful elected official since the 1930s. This individual initiated the centralization of, first, accounting information, and later, information on the clients of the county's social services (welfare, health, institutions, and probation agencies).

The technological instruments of centralization were the third generation computers that appeared in the early 1960s. The administrative agent of centralization was the newly formed Data Processing Center of the Auditor's Department, backed by the auditor, the county administrative officer (CAO), and indirectly by the six members of the county board of Supervisors.

It was the consensus of key decision makers in the early 1960s that the county faced demands for social services that exceeded its managerial capacities. Many believed that the problems could be solved by installing a central, computerized information system, linking the social service agencies and capable of providing almost instantaneous links between agencies and the Board of Supervisors.

The creation of a centralized data bank that pooled information among four social service agencies—welfare, health, institutions, and probation— aroused old suspicions with new vigor. The Institutions and Probations departments were frequently engaged in custodial activities and were not averse to using Welfare and Health agency information to locate their clients. The lack of trust among these four agencies before the computer arrived partly explains their resistance to participation in a centralized information system. The initial conditions were not favorable to an increase in the level of integration among the four agencies.

The manner in which the technology was introduced and organized—the process of reform—provides additional clues to the sources of resistance to the data bank. The county auditor and the administrative officer were the principal designers and initiators of the centralized information system. They were less interested in the problems of social service agencies and their clients than in the creation of a centralized, modern budgeting system. Participation of the social service agencies in the computer project is minimal, being largely restricted to supplying expertise and manpower. It is charged that the data bank is irrelevant to the needs of social service clients and to the professional ideals of the social service employees—thus one source of resistance.

The process of reform utilized in establishing the data bank helps explain why it has led to a centralization of administrative authority in the county. Designed by central administrative executives—the auditor and the CAO—the data bank has significantly increased the capacity of these officials to monitor and analyze agency budgets and expenditures. However, increased capacity to monitor budgets is perceived by agency personnel as interference with their jobs and as indicating a decline in their autonomy.

WESTERN COUNTY: AN INTRODUCTION

Western County is an urban county of more than a million inhabitants, 95% of whom live in densely populated cities and towns. Bordered on the east by the San Luis Mountains and on the west by the Pacific Ocean, the county hails itself as the "gateway to the Pacific." For the most part, the lush hills of the eastern region are unpopulated farming and grazing lands, the large population centers being spread along the western "ocean area."

Granted to a Mexican general in the early nineteenth century, the region remained largely agricultural until the building of the transcontinental railroads in the 1870s. Gradually Western County developed as an industrial, warehousing, and transportation center.

World War II, as perhaps no other event since the Gold Rush of 1849, transformed Western County into a relatively independent economic and social region. The expansion of a naval base, the building of a large naval supply depot, and the creation of an entire shipbuilding industry, spurred the development of a local tool and die industry, metals fabrication, and chemical factories.

Industrial expansion during the war necessitated the importation of additional labor. Naval and county officials made numerous trips to southern cities recruiting black labor, and to Mexico to secure agricultural workers.

Since the war, Western County has become the thirteenth most populous county in the nation. At the same time it has confronted all the social problems typical of urban counties elsewhere: (1) major structural shifts in its economy; (2) high unemployment, especially among unskilled minority groups; (3) a decline of the cities and their institutions, concomitant with the growth of the suburbs; (4) marked increases in demand for social services—welfare, health, police, and so on; and (5) increases in conflict between government and minority groups over the supply of urban social services.

The end of the war brought about the rapid decline of heavy industry in Western County, resulting in the release of large numbers of unskilled workers who were predominantly black. A similar decline in agriculture led to high unemployment among Mexican-Americans.

At present unemployment among blacks is two and three times that for whites, and similar conditions prevail for Mexican-Americans. In the largest city, unemployment for blacks is 15% and for Mexican-Americans 10%. Of the county's black households, 35% earn less than $4000, and 30% of the Mexican-American households are in this income range; but only 13% of the white households earn less than $4000.[1]

Demographic patterns in Western County display expected features: although the county grew faster than the nation between 1950 and 1960 (22% vs. 19%), the "core" cities declined by 4%. One typical suburban township quadrupled in size during this period.

During the 1950s the size of minority groups (black and Mexican-American) doubled. Most of this increase in minority population has been in the "core" cities, where minorities make up 35–40% of the population. A county Health Department survey reveals the extensive ethnic and class separation that developed during the 1950s (Table 6).[2]

In the core cities there are few upper-level SES census tracts, and these are predominantly in suburban areas.

The occupational structure of the county presents an equally familiar picture (Table 7).[3]

While the needs of urban residents were increasing during the 1950s, the tax base to support these demands was actually declining.

The declining capacity of city and county government to meet urban needs is revealed in the results of a county health Department survey of

Table 6   Ethnic Composition of Socioeconomic
Status Census Tracts in Western County

Ethnic group	Lower	Middle	Upper
White	34.7%	71.9%	91.0%
Black	61.8%	25.4%	6.6%
Other	3.5%	2.7%	2.4%
Total	100%	100%	100%

Table 7   Occupational   Structure   of   Western
County*

Group	UBC	SBC	WC
All-county	15.8%	34.1%	50.2%
White	12%	34%	53.8%
Black	40%	34%	26%

*Abbreviations as follows: UBC, unskilled blue
collar; SBC, skilled blue collar; WC, white collar.

1965: only 45% of the blacks were graduating from high school, although
67% of the whites completed high school; For the Mexican-Americans the
picture was worse with only 24% of the Spanish-surname population
completing high school.[4]

The health needs of the minority groups, and of the residents of lower
SES tracts in general, were equally staggering. Minority groups, and indeed
all low-SES neighborhoods, had critically high infant death rates, fetal
death rates, and rates of incidence of tuberculosis, gonorrhea, syphilis, and
other communicable diseases. Rates three and four times higher than other
areas of the county (principally suburban) were not uncommon. Yet the
1965 statistics of the county Health Department indicated that the most
pathological areas served by the department received two to five times less
service than "healthy" areas.

The welfare budget of the county, tied to federal and state programs,
exploded rapidly after the war: in 1947 welfare was 10% of the budget;
it was 20% in 1952, 50% in 1960, and 66% in 1969. From 1960 to 1970
Western's population increased by 24.4%, but its welfare population increased 175%. In 1970 the CAO stated that approximately 10% of the

county population received welfare payments, the largest number of recipients coming under the Aid to Families with Dependent Children program.

Government, Politics, and Policy: 1950–1970

Until recently local city and county governments have not generated much scholarly or public interest in the United States because of the belief that little of real consequence occurs there. National politics has for a long time commanded most of the nation's attention. Local politics in Western tended to raise "nonissues" typical of nonpartisan politics: "honest government," "public decency," public service records, personalities, and so on. Policies, when there were any, embraced avoidance of action to prevent open "public" controversy. The sole prerequisite policy of local government was to keep the wheels turning with as little fuss as possible.[5]

Although the foregoing caricature amply suits Western County in the 1950s, by 1960 the politics of the nonissue and its accompanying policies of inaction were no longer tenable. It was politically feasible to neglect the backlog of unmet urban needs and the failure of key urban institutions only so long as those in need accepted their position. Beginning in the 1960s, however, the NAACP and CORE, followed by the Black Panthers and various welfare rights organizations, and later Community Action Projects, emerged to organize and articulate the interests of the urban minorities and urban poor in Western County. Area newspapers in late 1964 and throughout 1965 reported frequent confrontations between these groups and police, welfare administrators, school officials, and others in local government.

The rising costs of the social service budget and expenses of general administration, coupled with the increasing observability of the urban poor, led to the activation of conservative suburban groups. These groups confronted government officials largely through quasi-governmental bodies charged with making investigations and recommendations to county government: the Welfare Citizens' Committee, the Penal Institutions Citizens' Committee, the Health Citizens' Committee.

The most important of the quasi-governmental bodies at the county level is the grand jury, whose members are generally retired professionals or their wives. The body is self-selecting, with little review by any other agency, and it has the power to issue subpoenas and to direct its own investigations.

With the exception of confrontations between city police forces and local community groups, the center of political attention in the 1960's was the county government. City government in the western United States is far more circumscribed than in the East: city functions are limited to parks and playgrounds, police, city streets, and auditing municipal operations.

The urban type of social services in Western County (welfare, health, probation, hospital) are delivered by county government and paid for by county government. The property tax authority resides with county government.

Fifty-six special districts in the county provide fire, sanitation, educational, and pollution control services. Each district levies its own assessments to finance operations, operating independently from other governments in the region.

Beginning in 1960 many of these governmental bodies within the county were coming under increasing political pressure to deliver more services and to reduce taxes. This was especially true for city and county government. And it became increasingly apparent that traditional responses were either failing or exacerbating the problems.

From Poverty and Crime, Good Lord Deliver Us

Brighton, the largest city of Western County, typifies the failure of public policy in urban America. Faced with a lowered tax base due to flight to the suburbs, inadequate schools, declining job opportunities, and increasing militance on the part of the urban poor, the city government adopted two major policies in the late 1950s: "Downtown Renewal" and "Law and Order." Although both policies were presumably intended to make the city more livable for the poor and the suburban working force alike, they had opposite effects.

"Downtown Renewal" is a catchall phrase that can mean many things to many people.[6] In Brighton, Downtown Renewal encompassed the destruction of dilapidated housing to make way for superhighways, luxury apartment buildings, new county government buildings, and the steel-glass skyscrapers of large corporations and convention hotels.

Extensive public relations campaigns were undertaken to encourage the building of chain store retail outlets, convention centers, and a $12.5 million dollar coliseum. The plum on the pudding was the proposed construction of the Rapid Transit System designed to whisk visitors and workers to and from their jobs at speeds up to 90 miles per hour.

The results of Downtown Renewal, although favorable for some, were disastrous for many residents of the city. Lamenting the fact that 75,000 families in Brighton were living below the poverty level of $4000 in 1967 (an increase porportionately from the 1960 level), the mayor of Brighton in his 1968 "State of the City" address was still looking to revitalization of the downtown area as a "solution":

> We intend to make this project [a $4 million federal grant] another catalyst for the revitalization of the entire downtown area including convention facilities, adequate parking and new commercial spaces adjacent to the Rapid Transit Station.
>
> Resulting economic and employment benefits—including 700 jobs at the proposed hotel project—will have meaning far greater than merely physical renewal of the heart of the city. . . . Related to this downtown renewal is the fact that Brighton is in demand as a convention and tourist center. The 1967 investment of Motel–Hotel tax revenues into promotion and services resulted in our hosting 54 conventions involving 20,000 delegates and an estimated spending of 4 million dollars in the city. At this early date, last year's record has already been surpassed by the booking of 57 conventions and we expect some 20 more, with related economic and good will benefits.

In the same speech, the mayor noted that 2500 jobs had been created by the downtown renewal project, since 1960. However, these jobs demanded special skills, and the urban poor were eligible for fewer than half of them. The 1960 census showed that of the 30% minority population, 14% were unemployed. Minority job requirements called for the creation of 12,500 jobs in 1960.

During the 1960s continued net in-migration of unskilled workers, predominantly black and Mexican-American, caused unemployment among this group to remain constant. In 1969, a State Department of Employment bulletin indicated that the vast majority of new jobs created by Downtown Renewal were going to suburban commuters in outlying districts.

Housing was another area adversely affected by downtown renewal. The 1960 census estimated that Brighton required 50,000 new rental units to provide "adequate" housing for its 1960 population. From April 1960 to July 1965, 7000 housing units were lost in Brighton (net), principally because of demolition for purposes of "redevelopment" (i.e., highway and office building construction).[7] The same study also shows that during the downtown renewal programs of the 1960s the density of population living in the black and Mexican-American neighborhoods of Brighton increased, with a subsequent decline in quality of housing.

"Law and Order," the second major policy pursued in Brighton in the 1960s, involved three programs: professionalization of the police force, establishment of police–community relations programs, and implementation of the associated agencies projects.

Brighton has a reputation of possessing a "model" police force: patrolmen receive college course training during their careers, officers study criminology, and the department recruits nationwide for its younger officers. The city manager explained Brighton's professionalization program in 1964 at a meeting of civic groups:

> You recruit nation-wide; you insist on high standards of selection; you train and train and train them, in particular in the area of community and group relations. You insist on an organization that meets the realities of the situation. You introduce sound police administration and adopt effective procedures. . . . You stamp out racial bigotry or any other prejudice that interferes with professional police work. For a variety of reasons we need to recruit more minority group people into our police department. But there must be no lowering of standards. We must seek out those with the potential and encourage them to compete.

In 1968 only 4% of the Brighton Police Department came from minority groups, which composed 40% of the population.[8] Community relations were going from bad to worse: Brighton experienced riots in 1966, 1968, and 1969.[9] Several shoot-outs with the Black Panthers, 1968 and 1969, along with charges of police brutality brought by local civil rights associations, tarnished the professional reputation of the police department.

The riots and complaints of minority groups spawned new programs in the police department and new fears in the mayor's office:

> Brighton is experiencing an accelerated rate of crime which must have our immediate attention. A home or apartment burglary is enacted every three hours in Brighton. The 1967 total of 5700 such crimes was a 95% increase over the previous year. Crime is a crisis in this city.

> Let me make one thing absolutely clear: This City Council, through its Manager and its law enforcement department, will maintain law and order in Brighton and enforcement will be carried out with firmness and decisiveness. The Brighton Police Department proposes a partnership between the citizens and police.

> . . . To help build this partnership, I am hereby calling for a conference to be held in Brighton among businessmen, leaders of civic groups, and law enforcement officials. The purpose will be to design additional means of stopping crime. This group may consider ways of making home alarm systems more readily available to the average family.[10]

Police–community relations after 1967 became a program directed by business leaders to publicize the dangers of the crime problem and methods (e.g., burglar alarms) to cope with it.

Perhaps the most interesting program developed by the Brighton Police was the Associated Agencies Project–Elementary School Project. Both programs were designed to combine the intelligence resources of the many institutions that deal with actual or potential juvenile delinquents. In particular, racial disturbances and demonstrations were causing alarm among police officials. The city manager publicly voiced these fears in 1964:

> In facing the emergencies in these new areas [demonstrations, picketing, sit-ins, open conflicts] it became increasingly clear that our city government was not properly structured to take care of these critical problems.
>
> This was dramatically brought to our attention one day in 1967 when the Chief of Police came to me saying, "The 15 police cars we are sending to Technical High School everyday will never answer this problem." He was referring to the racial disturbances taking place in Brighton High School. Moreover, tensions which had grown between negro and white teen-agers had spread beyond the school ground to the entire neighborhood. The economic effects of this urban disease were already being felt by the merchants.
>
> It was obvious at this point that we need total community involvement in response to this explosive situation. As a start, the City Manager's Office called a meeting and invited the School Superintendent, the Police Chief, the Recreation Superintendent, the Chief County Probation Officr, and a representative of State Youth Authority.
>
> United we have been able to quickly identify the "leaders" and "catalysts" among juvenile gangs. Channels of communication both among agencies and between agencies and informants have allowed us to size up incipient situations rapidly, pool our knowledge, and act fast.

We have also been able to modify some institutional thinking that develops among agencies that are fragmented and isolated. For example, the recreation director in Brighton no longer attempts to "protect" the juvenile delinquent from the "bullying" and "heartless" police; and the officer no longer regards the recreation director as a "bleeding heart" and coddler of vicious juveniles. The schools have accepted full partnership in our coordinated approach by community problems. There is frankness and trust between the personnel of the police department and the schools that enables each to perform its mission more effectively.

. . . one demonstration project that the Brighton Police Department in involved in, as a member of the Associated Agencies, is the Elementary School Project. This project is designed to identify early the children who, for whatever reason, are tending towards delinquency, so that the community's resources can be brought to bear to modify their behavior patterns.

Thus by 1967 it had become necessary to send informants into high schools and to create informants out of teachers and recreation directors.

This cursory review of Brighton city government policies in the early 1960s leaves the impression of a city in deep trouble. A dwindling housing supply, poorly performing schools, falling job opportunities, increasing racial tensions, and a falling tax base, hardly argue for a bright future. Either by intention or through ignorance, city policies exacerbated the problems. Yet many of the city's problems—such as inadequate housing, welfare, and health care units—were beyond its powers to change. County, state, and ultimately federal governments by and large determined the supply of these services.

The Government Ganglion

The dismal situation facing Brighton in the early 1960s was hardly unique: the other "core" cities of the county, and other urban areas in the United States, confronted similar problems. City government was simply the first on-line agency to have to deal with the urban crisis, and it was the least equipped to do anything about the problems. City governments have always maintained lobbies at state and federal legislatures, as well as with county governments, but these channels of upward communication were notoriously weak and ineffective.

County Government

A standing joke among Western County officials is "minus lead time decision making," referring to the tendency of federal and state legislative and administrative bodies to make decisions with retroactive clauses without consulting county administrators.

Although less visible than city governments, the county government began to feel the urban crisis as early as 1958. Massive increases in the numbers of persons demanding the services it was charged to deliver, and more importantly, the growing complexity of state and federal programs in which the county participated, were overwhelming the available administrative machinery.

In one instance, the Institutions Department (hospitals, jails, county buildings) was unable to charge welfare recipients for hospital services simply because of the cost and difficulty of pursuing patient records from Hospitals to the Welfare Department. From 1954 to 1959, the accounts receivable at the Institutions Department grew from $600,000 to $1.2 million and prompted a grand jury investigation:

> Continued improvement was noted in the accounts receivable records. However, limitations of space and the number of personnel, as well as the lack of mechanized equipment, have handicapped the system. The importance of the utilization of machine accounting in this department is emphasized. . . . Under the present system the Social Service Department classified many patients as welfare cases at the time of admission, and no billing is made for services to these patients. With the help of electronic data processing or some alternative system of machine accounting, it should be practical to process charges for all services rendered.[11]

The ganglion was beginning to exhibit signs of stress and overload in the performance of its simplest task, accounting.

FORMATION OF THE DATA PROCESSING

In 1958 the Board of Supervisors, disturbed by the rapidly increasing number of clerical positions in county government, the growing amount of requests by departmental heads for more clerical aid and, not least, the out-and-out failure of many departments to keep up with demand, commissioned a study by an independent auditing firm, Lefeber and Company and the county auditor, Lawrence Walsh. The Lefeber company was also acting as consultant and advisor on this earliest electronic computerization program.

The Lefeber Company and Walsh were charged with finding new accounting methods and procedures that would cut administration costs, which began rapidly rising during the latter 1950s. The action of the Board of Supervisors reflected recommendations by previous grand juries to seek out new and more intensive applications of machine accounting.

Machine accounting and primitive computers had been used in the county since 1947, when Tab-card sorter equipment was used for the first time by the county treasurer in computing the tax roll. In the words of the auditor, the equipment was necessary if only because it was "impossible to hire more bodies to keep the tax rolls."

In the early 1950s other departments had introduced automatic calculating machines for use in preparation of payrolls and accounts. In 1955 the Road, Health, Welfare, Probation, Auditor, Clerk, and Treasurer Departments were all utilizing tab equipment independently.

The county auditor was undoubtedly the most powerful and influential computer advocate in county government. A county employee since the late 1930s, and the elected auditor since 1946, he was a master of "courthouse" politics.

Quick to point out that his wooden desk is a 1916 model, replete with roll-up top and innumerable cubicles, the auditor nevertheless welcomes and generally receives credit for bringing "electronic" computers to Western County. He said:

> Our office [the Auditor's] was the first to install real computers, and by that I mean the electronic jobs. We were always way ahead of any other departments in the use of computers. At that time, in 1955, our first machine was a huge RAND drum calculator. It was so huge because the memory unit was a metallic drum which rotated in a bath of liquid nitrogen.

> Reporters and government officials came from all over the county just to see it work. It was beautiful, but ugly as sin, a real contraption.

> It cost us $105,000 and took a real fight to get it. At that time you had to buy machines, you couldn't lease them like we do now. I always knew the thing would pay for itself, but the others, everyone was down on the machine.

> But I got my chance to show them when the State pulled one of its typical stunts by ordering a 20% increase in county property taxes, effective immediately.

I figured out, and presented to the Board of Supervisors, that it would have taken $70,000 just to recompute the tax parcels with nonautomated procedures. Even then it would have taken a year to do the job.

We did it here in a couple of months, the first county in the state to complete recomputing. That machine paid for itself literally in a couple years.

People just don't ask any more about the costs of computers.

In 1959 the Walsh-Lefeber Report on the possible remedies to "the alarming growth of paperwork and clerical positions in the county" was released. The report, entitled *Proposal for a County Data Processing Center,* recommended that electronic computers be installed in the Auditor's office and that all payroll and accounting functions of the individual county agencies should be transferred to the auditor.

The proposed centralization of accounting and billing would necessitate the removal of present rented tab equipment from the individual departments and its replacement by "more efficient and modern high speed equipment." The report claimed that present decentralized equipment was 70% underutilized.

Personnel changes and costs savings projected in the report were so drastic that the grand jury was euphoric. The "paper dragon" was about to be slain:

> The Grand Jury recommends that the County payrolls be reduced as contemplated with the installation of the *Data Processing Center*. The study, *Proposal for a County Data Processing Center. . . .* It developed that the above report, with its recommendations was approved by the County Board of Supervisors, September 22, 1959.
>
> This report was stated to be the results of studies by Department of the Auditor-Controller for over ten years, in line with recommendations for automation by preceding Grand Juries for at least five years. Since it appears that gradual approach and development is planned, with full use of existing rented equipment and additional machines to be added only as required, this Grand Jury concurred in previous recommendations of the Grand Jury.
>
> While the Audit Committee questions the availability of personnel in the first three grades at the salaries set forth in schedule A of the report, and the ability, under Civil Service, to reduce other personnel as rapidly as projected, the recom-

> mendations and planning in the report appeared sound, and
> the Audit Committee is impressed by the work of Messrs.
> Walsh and Lefeber on their study. The Board of Supervisors
> is urged to exercise full diligence in seeing that the County
> Payrolls are reduced as rapidly as contemplated by the
> Auditor-Controller and that displaced persons are not re-
> placed.[12]

Despite the glowing predictions in the report, the grand jury's doubts were
well founded. As the Data Processing Center developed in the 1960s,
clerical costs of government continued to rise as fast as before, and the
county has had much difficulty in hiring competent personnel to run the
computers at Civil Service wage levels. Worse yet, no one seemed to be
able to measure the actual impact of the computers or their relative
efficiency.[13]

Despite the tongue-in-cheek doubts of the grand jury, the auditing report
carried the day, and in 1960 the Board of Supervisors established and
funded the Data Processing Center, a bureau within the Auditor's office.
Since 1960, the Center has expanded its initial assignment to automate
county tax rolls and now includes more than 1700 separate programs,
which service all county departments.

Since 1960, the Center has gone through five equipment conversions
because of heavier demands on its services and changes in computer technology. Equipment rental costs of up to $90,000 per month, coupled with
failures and conversion costs, have chastened the utopian dreams that
characterized the "feasibility study" period. In an interview, the county
auditor recalled his early learning experiences:

> Our first equipment change over occurred shortly after the
> Center was established. The tab equipment was clearly out-
> dated and the repairs on the equipment were becoming too
> costly. In addition, it was simply too slow to accommodate
> our needs. In late 1960 we converted all of our card equip-
> ment to tapes using a Rand Solid State 80. Our first job was
> centralizing the county payroll.
>
> Here I made my first mistake, a real whopper: I believed the
> fancy-dan planners and systems people when they told me
> things were all ready. Fantastic, we had payroll checks going
> to all the wrong people for the wrong amounts. Twenty
> thousand wrong payroll checks worth millions!!
>
> Anyway since then I've learned my lesson, and I personally
> check out the system with a trial run. In 1962 we had out-

grown the capacity of the Solid State 80 and switched to the latest Solid State 90. Then in 1964 we took on a great many new functions which required "real-time" access and far more complex equipment than the Solid State 90. This was when we leased our first IBM machine, a 7040. In 1964 we closed out the Welfare Tab unit and other still separate computer operations in other departments. We added Health, Probation, and Institutions accounting and information retrieval needs.

In 1965 we switched to IBM 7040 equipment. Finally in 1966 we changed to the new third generation IBM 360 models 40 and 50, plus a Univac 9300.

All of these conversions have involved incalculable and unforeseen costs for programmer and other professional talents. Often, the Board of Supervisors would ask me if it was worth the costs. They always want to know if the payroll of the county will go down.

I always respond, "No, it will go up!" They don't like to hear that so they ask if it will go up slower. All I can reply is that its impossible to tell.

I have the feeling that all this equipment pays for itself. It would just be impossible for humans to work as fast and efficiently as these machines for such low costs. But there really is no way to tell how much time and money is saved, especially with new programs being launched all the time.

For those associated with the feasibility study, it is perhaps fortunate that copies of that report are no longer available either from the county government or the issuing company. The procedures used to measure the cost-effectiveness of traditional administrative arrangements are not applied to computers.

SOCIAL SERVICES: THE WELFARE BONANZA

Although all government services can be described as social services, it is more common to identify the agencies that perform welfare functions as "social service agencies" (e.g., welfare, health, institutions—hospitals, jails, clinics, etc.—and probation). This is the typical usage in Western County.

Political observers often note that the social service sector of local governments is not a popular government activity. Indeed, the social service sector is a popular target of the party out of power and of taxpayer and citizen committees.[14]

In Western County public attacks on the social service sector reached fever pitch between 1961 and 1965. The editorial page of the largest and most conservative newspaper in the state was applauding the auditor in 1961 for his "progressive application of business methods to county administration." The reporting staff was quietly digging up another in a series of "welfare scandals."[15]

A casual visitor to the county would have concluded over the years that the Welfare Department was one of the most corrupt and venal organizations in the state. For instance, in 1961 the Welfare Citizens' Committee, following the leads provided by *The Western Herald*, published its own list of welfare fraud cases:

Case F

Mrs. X mother of 12 children, separated from husband in 1954. Since then has had 5 illegitimate children. Named one man as father of first two, which the man denied. Named one other father of the last 3.

Mr. X, the husband, had admitted fathering illegitimate children in other welfare cases. Mother of that child has never married, has three illegitimate children by 3 different fathers. The oldest daughter, 17, had illegitimate child in 1961. Both daughter and grandchild included in Mrs. X's welfare budget.

Case G

Inspector in checking home on a tip there was a man there in the home found not one but two men! Mrs. X's daughter, 12 years old, was sleeping on the couch. Mrs. X's 16 year old daughter came out of the front bedroom and on the bed, in a completely undressed condition, was a Mr. Y, 23 years old.

Checked back bedroom and found a Mr. Z asleep in bed. Mr. Z readily admitted sleeping with Mrs. X every night for the past three weeks. Mr. Z stated that Mr. Y had been sleeping with Mrs. X's daughter longer than Mr. Z had been sleeping with Mrs. X.

Case H

Following is a list compiled November 16, 1961, of police reports (contacts in a 10-year period by a local police department) for this one welfare family:

Contacts

Mother:	51
Father:	30
Child 1:	11
Child 2:	28
Child 3:	52
Child 4:	39
Child 5:	25

Total: 236 police contacts

All of the children have been in almost every conceivable type of trouble with the police during the last ten years:

MOTHER: Presently on probation with restitution to repay the County Welfare Department $1200 at $50 per month.

FATHER: On 3 years' probation for failing to provide for his minor children. He has lived in a common-law marriage since his separation from his family.

CHILD 1:   Presently on probation for forgery. Has two children by Mr. X who never supported his family while she was receiving ANC (Aid to Needy Children's Program) funds because he was in a state prison. She has another child by Mr. Z, for whom she received ANC funds because of the father's lack of support. Mr. Z has since taken custody of this child and moved to another county.

CHILD 3:   Presently awaiting trial for armed robbery. Was placed on probation in 1961 for failure to provide for his illegitimate child who was receiving ANC funds. He later married another girl after causing her to become pregnant. They have since separated.[16]

Even the most enthusiastic supporters of the ANC program concluded that something was wrong. Instead of preserving a family structure and creating stability, the program appeared to be having opposite affect in many cases. How many cases? No one knew:

Philosophically, the purpose of the ANC program is to maintain and strengthen family life—help towards the attainment of self-support and personal independence consistent with maintenance of continuing parental care.

Ironically enough, the administration of the program, in many instances, not only defeats its own purpose but actually appears to create the very conditions it would seek to resolve.

Thus "apparent parent" figures are accepted (without benefit of a marriage) within the home by social workers. One generation of a family upon Welfare is succeeded by another generation.[17]

Along with possible deleterious social consequences, the ANC program and its clients were absorbing the resources of four separate agencies: Welfare, Health, Probation, and Institutions:

The local administration of the program is likewise encumbered by the duplication of services by the various involved departments and by a distinct lack of communication between them in relation to mutual cases. Thus it is not unusual to find from two to four of the named departments servicing the same family or individual members thereof; each setting up its own forms, rendering its own or some service common to other departments and maintaining its own exclusive files.[18]

One consequence of separate departmental files and program involvement was the lack of any coherent body of information or knowledge regarding the welfare population:

In seeking facts which will permit an analysis of the problems and an evaluation of the programs, we find that reliable statistics (other than for budgeting and staffing) are conspicuous by their absence.

Valuable IBM statistical information maintained by the Family Support Division was recently discontinued although no other department kept these statistics.

It appears that stock answers to many pertinent questions, which are the basis of administrative decisions, are based upon conjecture or an outdated, insufficient sampling in areas which may or may not be comparable to local conditions.[19]

Increasing Interdependence

The attacks on the administration and policy of the social service agencies by the county grand jury just cited are only in part politically motivated. In an important respect they reflect accurately the confusion that did exist within the administrative complex of social services.

State and federal legislation in the early 1960s broadened the scope and increased the size of social service programs.[20] Besides adding to the number of persons eligible for social services, this legislation increased the numbers and types of service available. Welfare clients became eligible for hospital care, and patients in the county hospitals became eligible for certain welfare payments. New regulations declared that arrested welfare clients should have their payments stopped, and illegitimate children born in county hospitals were to be reported to the Welfare Department. It was discovered that the Welfare, Health, Probation, and Institutions departments were sharing clients, and decisions made in one department were affecting the clients of other departments.

However, while state and federal legislation and regulations were taking account of this interdependence in their broad policy-setting actions, local administrative agencies were operating independently from one another. That is, there was no efficient, systematic arrangement for transferring information about clients back and forth between agencies at the local level.[21]

As long as the *de facto* interdependence of local social service agencies was low (e.g., as long as Welfare, Health, and Probation clients were indeed different people), then written exchanges of information were feasible. As interdependence increased, as it did during the 1950s and early 1960s, ad hoc and manual means of transferring information became strained. Errors, fraud, and rapidly increasing costs of administration resulted.

Jurisdiction, Autonomy, and Professionalism

Although nominally within the political jurisdiction of county government, the social service agencies in Western County are subject to such control only regarding the administration of policy decided on by federal and state government bodies. In the case of Welfare and Health, the federal government enacts enabling legislation, and the state government passes laws concerning specific administration, disbursement, and enforcement of such legislation.[22]

The county Probation and Institutions departments are almost totally controlled and regulated by state government. All the social service agencies perform special tasks funded by grants from federal, state, or local government. The care of indigents is traditionally a county program, for instance, and preschool health programs in the county operate under special grants from the U.S. Public Health Service.

Social service agencies in general, and certainly in Western County, have rarely developed the kind of autonomy, self-supervision, and localism that can be found in, say, municipal police departments. The operations of social service agencies in Western County have always been closely scrutinized by local conservative interests who dominate the citizens' commissions and grand juries which investigate these agencies.[23]

Local interests in Western have consistently attempted to shift the burden of social service functions to state and federal government. An increase in federal income taxes is preferable to an increase in property taxes.[24]

The large policy role played by state and federal governments, the close supervision and intervention by local interests, and the low popularity of social service programs in general all serve to decrease the internal integration of social service agencies.[25]

The same factors contribute to conflict between managers and professional staffs. The Probation, Health, and Welfare departments in Western County are directed by managers appointed by and responsible to the Board of Supervisors. To keep their jobs, managers are frequently forced to implement policies that run counter to their own professional ideals and those of their subordinates.[26]

For instance, in 1970 the Welfare Director, acting under pressure from the Board of Supervisors, requested a list of all county employees who were receiving welfare payments. This list, which was to be revealed at a public meeting of the Welfare Commission, was compiled in response to previous allegations of welfare fraud. The professional staff threatened a job slowdown; they were quickly disciplined. The list was published in a newspaper serving the area on May 15, 1970.

The low integration of the social service departments (lack of self-direction and low employee loyalty), and the prevalent conflict between managers and professional staffs, serve to shift loyalties of employees away from the organization. In interviews, clerical personnel indicated a low identification with their jobs (to be expected), but so also do the professional case workers. A not untypical remark of a welfare caseworker is illustrative:

> About the only difference the computer makes is that it's harder for me to give the client more money and more services simply because everything is more closely watched. . . . The computers are just a part of their [Board of Supervisors] efforts to save money and cut back welfare. It's all pretty cut and

> dried now how much the person can get and we just fill in the information and submit the form.
>
> When I'm at parties and I tell people I work for Welfare, they most often launch into a tirade about how we are the ones putting people on the dole. I just tell them the computer does all the work and we just follow orders. That usually calms them down.

Moreover, welfare personnel frequently work against the interests of the department by distorting records to increase the allotments given to clients: "Some Social Workers would prefer to accept blame for an error, rather than see the client suffer the consequences of an unreported change in circumstances."[27]

Subject to attack from powerful outside political forces, directed by legislators distant from local situations, and bereft of employee loyalty, the social service agencies in Western County are the first to be reformed and the last to be consulted about the proposed reform. The computer reform projects in the county continued this pattern.

EXTERNAL ELITES: INITIATION OF THE COMPUTER REFORM

In Western County the Social Service Information System (SSIS) originated with and is implemented by a group of external elites: the auditor, the county administrative officer, the director of Data Processing, and the Board of Supervisors. The social service agencies are the object of reform.

In 1963, following the recommendations by previous grand juries and welfare citizens' committees, harassment from local conservative interests, and encouragement from the Data Processing Center, the Board of Supervisors authorized the Data Center and the county auditor to begin work on a centralized information system called the Social Services Information System. The announced purpose of the SSIS system was the creation of a central storage "bank" and exchange network for information collected by the social service agencies.

In public statements, the Board of Supervisors claimed that the SSIS system would reduce fraud, error, and inefficiency in social services, and that it would provide the tools required for effective administration of the new, more complex social legislation originating at federal and state levels.

The Auditor

The most direct influence on the decision to adopt the SSIS system was the aggressive salesmanship of the county auditor, who was a key advisor to the Board of Supervisors, most of whom are elected for short terms. Under his management, the Data Processing Center (DPC) had gained the respect of the supervisors, the press, and the public, for its contribution to "sound government." As an accounting tool, the DPC computers were in the eyes of most a good investment.

However, the auditor and his allies in county government believed that the computer was destined for greater tasks than those of a mere accounting tool. Rising welfare costs and fraud were the pressing political issues in 1963, and the auditor argued that the DPC computers could "rationalize" the social services just as they had "rationalized" accounting and bills:

> Our department was the only one that could alleviate the problems in that whole social service sector. It wasn't just that they couldn't do the complex accounting their jobs and programs required, exchanging information and so forth, but they had fraud and identity problems. They didn't know who was getting welfare, if it was legitimate, what the history of the person was, where he was receiving outside funds from, etcetera, etcetera.

> At the same time, they (the social service agencies) just kept hiring more bodies to do the clerical work, falling behind, and asking for more. The supervisors used to get angry just hearing the name Health or Welfare.

> Anyway, the solution was automation, but if each department bought its own sophisticated computers the costs would be prohibitive, and the exchange of information not guaranteed.

> But in one central computer we could make the operation worth the costs. Of course, we would have to get the latest equipment in our Data Center. But what else was there to do? No one else came up with a better suggestion, so our ideas on the matter were adopted. It's as simple as that.

> Of course the departments didn't like this idea from the start. Taking away their little computers was like pulling teeth from a baby. They've gotten used to it by now, and they receive whatever they pay for.

More candor was expressed by the Assistant Director of the Data Center, also a 30-year employee of the county, who took part in the decisions involving SSIS:

> Oh yes, our SSIS and PRIS [Police Regional Information System] systems are a big part of our job here at the Center.

> PRIS allows police departments in the county to serve warrants more effectively, and SSIS provides identification information to the social service departments. Actually though, both were considered a good thing for us here at the Data Center because there was money in warrants and money in the SSIS programs.

> At that time the DPC had outgrown its early equipment and was attempting to expand into more expensive and larger machines. PRIS and SSIS were really taken on in order to obtain funds for these conversions.

Expansion of the equipment and functions of the Data Center promised a number of political gains for top administrators in the county. Lobbying for the addition of social service client information to his Data Processing Center, the auditor assured himself of receiving the latest IBM 360-40 computers, which in turn could be used to extend Data Center functions even more.

If successful competition for scarce tax dollars in the budgetary process of government be taken as a measure of power and influence, the auditor was increasing his relative accumulation of both. If public acclaim in newspapers and government journals be taken as a measure of eminence and prestige, favorable area press reports in 1965 indicated that here too the auditor was a rising star—albeit an elderly one.

The Professional Manager: County Administrative Officer

An important and necessary ally of the county auditor in the initiation and design of the SSIS system was the county administrative officer (CAO). Appointed to an indefinite term by the Board of Supervisors, the CAO is the most powerful administrative–executive officer in county government. The CAO, who was responsible for preparing the annual budget, supervising and reviewing all county programs, executing the directives of the supervisors, and initiating changes in administrative procedures, gave his early and enthusiastic support to the SSIS project. A brief historical sketch of the role of county administrative officers in local government is helpful to an understanding of origins of the SSIS project in Western.

The county administrative officer plan is a younger relative of the council–manager form of city government which appeared first in 1911.[28] Both forms of government were the products of the period of reform in America that began toward the end of the nineteenth century and continues almost unabated to this day. In its typical manifestation, professional politicians and urban political machines came under intense political attack by various "good government" movements supported predominantly by middle-class citizens and informed largely by their political values.[29]

The broad goals of these municipal reform movements included the elimination of corruption, the achievement of greater efficiency of government, and the increased democratization of government by ensuring that its administration was conducted according to universalistic rules.[30]

Whether federal, state, or local government, the reform movements proposed common remedies: consolidation of offices; reduction in the number of elective positions; creation of a strong, central executive on the "business model"; and strict separation of legislative and administrative functions.[31]

In county government the reform ethos is represented in the county administrative officer plan, which appeared first in the 1930s, supported by the same advocates of the council–manager plans—the National Municipal League and the International City Managers' Association.[32] Arguing that the prevailing decentralization of authority made county government incapable of efficiently delivering services to the citizens, hence less responsive, the CAO plan advocated placing all authority over public policy in the hands of an elected board of supervisors, who in turn would delegate all administrative matters to one professional functionary. The goal was a more perfect union of democracy and efficiency in which the public interest would be served by expert technicians and protected by elected officials.

The spread of the CAO plan has been slower than that of the council–manager plan. In some states, notably California, however, the CAO plan has recently grown rapidly: beginning in 1950, twenty-three counties in California had some form of CAO government. Western County adopted the CAO plan in 1955.[33]

Like the typical city manager, the typical CAO holds a bachelor's degree in engineering and an advanced degree in public administration, or he has acquired similar experience in private enterprise. He considers himself to be a professional manager. Guided strictly by his profession's code of ethics and his own sense of rationality, the CAO is in theory above politics—neither advocate nor adversary.[34]

In practice, the CAO is an advocate of administrative reform policies; as such, he is a powerful adversary of county line agencies. Possessing a virtual monopoly over technical information, complex governmental rules, and procedures, and aided by a highly trained staff, the CAO exercises considerable control over amateur politicians who temporarily compose the Board of Supervisors. While the Board of Supervisors, for instance, may believe it incumbent on themselves to "do something about rising social service costs," it is the CAO who defines just what, in the event, is possible, practical, and desirable to do.

The policy-making role of the CAO is not often objected to by boards of supervisors for its serves as a buffer between the citizenry and the elected officials. If the CAO's policies create unusual criticism, the supervisors may publicly denounce him, replace him, or change policies. When his policies are successful, the supervisors may share the credit with the CAO. For these technical and political reasons, the CAO is encouraged to assume an important advocacy role in county government. As an advocate of specific policies, however, the CAO becomes an adversary of the county line agencies subject to those policies. Nowhere is this conflict more apparent than in the politics of the county budgetary process.

BUDGETARY POLITICS: CONTROL OF LINE AGENCIES

The Board of Supervisors, who are county elected officials, attempt to control line agency policies and administrative procedures through two mechanisms: the power of appointment and the power of the budget. The power of appointment extends only to agency directors and is a most inexact means of control. Candidates for agency directorships are submitted to the Supervisors by the Civil Service Commission and professional groups (e.g., state associations of county welfare directors). Once appointed, an agency director can be formally removed only for gross negligence, illegal actions, or insubordination. Directors may of course also be removed for a variety of reasons through exertion of informal pressure. However, this device is likely to meet with resistance from the Civil Service Commission and professional groups. In the nonpartisan politics of Western, agency directors are appointed largely according to their professional competence, and their offices are considered to be above politics. In turn, the professional norms ascribed to by agency directors encourage them to remain out of politics.

Thus in the short term the power of appointment is a weak means of control over the line agencies and control of the budget necessarily becomes the principal mechanism through which elected officials seek to dominate agencies.

Political control of county social service agencies by county officials is vitiated because many social service programs are mandated by federal and state law. County government is charged with the administration of programs and policies and must also pay the costs of administration. Hence, with special regard to social service agencies, the policy discretion of elected county officials is restricted to matters of administrative procedure (e.g., numbers of clients per caseworker, location of a new welfare or health facility, choice of procedures to prevent fraud, choice of accounting methods, and indirectly, the availability and distribution of social services in the county).

As noted earlier, the social services—especially welfare—are the least popular governmental activity in the county. Considerable pressure is placed on the supervisors to reduce the costs of social service. Lacking the capacity to influence social service policies, the elected supervisors' most frequent blanket criticism of social service agencies is inefficiency, fraud, and ineffective administration. In turn, the public policy of the supervisors is close surveillance of social service procedures and intensive review of agency expenditures in the annual budget hearings.[35]

Although social service professional managers are expected to remain above politics, ineluctably they are drawn into the political arena. First, administrative decisions, regardless of their intent, have political consequences insofar as they affect the distribution of social services in the county. The decision, for instance, to place a birth control clinic in a black neighborhood instead of in a white, middle-class suburb has political ramifications. Second, agency administrative decisions have political consequences for elected supervisors. For instance, the decision to reduce social caseworkers' client loads from 100 to 75 is likely to be seen by conservative political groups as a decline in efficiency, signaling an increase in costs.

Historically, and especially with the decline in public acceptance of social service programs, the Board of Supervisors has tried to decrease the autonomy of social service agencies from close supervision and to reduce the discretionary control of agency managers over public funds. Apart from the consequences of this policy for the actual efficiency and costs of social service administration, political expedience alone would have dictated such a course.

The supervisors' attempts at close supervision and administrative control of the social service agencies are interpreted by the directors and staff of these agencies, and in many instances by the nurses and social workers, as political interference with their professional activities. The social service agencies are managed by "professionals"—doctors in the case of the Health Department, and in Welfare and Probation, career social workers who have risen to managerial positions through long service and the acquisition of advanced degrees in public administration and social work. Because of commitment to professional norms and to the goals of their respective agencies, social service managers want autonomy from close supervision by politicians, and they try to maximize their discretionary control over the use of public monies.[36]

Before the advent of CAO government in 1955, the maintenance of agency autonomy and managerial discretion was aided by the absence of any central budgetary authority, the inability of amateur politicians to systematically probe and understand agency budgets, and the use of antiquated line-item budgets that concealed an agency's specific uses of public monies. The adoption of a CAO form of government threatened to change, in theory at least, the delicate balance between central control and agency autonomy. In practice, the formal powers of the CAO could not be exercised, as the CAO himself recounts:

> From my view in the late fifties and early sixties things were getting worse by the minute here. We had no control over the budget except after-the-fact. That meant no control over simple but important things like how many people to hire, how many new desks to buy, how much building space to allocate. There was no concept of planning around here, mostly because we didn't possess any criteria, let alone information, to determine the next year's budget.

> Each department would prepare its budget, raise it by a certain percentage each year, but they could never tell us what we got for our money. The Board of Supervisors obviously couldn't investigate every budget item thoroughly, so they passed whatever the departments recommended. We were flying blind as a bat.

> For example, it used to take us nine months, sometimes a year, to determine next year's budget. It took that long to put together the individual departmental accounts.

> We needed two things: new accounting procedures, changing over to functional budgeting from project budgeting, and second, we needed computers to speed up the process. More, we needed tremendously big, sophisticated computers that could get us the information on time. "Timely information"— that was the key.

The CAO was thwarted in his efforts to achieve greater control over departmental budgets by the expense in time and money inherent in any intensive review of budgets. Agency directors considered it a blessing that the CAO had neither time, money, nor machinery to subject agency budgets to complete review. Even under the CAO, budget came but once a year, frequently after the fiscal year had begun; it was relatively easy for agency managers to juggle new personnel into old programs, to spend excess funds for "general administrative purposes," and to obtain yearly increments in budgets based on some politically acceptable formula (e.g., up to 1965 managers could expect to receive a 6–10% increase in county funds). In the words of one social service manager, "Government was tolerable here so long as it was ineffective."

THE SSIS PROJECT AND BUDGET REFORM

The addition of the SSIS project to the Data Center's responsibility required the leasing of large, sophisticated, and very expensive computers. (Lease costs of the IBM 360-40 computers used by SSIS, with peripheral equipment such as remote access terminals, were approximately $70,000 per month.) These expenses were justifiable to the CAO only if his office would receive sufficient computer time to carry out a thorough budget reform. Although welfare fraud and waste were politically more pressing issues, the CAO argued that the new equipment designed to solve these problems should also be used to "rationalize administration in the county."

Budget reform in Western County was introduced under the rubric, "Administrative Services Package." Designed by the CAO, the Administrative Services Package involved three changes in budgetary procedures: (1) a change to functional budgeting in all county agencies, (2) monthly updating of all agency expenditures, and (3) mandatory submission of proposed agency budgets six months in advance of budget hearings. According to the CAO, the "timely information" provided by the computer-driven budget procedures has brought the following changes:

> Since we've had the 360-40s, we can do the following: prepare a total county budget in one month, prepare monthly budget analyses of each department, and prepare and review the budgets of individual programs within departments monthly.

> We've tightened up the ship. If it looks like we'll run a deficit in July, we can cut back programs and personnel for the next month. If a department spends too much in one month, we can pull them in here and get an explanation. For the first time we can analyze a whole budget and begin to ask, What are we getting? and What's the proof?

> Without computers in a centralized department like [the auditor], we'd be spending a hell of a lot more money. The departments would be running government not the Board of Supervisors.

The "lead time" given the CAO allows item-by-item review of agency budgets. Each proposed change in personnel or resources suggested by an agency becomes a point of issue in the County Budget Message, which is presented to the Board Supervisors one month before the budget hearings.

In the past agency managers used the budget hearings not to convey information but rather to present the picture of an agency overworked, understaffed, and desperately in need of additional funds. Now, however, the agency directors must defend even minute changes in their budgets. Armed with a complete, detailed breakdown of agency expenditures, annotated by the critical remarks of the CAO, the Board of Supervisors has assumed a more aggressive role in the budget hearings. An example of the new procedures is provided by the *Budget Message of 1970,* used to review the proposed Welfare Department budget of 1971.

Point of Issue No. 3

Food Stamps	3 positions	Cost	$23,829
		Less revenue	14,324
		Net county cost	$ 9,505

The recommended budget for this unit includes three additional positions, including one added supervisor, which would increase the staffing from 16 to 19 positions. A further increase, including two more supervisors and a Clerk I or II is requested by the Department.

Point of Issue No. 4

State Medical Care Unit	1 position	Cost	$11,326
		Less revenue	5,663
		Net county cost	$ 5,663

An increase of one position is requested by the Department. The "justification" for the increase was inconclusive, particularly with regard to the ability, or inability, of the Department to impose controls on this activity.

Point of Issue No. 5

State Medical Unit	8 positions	Cost	$63,504
		Less revenue	63,504
		Net county cost	$ 0

Although this item is submitted as a "no County cost" matter, the subject is presented for a determination of the proper organization for handling "no cash grant" caseloads.

Point of Issue No. 6

Appeals Program Validation	11 positions	Cost	$96,624
		Less revenue	48,312
		Net county cost	$48,312

> The Department requested a 57.9% increase in staffing of this unit—from 19 to 30 positions. It is a significant problem area and one where no standards have been established. It relates to the problem of "administrative error," but as noted by the Welfare Director, "Some Social Workers would prefer to accept the blame for an error, rather than see the client suffer the consequences of an unreported change in circumstances." Although the Department states that program validation is required in AFDC, no information was supplied on the level of such services, nor were any data provided to indicate the worth, if any, of this activity.[37]

Thus one of the more significant functions of the SSIS project is to shift the balance of central control and departmental autonomy in favor of the County Administrative Officer and the Board of Supervisors. And although this result was an intentional goal of the CAO, it was largely unexpected by the managers of agencies. For the latter group, especially the social service managers, the SSIS project has served to increase the visibility of what they regard as professional decisions taken to better serve their clients. As these decisions become more visible to central budgetary authorities, the agency managers experience a decline in autonomy and discretion. Indeed, this result becomes the principal focus of resistance to the SSIS project which is described later in our study.

NEW TOOLS AND NEW MISSIONS: THE PROFESSIONAL DATA PROCESSORS

As a third and last initiator of the SSIS project in Western County, we have the successive incumbents of the Data Center director's office.

Through a process only dimly understood by sociologists, new tools and techniques quickly gather about them a coterie of persons—some users, suppliers, and potential users, a good number of crackpots, and not a few who stand to gain by the application of the new tool.

At first this coterie is a loosely defined group of believers, a sort of cult, but in time and depending on the level of societal utilization of the tool, the cult takes steps to institutionalize the use and the users of the tool.[38] When the level of expertise required to use the tool is moderate, the cult becomes a guild. When the level of expertise is high, the cult forms a profession, usually with its own "association" and training schools.[39]

One function of the guild or profession is to restrict entrance to certified persons only, thereby to regulate the use of the tool. In time, more and more communications are directed from the association to outside groups, in part to legitimate the association's monopoly of expertise, in part to enlarge the societal application of the tool.[40]

In California since the late 1950s, a number of county and state data processing organizations of different types have played an important role in propagating, regulating, and standardizing the use of computers by government agencies. Composed as they were of government employees engaged in the use of data processing, these organizations had direct access to the decision-making councils of government at city, county, and state levels.

The first and largest of these organizations is the California Association of County Data Processors (CACDP). Formed in 1957 by directors of county data processing bureaus in ten counties, by 1967 the CACDP included data processors from more than thirty-five counties. County government in California was spending $12 million per year for data processing and $4.5 million on computer equipment.

Other organizations of data processors formed following the lead of the county employees: State Data Processing Association (1964), League of California Cities–EDP Committee (1968).

Computers at virtually all levels of government, but especially at county and state levels, were becoming a cause célèbre in the early 1960s. Between 1960 and 1965 in California, the number of computers used by state government grew from five to fifty-five.[42]

PROFESSIONAL UTOPIAS: A UNIFIED INFORMATION SYSTEM

Political scientists may dream of a world in which politicians make "rational" decisions, and sociologists of a world of social equality. Professional data processors dream of an electronic utopia, where fragmented and feuding governments are replaced by a rational administration of "people, places, and things" and the inherent inequality of a managerial society is replaced by a "management information system"—a sort of reasoning leviathan before which, presumably, all are equal.[43]

Clearly one of the fashionable ideas about the role of computers in government created by the data processing profession was the "Total Unified

State Information System." Originally the idea of two RAND Corporation systems analysts, the "Unified Information System" became the accepted goal of prominent county data processors in California.[44]

Hearle and Mason published in 1962 an expanded account of their "Unified Information System." Citing localism, decentralization, and multiple jurisdictions as contributing to the paralysis of American government, the authors urged the adoption of computerized information systems:

> In essence the Unified Information System provides an information center to store and process data that are gathered and used by state and local governments within a particular state. The system is designed primarily to enable environmental data to be efficiently organized into records about persons and about properties.
>
> These data would be gathered in the regular operations of government agencies and transmitted to the information center via a communication channel, often conventional telephone networks. Similarly, agencies could obtain from the center either raw or processed data.
>
> The system does not require the collection of any new data and is entirely independent of the purposes or procedure for which the data are used. It simply provides for a technological facility to file these data and to process them according to the instructions of participating agencies.
>
> Therefore, it does not alter the present relationships between any citizen and the government or those between government agencies.[45]

The system proposed by Hearle and Mason would reduce duplication of record keeping, increase the accessibility and usefulness of information to government managers, and presumably overcome the fragmentation of American government.

WESTERN COUNTY: DREAM AND REALITY

The benefits of the electronic utopia are forthcoming if only those fragmented, localistic agencies of government will allow the development of a statewide information system. Furthermore, the same agencies would have to agree on the nature of the information to be stored. But the trouble with all utopias, and their advocates, is the lack of a plan telling how to proceed from dream to reality. Thus by 1964, Santa Clara, Los Angeles, San Francisco, and Alameda counties had all announced plans to build their own separate, autonomous, and "local" unified information systems. The growth of the Unified Information System was itself becoming as fragmented and decentralized as local government.

The Western County SSIS system is the first attempt to implement a Unified Information System on a local level. The core idea of SSIS is the construction of three connected electronic data files on persons. A central file contains the names of all persons who have had contact with the Welfare, Health, Institutions, and Probation departments, and each of these agencies will have access to the file. The second file is an agency file containing confidential information on clients; only the appropriate agency will have access to these data.

The first Chief of Data Processing in Western began to promote the Unified Information System idea in the county during 1962. At the 1964 meetings of the CACDP, he announced Western County's decision to build such a system:

> The general agreement is that 5% of the population requires 95% of the services, however, no one knows for sure. At least here in Western County no one can prove that the ones known to Welfare are also known to Health, Probation, and the Police. One of the greatest benefits we are looking for is that once we are in a position to present this information to the appropriate agency they can do a better job. . . . I want to convey this philosophy very clearly and precisely that these systems are the beginnings of the so-called Unified Information System but it will be built one block at a time and according to the operational needs of our line departments.[46]

These remarks imply that no one at the county level of government was interested in building an electronic utopia. County supervisors and administrative officers were more interested in increasing the efficiency of operating line agencies, in closer control over expenditures than in the needs of state government or any other government for a Unified Information System.

Many professional data processors reject utopian visions in which managers and officials are replaced by computers, but the notion of a single, centralized repository for local government information is seen as a necessary condition for solving the "urban crisis," which is perceived as synonymous with the "information crisis." This view is typical of the professional data processors as indicated in an interview with the director of the Los Angeles County Data Processing Center:

> You have to understand one overwhelming fact: local county government was then and is now in a state of crisis. The increased mobility of the population, the rising rate of crime, the growth in welfare and health programs, and the sheer growth of population, all these factors meant that going into the 1960s county government just couldn't keep up with the demands being made upon it to administer people and property.
>
> County supervisors aren't interested in fancy plans for Unified Information Systems or management information systems. They don't exist now and probably never will. They want to know how to keep taxes and budgets down, they want to know what's happening in their counties. The CAOs want better budgeting procedures, more central control over departments the auditors want tax parcel automation, the clerk wants automatic vote tabulation, etcetera, even the dog catcher wants automatic licensing. . . .
>
> The answer to these real needs, and to crisis in government, is electronic data processing carried on by specialized centers. Without centralized data centers in county government, you end up with a hodgepodge of computers. Here . . . they had eleven computer centers, each with different equipment, each serving different needs, and they couldn't even talk with one another. My task here, as it was in Western County, is to pull these centers together into one centralized operation so that the information stored by one agency can be transferred to another agency that needs that information.

The idea of a county information system appeared in Western County in 1961 and 1962. The central element of the proposed information system was the SSIS system, which would centralize the record-keeping and accounting files of these agencies under the aegis of the Data Center. The two subunits of the Social Services Information System are the Central Index and the agency file, both in *real time*.

The second element of the proposed information system was loosely termed an "Administrative Services Package." This system would centralize the budgeting information of departments in one computer file. Access to this file was restricted to the county administrative officer and the auditor, although other departments could use it when necessary.

The third element of the system was a "things" or property file that would serve the auditor and the Tax Department by listing all taxable and assessable pieces of property in the county. The property file could also be used for planning and zoning studies.

Armed with an expertise, a new tool, and a mission (centralized data processing), the professional data processor offered new hope to the beleaguered county public official. Faced with protests from taxpayers and rising discontent of urban populations over the lack of public services, the county supervisors received with enthusiasm the promises of the data processor: a new man–machine technology could deliver more services for less cost, and in the long run, reduce the demand for services through greater knowledge and understanding.

PRECOMPUTER CHARACTERISTICS: THE INITIAL CONDITIONS

The initial characteristics of the SSIS agencies were not especially favorable for effective integration of their information storage and processing facilities into the proposed system. The agencies differed markedly in terms of the kinds of activities each performed, the values that informed those activities, and the personnel employed. However, the increasing levels of interpendence among the agencies, and their low internal integration, were favorable to their closer integration.

Increasing Levels of Interdependence

We have noted earlier that legislation written in the early 1960s at state and federal levels increased the interdependence of public social service agencies in the county. Thus a functional requisite of administering welfare programs, for instance, was information on the clients' health records and eligibility for a Medicaid grant. A commonly cited figure in Western County during the initiation of the SSIS system was that 95% of the social services were delivered to 5% of the population in the county.

Not all functional requisites are consciously or accurately perceived, of course. However, in Western County during the initiation stage of the SSIS project, county managers and agency managers alike both recognized the need for an innovation that could systematically transfer selected bits of information about clients across agency boundaries. Increasing interdependence created an objective need for information sharing; the subjective perception of increasing interdependence by all parties created the necessary consensus for the initiation of the SSIS project. As one welfare director remarked:

> We had run out of solutions by 1964. Ad hoc interagency conferences could handle only a few multiproblem cases, but there were thousands. Obviously we needed some new arrangement, and in 1964 the SSIS project appeared to be the only feasible solution.

A Low Level of Internal Integration

We know that welfare workers are the subject of frequent and intensive reviews by external political actors, such as the county administrative officer, the Board of Supervisors, and even private groups such as the Taxpayers' Association of Western County. A social workers' union in the county serves to lessen the control of supervisors over their workers, and there are a number of state regulations that determine the caseload of social workers. Complex federal and state regulations set the amount of monetary grants to Health and Welfare clients. Knowledge acquired during caseworker–client interactions is considered to be privileged information, thus is removed from influence of supervisors and agency directors. One welfare official remarked, "About the only control we have over caseworkers is the number of hours they work." A Probation Department director found after an informal investigation that many long-term clients of the department became so "because the social workers liked them personally."

Thus when compared, for instance, with police departments or other criminal justice agencies, social service organizations are seen to possess far less control over their members and to be less able politically to defend them against external control.[47]

Partly because of these features of social service agencies, they are less likely to become the predominant focus of members' occupational and political identification. Impressions gained in interviews with caseworkers from the SSIS agencies lead to the conclusion that caseworkers identify with their profession, not the specific agency.

A multiagency data bank such as SSIS involves the systematic exchange of information among relatively autonomous organizations. Low or moderate internal integration of participating organizations is conducive to the successful initiation of a shared data bank for a number of reasons. First, the lower internal integration, the more sensitive—even vulnerable—are agencies to such externally initiated reforms as shared data banks. Second, the lower internal integration, the less competition, hostility, and suspicion among agencies, and the more likely will be their cooperation. Third, the lower internal integration, the less likely it is that agency personnel will define their information needs as unique; hence sharing certain pieces of information about clients will generate less internal opposition. As the section, "The Advisory Committee," reveals, directors and professional personnel of the SSIS agencies welcomed the concept of a shared data bank as a device to provide more social services to the so-called multiproblem families of the county.

Low Homogeneity

The SSIS system was to be composed of agencies that did not perform the same tasks or employ the same personnel. Two of the SSIS agencies, the Probation and Institutions departments, engage primarily in custodial activities. The Probations Department employs a large staff of probation officers whose principal task is the surveillance of former prisoners and convicted criminals. The Institutions Department operates the county's jails and reformatories and employs the correctional staffs of these institutions. The activities of the Probation and Institutions departments have frequently led to conflict between these agencies and the Welfare and Health departments.

Caseworkers from the SSIS agencies frequently participate in interagency conferences on "multiproblem" families (i.e., those served by more than one agency). According to one Welfare official who coordinates these meetings, patterned and frequent conflicts occur between Probation caseworkers on the one hand and Welfare and Health workers on the other. What is viewed in the Welfare and Health departments as a family problem, solvable through counseling, is considered by Probation workers to be a criminal problem. "One wants to put the man in jail for violating probation, and the others want to give the man therapy," remarked a Welfare official. Thus the custodial and law enforcement functions of probation workers conflict with the therapeutic orientation of Health and Welfare workers.

Yet another source of conflict among these agencies had been the use of information about clients. Police and probation workers used to try to acquire the addresses of wanted persons through informal inquiries to "friendly caseworkers" in the Welfare Department—assuming that a wanted person will avoid the police, but he will certainly be having his welfare check sent to his current address. The SSIS system caused managers and caseworkers in the Welfare Department to fear that personal

client information would be made available to probation workers. They
were also afraid that the Health Department would use the welfare information to track and record illegitimate births.

The low homogeneity of the SSIS agencies in terms of the tasks they
performed, the values that informed their activities, and the different kinds
of personnel they employed, was not conducive to initial consensus among
the organizations participating in the centralized data bank. The low
homogeneity of the agencies was instead responsible for an atmosphere
of distrust.

THE REFORM PROCESS: MECHANISMS OF LEGITIMATION

In theory the CAO and the Board of Supervisors could have established
and implemented the SSIS project by executive fiat. For a variety of reasons, however, large-scale administrative reform projects in local government are implemented in this manner only as a last resort. In jurisdictions
in which agency directors possess a measure of independence from elected
officials (e.g., Civil Service appointment or professional group strength),
reform projects can be resisted and either forestalled or scuttled completely. The history of police civilian review boards and the resistance
mounted by police unions, professional groups, and agency directors gives
ample testimony to this possibility.[48] In addition, broadly based reform
projects—such as information systems—cannot be implemeted and put
into operation without many technically trained personnel who are also
familiar with the workings of participating organizations. This expertise
cannot readily be imported or bought on an open market but instead must
generally be recruited from participating groups. The potential adverse
consequences of the importation of expertise in this crucial initiation stage
are illustrated in Chapter 9.

The Notables Model of Legitimation

Largely for the two reasons just named, external initiating elites of a reform attempt to involve the participating groups in the reform at some
point in the planning, implementation and/or operational stages. It is
hoped that this involvement will help create the necessary degree of consensus regarding the ends and means of the reform, leading also to the
identification of a pool of technically trained experts to operate the project.

The mechanisms of legitimation utilized by the SSIS initiating elites
developed in two stages. Once the decision to establish a shared data bank

for the social services was made in 1963, an advisory committee of representatives from the involved agencies was selected by the CAO. Besides the director of the Data Center and the county auditor, the Advisory Committee was composed largely of assistant managers from the SSIS agencies and their respective agency systems experts who operated the separate agency computers.

This period corresponds in our typology to the Notables model of legitimation, in which external initiating elites select members from the groups to be reformed, claiming that this select body of notables is "representative" of the interests affected by the reform. In fact, since the selection of notables is made by external elites, usually before nonelite groups have the time to arrive at a consensus among themselves through discussion and debate, the body of notables tends to reflect the initiating elite's notion of those who would be most "useful" to the success of the reform. "Usefulness" to the reform depends generally on three factors: (*a*) familiarity with the operations of the nonelite groups, (*b*) influence within the nonelite groups, and (*c*) favorable disposition toward the reform.

A Notables model of legitimation was a logical choice in the SSIS project for two reasons. First, the 1963 Board of Supervisors decision authorized the creation of a social services data bank that would utilize the computer facilities of the Data Center in the Auditor's Department. Second, although the SSIS agencies were favorably disposed to data sharing among themselves, they did not wish to lose their own computer operations to the Data Center, nor to concede control of certain kinds of agency information to a separate, autonomous data center.

If a Pluralist or Collegial model of legitimation were adopted, with nonelite groups exercising veto power or total control, respectively, over the reform, chances were very great that the SSIS project would have disintegrated—or, at the very least, that it would have assumed a character different from that desired by the elite groups. Specifically, the SSIS agencies desired to maintain separate computer faculties and to establish tie-lines among computers for exchange of selected client information. Such a prospect was anathema to the professional interests of the Data Center director, who was interested in building the Total Centralized Information System, to the county auditor interested in obtaining new equipment for his center, to the CAO interested in building his Administrative Services Package, and to the Board of Supervisors interested in reducing the costs of social service administration.

At the same time, a Reputational Elite model was inappropriate to the SSIS project in its initial stages. The SSIS project was envisaged by its designers as a real-time, instantaneous update and retrieval data bank. Both the input and output from the computer would depend on the willing and accurate compliance of hundreds of field and lower-level managers in the SSIS agencies to new and complex computer instructions, forms, and rules. Virtually every employee, some more than others, would have to undergo a certain amount of retraining to accommodate the demands of the information system. Personnel of the agencies could be ordered, or induced by higher pay, to follow a new set of procedures, but enforcing the new procedures against unwilling, resistant field workers and lower-level supervisors would be extremely costly. Responsibility would be difficult to ascertain. Willful or accidental misplacement of a pencil mark on a computer form would require a manual investigation of a welfare case, for instance. Deletion, failure to record, or distortion of a piece of information, such as correct address or mother's maiden name, could not be detected by the computer, which was blind without the willing cooperation of clerks and social workers.

Given the large scale and scope of the SSIS project and its sensitivity to resistance and sabotage, it was essential that the project possess some degree of legitimacy with social service management, middle-level supervisors, clerks, and caseworkers. A Reputational Elite model, featuring a small number of notable members bought or hired into the reform, would be unlikely to produce the requisite initial legitimacy. As it happened, a Notables model of legitimation was necessitated by the uncompromising intentions of the initiating elites, and even this model proved barely adequate as a mechanism of legitimation.

The Advisory Committee

The task of the Advisory Committee was twofold. First members decided which specific pieces of information about their clients were to be shared. In addition to legal restrictions on the flow of information among agencies, professional norms and agency political interests were factors that restricted information stored in agency exposure files. Second, the Advisory Committee designed a program to implement the SSIS project.

Interviews with members of the committee indicate that the basic cleavage was between the central administration group (the Data Center director, the county auditor, and the CAO) and the social service agencies. Among other results, this split produced different views on the purpose and form of information sharing. The central administration group was interested in the data bank concept as a means to reduce costs of administration, to reduce fraud—especially in welfare—and to better coordinate the actions of the SSIS agencies vis-à-vis "multiproblem" families. This could best be accomplished, it was argued, by the creation of a centralized information system under the auspices of the Data Center.

The social services agencies were primarily concerned with identifying and providing more comprehensive services to "multiproblem" families; the elimination of fraud and inefficiency was clearly of secondary interest. Identification of the needy families could be accomplished through expansion of existing agency computers and tying them together into a network.

Since the decision to centralize computer operations had already been taken, the agencies' proposals was not even considered to be an option by the central administration. This body argued that efficiency, fraud prevention, and better service all required a system of shared intelligence with regard to social service clients. Moreover, the SSIS agencies were assured that once the Central Index was established, funds would be provided to write research computer programs that would allow the agencies to identify the "multiproblem" families and to establish interagency programs aimed specifically at this group. At the time, these arguments appeared reasonable to the SSIS agencies, and agreement was reached on the use of personal identifying information in the Central Index (e.g., name, address, maiden name, social security number, case number, agency exposure, and social worker number). As one participant from the Probation Department confided, "In those early days we didn't know a computer from an adding machine. They [the central administration group] could have told us anything and we would have had to believe it."

Transition to a Reputational Elite Model

Reform projects of long duration and large scope require a relatively permanent group of trained experts for their implementation and operation. Once the SSIS project was clearly defined and had received the support of the agency managers, it faced two generic problems: first, to obtain the support of the much larger staffs of the various agencies, and second, to train a group of experts who could run the system. The typical solution to both problems is the hiring (and promoting) of well-known and respected personnel from the nonelite groups into the leadership of the reform project. The reputational elite thus produced is intimately familiar with the politics and operations of the nonelite groups, is committed to the success of the reform, and can be expected to use its influence within nonelite groups to foster the reform. The reputational elite, besides providing the reform with knowledge and guidance appropriate to its purpose furnishes an aura of legitimacy to the project. Nonelite groups, and their personnel, are able to take consolation in the feeling that "one of them" is representing their interests.

The building of the reputational elite was itself a matter of contention in the SSIS project. The social service agencies argued that trained personnel, (e.g., systems designers and programmers), should be responsible to them as principal users of the system. The central administration and the Data Center argued that since the ultimate responsibility for the project lay with the Data Center, the experts should be responsible to it.

The central administration view won out, and thus began a process of recruitment and training of personnel from the ranks of the agencies to the Data Center staff. From the Welfare Department, the largest component of the system and potentially the most troublesome, the director of the Central Index was selected. A 12-year veteran of Welfare, he had risen from caseworker to manager and was highly respected by welfare managers and social workers alike. Ten welfare caseworkers were chosen by examination to participate in a computer programming course operated by the vendor, IBM. The best of these was hired by the Data Center to act as liaison between the Center and the Welfare Department; the remainder were promoted within the Welfare Department to programmer positions. From the Health Department, the second largest component of the system, five recently trained programmers were hired by the Center to "help bring Health into the program."

In the short span of the year 1964 the social service agencies had been relieved of their data processing facilities and the personnel required to use electronic data processing. A significant part of the SSIS agencies' information storage and retrieval capacities now was controlled by an autonomous bureau, the Data Center. All research requiring the use of electronic equipment was subject to the approval of the Center. Simultaneously, the central administration's capacity for information processing, largely budgetary information, expanded in the form of the CAO's Administrative Services Package. The consequences of these features of the SSIS system were not immediately apparent, however.

1965: On the Air in Real Time

In early 1965 the design and implementation of the SSIS system was completed, and, in systems analyst's argot, SSIS was "on the air," or operational. Beginning with 100,000 persons on Central Index, the system has multiplied five times between 1965 and 1969: 500,000 persons were on the file, according to 1969 Data Center figures.

Despite the size and complexity of the system, little attention was given in the public press to the arrival of the technetronic age. Most of the attention in the print media was devoted to another system that was being promoted by the Data Center; namely, the Police Regional Information System (PRIS). Welfare scandals continued to "be discovered" by one area newspaper, and perhaps because of its overall hostility to the Welfare Department, the paper did not publicize the agency's "modernization" of welfare. Indeed, the only Data Center news to appear in that paper during 1965 concerned PRIS.

The first director of the Data Center left Western in 1965 for another county, where he later created a Uniform Information System, and the assistant director was appointed the new Director of the Data Center.

An inveterate showman, the new director was always willing to perform yet another demonstration of the wonders of modern technology. At the 1965 meeting of the state Association of County Data Processors the director presented to his professional peers the long-awaited prototype Uniform Information System:

> Press keyboard request key. Wait for response. The response in this case is M-1, indicating that there is one record in file that matches the data entered, followed by the name, sex, first four characters of street, month, day and year of birth, case number, social worker position number, status of the case (open or closed), and a reference to the degree of match.

> In the second example we entered the inquiry code, last name, first initial, and first four characters of street address. . . . In this response we obtained two possible cases. . . .

> In the third example we purposely misspelled the subject's last name and entered full first name and sex. . . . The response is the correct record with a degree of match of 071/171 because the spelling of the name is different.

> To further demonstrate the flexibility of the inquiry program, assume that we know only the last name, and that the subject is about 64 years old (born in 1901). We enter inquiry code . . . the response is a match.

> Assume that as a result of one or more earlier inquiries, we have determined that Axel Anderson is the case we want, but we would like more information. We use a different inquiry code, 3053, tab once, and center the case number from the previous response. . . . The response now includes the complete address of the subject, the year in which the status of

the case last changed, the census tract in which he resides, social worker position number, and status of the case.

If we are interested in other records, in the files, that are associated with the Anderson case, we use another inquiry code (3054) and the case number. The response lists the phonetic code and indentification serial number of each person related to the master case. The phonetic code is machine developed and consists of the first letter of the last name— a three-digit numeric code and first letter of last name. Note the system will chain together related cases, even though the names are completely different.

Note that you are inquiring against a file of approximately 30,000 cases involving nearly 100,000 persons, and that, while you are doing this demonstration, several other terminals are also inquiring into the file, and the mainline processing of Western County is proceeding.[49]

Other demonstrations in 1965 included a 6000-mile remote inquiry into the prototype Police Regional Information System from West Germany to Western County by trans-Atlantic cable. Even Scotland Yard paid a visit to the Western County Data Center.

For the social service departments' new information system, 1965 was not a year of demonstrations. The agencies were too busy trying to make the "infernal machine" work on a day-to-day basis. The promises of the new technology were about to be tested in the field. And the results were neither expected nor encouraging.

THE PARTISAN VIEW

For the partisans in Western County, the SSIS agencies, the computer center expansion is now perceived and criticized as decreasing their command over vital resources and impairing the pursuit of agency goals.

In all organizations the control over information collection, flow, and storage, whether pertaining to clients or to internal administrative matters, is held to be essential for preserving the integrity of the organization with respect to the public, other competing agencies, and politicians of all stripes. Control over information functions serves organizations as an important boundary-maintaining device against potentially disruptive external inquires and is a requisite for self-evaluation and planning. Organizations establish mechanisms to preserve their control over internal information (e.g., rules and guidelines about public disclosure, informal written communications, limited access to files and records); in turn, organizations resist any threat to impair its control over information.[50]

In Western County resistance to the SSIS project developed among the social service agencies along two lines. First, the agencies did not want to lose control over a vital organization process (client information storage and retrieval) to an autonomous data center which, it was feared, had different goals and priorities. As one Welfare manager remarked:

> It all sounded pretty rosy in 1963. If you want to know why we joined the system it was because we were so impressed with what they promised us.
>
> They were practically going to do the casework for us. There were promises that our clerical staff would be cut in half, and that a good part of our paper work would simply disappear.
>
> At least that is what IBM, the computer vendors, and their allies over at the County Auditor's office were telling us then.
>
> The promises simply haven't been realized. Our fears have been realized. It's probably cost us more to get into this thing than if we had built our own computer operation right here.
>
> So far the computer center just hasn't been able to live up to our expectations of helping us to provide better service to our clients. Sure we've continued to expand and the data center has been able to keep up with our operation, but just barely. If anything, quality has suffered.
>
> The first mistake was taking our computer facilities out of our hands and putting them into the hands of the Data Center.

As described below, welfare workers and supervisors believe that the SSIS project has decreased the ability of the agency to cope with "multiproblem" families and has transformed the department into something akin to an insurance company.

The second line of resistance to the SSIS project centers around the threat of confidential welfare or medical information reaching the wrong hands. This prospect causes political problems within the agencies, where professional caseworkers view the computer project as detrimental to their clients' interests. But the question of the confidentiality of client information is raised by any procedure for exchanging information among agencies—computer or no computer. The Administrative Code of Western State prohibits the release of personal client information to any outside source—

private or public. However, a good deal of information kept in Central Index is not considered to be "personal" information. According to a Central Index official:

> In practice, for instance, Welfare does not pay much attention to additional information printed out on its clients which have been involved with other agencies. However, Probation does use Central Index fairly regularly to obtain information on addresses of its clients who may be involved with Welfare. The idea is that a person on welfare would always update his address accurately in order to receive welfare checks.
>
> Probation then takes advantage of this latest welfare address. Also the Health Department uses welfare addresses to keep track of persons with contagious diseases like TB and VD.

Although through the Central Index the SSIS system permits formal exchange of information which previously was not possible, there had also been an increase in informal exchanges. According to the official just quoted:

> Each agency makes an agreement with the other agencies about formal information exchange. On the other hand, once an agency knows the number of a person on welfare—which it can get from the Central Index—the agency can then inquire by private telephone to a friendly welfare worker or supervisors about the status of that person with welfare.
>
> Of course this kind of informal exchange took place before the computer as well. The difference is that such exchanges are now more probable and efficient.
>
> So there are indeed real problems of confidentiality with Central Index, even though we try to minimize them. Each agency tries to guard the integrity of its files, but by virtue of participation in Central Index it is impossible to do that completely. Before the computer it was much effort for the police to follow up a welfare case. Now it is easy, so it's done.
>
> Because of this, there has been a period of hostile relations between the police, probation and welfare due to probation's use, and police as well, of Welfare Department's address information.

The participating agencies in the Central Index do not consider confidentiality of information to be a fundamental problem, but as the next section reveals, the issue does occasionally surface to claim public attention.

During these periods of public interest, the Data Center points to the official agreements arrived at between agencies as evidence that information exchange is strictly controlled by the agencies and by state law. The reality is quite different, but the public is not aware of how police and Probation use the Central Index welfare information to find, arrest, and prosecute their clients.

Is Anybody Listening?

> The urgency was twofold: first to provide better service to truly needy families served by multiple agencies; and second, to avoid misuse of these services with the resultant drain on taxpayer dollars.
>
> Data Processing Center pamphlet, 1968

The reaction and behavior of the line agencies involved in the SSIS system can best be characterized as alienated acquiescence. The expression of alienation takes the form of complaints: (1) the loss of agency information processing equipment has reduced the flexibility of the agencies, (2) the agencies have become dependent on a bureau that does not share their commitment to professional goals, (3) inability to meet the needs of agency clients results, and (4) there is resistance to computerization from professional and semiprofessional staff who fail to see the "relevance" of the computer for their clients.

In the eyes of the managers and staff on the line agencies, the centralization of information processing equipment has resulted in the Board of Supervisors being less responsive to the needs of the agencies.

The bitterness toward the Data Center is most pronounced in the Welfare Department, which has the largest budget and the largest client population of all the social service agencies. As one welfare director remarked:

> . . . the promises have not been realized. . . . So far the machine has just not been able to live up to our expectations of helping us provide better service to our clients. . . . If anything, quality has suffered.
>
> The first mistake was taking our computer facilities out of our hands and putting them into the hands of the Data Center.
>
> Second, there is a tremendous unsolved problem of programming and staffing over there. We had a number of programmers with us in the early 1960s who really knew our opera-

tion in Welfare. And they worked for us!!! But when the Data Center came along they got hold not only of our equipment, but also they took our programmers.

They put our programmers to work on the problems of other agencies, such as Probation. This dispersion of talent hurt us badly. We get inexperienced programmers as a result.

It takes a long time to train a programmer to do a certain job well. It takes even longer to convince him he is doing something important, something that will help out people. As soon as you train them they move on to better jobs nowadays. In the old days the programmers would be loyal to us here at Welfare. It wasn't just the money they were out for.

The unfilled need for trained programmer personnel committed to Welfare goals is seen as a partial explanation for the absence of coordination among social service agencies and the lack of knowledge pertaining to the impact of welfare policies. According to another manager in the Welfare Department:

We've wanted for years to do research programs on our case studies, and we've tried to get program development studies. For the last four years we've been limited by the low resources of the Data Center and the low priority these programs receive over there. It isn't just a matter of money: given the money we still can't get things done for us.

This all relates to the question of why there isn't more coordination and integration of social services here. I've sat in on case conferences involving many agency caseworkers, and you'd be surprised how often the policy of one agency contradicts that of another in reference to a single client.

Sometimes police want a man arrested, probation wants the man on parole, and Welfare is trying to increase his welfare check. We can get the total picture of a man and make a better judgment when we have cooperation between agencies.

But, and this is a big "but," we need new kinds of information and processing to bring coordination about. We need housing information; police should contribute; and schools should be added. I mean the teacher of a class should know whether Johnny's mother beats him, his father is out of work, etcetera. As yet we don't have this sort of coordination of information.

Although some might attribute the lack of coordination among agencies to insufficient funds, the management of the Welfare Department emphasizes the lack of usable knowledge and appropriate information as the basic causes of fragmentation at the local level. The official just quoted said:

> Certainly the Central Index and other components of the Data Center (Accounting Information System) have improved budgeting procedures and enforcement of eligibility rules. On the other hand, despite what the newspapers and the public believe, fraud is not any more significant in welfare than say, a large insurance company.

> So what if you exchange that kind of information? The jealousy of schools, police, and the SSIS agencies prevents much useful information coming to Welfare. As long as each agency has its own philosophy about how to help or change people, the increased information exchange has little effect on decisions actually taken.

> More money alone is not the answer. More knowledge would certainly help to solve disputes over how to treat the so-called multiple problem family. You see we still do not know what we are doing in Welfare.

> Take, for instance, the case of illegitimate children, and the AFDC program. What is its impact? Do we create more illegitimate children? Does it cause people to avoid employment?

> We just don't know the answers because we have done no research, we have no direction. And we haven't been able to get the Data Center to let us do the research—it is too low in priority for them and the Board of Supervisors. For two years they have sat on our research proposals. . . .

At this point we must ask whether local county agencies in the social services could use more knowledge to exert genuine impact on state and federal programs. The Welfare Department, for instance, has few policy options: it is a regulated arm of state and federal welfare policies; an administrative not a policy unit. To this question, the Welfare official responded:

> It's true we are more subject to federal and state regulation than some of the other agencies, but if we could prove certain points we could change many welfare policies at the federal and state levels.

> The County Board of Supervisors, with other counties, main-
> tains a lobby in [the state capital] and there is a National
> Association of Counties in Washington. Welfare directors
> have a statewide association with a lobby in [the capital] and
> so do the caseworkers.

> The channels for change exist. If we could show, for instance,
> that the AFDC program is causing more families to deteri-
> orate than it is helping, or if we could show that more money
> should be pumped into family planning and planned parent-
> hood programs, then I feel more than confident that we could
> bring about important changes in welfare.

In a subsequent interview with a systems analyst of the Welfare Department,
an interesting distinction between administrative and social information
emerged:

> The present system is good at shuffling large numbers of
> similar cases through the welfare process, preventing fraud,
> and stringently enforcing criteria for eligibility. Fine, but the
> point is we still do not know our own cases.

> The population we deal with is for all intents and purposes
> unknown to us. We don't know the family size, ages of chil-
> dren, education of children, schools attended, income of
> family, education of parents, origins of family, jobs held by
> the male or female, educational potentials of parents, et cetera,
> et cetera. We don't know the caseloads of caseworkers despite
> the fact that the law says no more than 80 cases per worker is
> permissible.

> All of these items could be obtained by simple counting
> procedures—but they are necessary to any fruitful analyses
> of the population. But the Data Center does not have the
> programmers to write the programs. All of their programmers
> are either busy with some urgent problems of entry, update,
> and clearing functions, or they have left their jobs. What can
> you expect on Civil Service wages?

Thus in the eyes of management in Welfare, the information system functions to increase the instrumental control features of the agency. This
emphasis on instrumental-control information appears to conflict with a
desire to gather information about clients for the purpose of attaining the
expressive goals of the agency, variously described as "helping people,"
"intervening in the poverty cycle," and so on. As a welfare caseworker
pointed out, "We aren't just an insurance company passing out checks."

The lack of commitment to the expressive goals of Welfare is exemplified in an interview with the Data Center's welfare liaison officer. Formerly one of the bright young programmers of the Welfare Department, he was transferred to the Data Center in 1964 when the SSIS system was approved.

> I've been with the welfare section of the Data Center since its inception. You see I was a social worker in the beginning. Actually my college degree was in music. At any rate I became a social worker like a lot of young college graduates— sort of in the hope that I could do something about the social condition of the country, but also in part because I didn't want to go to graduate school.

> Like most of the young recruits to Welfare I quickly became dissatisfied with the sort of work I was doing and soon became frustrated with the whole welfare approach. That was in 1958.

> A couple years later I was one of ten social workers chosen on the basis of aptitude tests to be trained in elementary programming and card sorter operation, for the Welfare computers.

> After a year at that I became very dissatisfied—it seemed I was even further away from doing something which I felt was meaningful. Five of my fellow workers had left the training program and the Welfare Department. About that time the county had decided to install this much bigger Data Processing Center to replace the agency computers. I applied for the job to work here at the Data Center and was chosen from among five applicants. IBM then gave me further training in programming. . . .

> Welfare actually doesn't do any policy research. Actually, a few months ago, no I guess it was a year or so, they did request to be assigned a statistician to do some compilations for them and extra computer time to run them. (Looks for request in back of file; fails to find it; shrugs shoulders.) . . . But I don't think they will get an OK on that anyway. We just don't have the funds or time to do that kind of stuff.

> Besides, what would they do with it anyway? They don't make decisions about welfare, the state and federal government is more important in that area.

The unresponsiveness of the Data Center and its personnel to the expressed needs of the welfare agency is reflected in the resistance of "professional" caseworkers to the SSIS project. In the view of the Data Center liaison officer, caseworker resistance is caused by the immaturity and personal instability of the workers. According to the workers, the computer project is resisted because it does not seem to bear any relation to "helping the client":

> There is a great deal of resistance to computerization within Welfare, especially in the Aid to Dependent Children program. I remember in particular that the director of the program was very much against the computer in general and opposed the use of it in his ADC program. He would always make snide remarks to us at the Data Center about the computer not being able to process the "odd-ball" case. Which is true, we always have some special cases which for one reason or another cannot be handled by the computer and must be processed manually. But he would always go out of his way to tell us when this happened. . . . Often the problem was that the workers in his division, the caseworkers, incorrectly filled out the information sheets, and the computer would reject these and send them back to the caseworker for correction.

> The largest amount of resistance is found not in management, but among the caseworkers or so-called professionals. I call them professionals because they have been fighting for professional status for the last two years here in the county, but actually they are just caseworkers, most with B.A.'s and a few with a Master's in social work.

> The caseworkers just don't see how filling out a computer form correctly relates to the problems of their clients. Consequently we have a large problem with Welfare in getting them to properly administer the Data Processing Center's operations within their own organization.

> The clerical workers don't mind the system at all—I think they feel that being associated with the computer improves their status and image.

> The "professionals," however, point to the depersonalization of the professional-client relationship. I suppose they dislike the limiting of their discretion by the computer, which makes certain decisions for them, such as the amount of aid given to the client. Their authority is reduced.

> Actually though, the real problem is that they are generally young kids just out of college who are very idealistic, insecure about both present and future. The job is frustrating I admit.

> The turnover is very high in Welfare, about 30% per year. In other words, the inability of the social workers themselves is the major cause of resistance.

Interviews with the caseworkers confirm the impression that they oppose or are indifferent to computerization because it does not help them help their clients. In the caseworkers' view, the SSIS system is part of an economy drive by the Board of Supervisors:

> No one likes that damn machine. Every time you fill out one form, you get two more forms back from the machine telling you about your mistakes on the first form. Before the computer, we kept our own records and we didn't have all these forms to keep filling out.

> I'd say most of us feel indifferent to it. After all it doesn't really make any difference to my clients if the computer or a man prints out the check. On the other hand, it doesn't help our clients any more than the old system of records. About the only impact I suppose is that it saves the county some money, maybe. They're always on an austerity kick of one kind or another.

> For us the question is, how do we get jobs for welfare people? How do we keep them fed with the small welfare budgets? What do we do about their kids dropping out of school, getting arrested, jailed, et cetera? And why spend the money on a computer if you can't help your clients in the process? It's a farce.

In two recent instances, the use of the computer has been vigorously protested by Western County welfare workers. In 1969 the state Department of Welfare ordered the county Welfare Department to administer and process a battery of psychological tests to a sample of persons receiving public assistance. The information was to be processed by the Data Center and later filed in the state Welfare Department's computers in the capital.

In one office of the county Welfare Department twenty caseworkers refused to cooperate with the state's orders. Arguing that the tests and subsequent computer filing of results constituted an invasion of privacy, the caseworkers staged a walkout.

The county Welfare Department threatened to suspend the workers permanently for failing to comply, and eventually they were coaxed back to work. Newspaper reports indicated that five workers, the "ringleaders," were suspended for one week without pay for insubordination.

A second protest involving the computer occurred during the summer of 1970. A newspaper had uncovered yet another "welfare scandal." This time, it was learned that a $14,000 per year county employee was receiving $500 per month in welfare grants. Investigation revealed that the person had five children, four of whom were mentally retarded and were receiving county assistance to pay for institutional care and doctor bills. Nevertheless, a county grand jury ordered the Welfare Department to compile a list from the Central Index file of all county employees who were receiving welfare of any kind. Caseworkers publicly protested the use of the computer files as an invasion of privacy, but no suspensions resulted.

Summary of the Welfare Experience with SSIS

One is hard pressed to find welfare workers at any level who are satisfied with the SSIS system or who feel that it makes a positive contribution to their work. Directors of five local offices in the county point to the efficiency of the computer, but they quickly add that it takes more clerical workers just to keep up with the machine output. In the long run, the feeling is expressed that the computer has not made any substantial impact on the costs of administering the programs of the Department.

The supervisor of the AFDC program in the Brighton city office made one of the most positive assessments of the computer project: "I'm tired of being attacked at cocktail parties for being a coddler of poor people on the dole. So when I tell them a computer runs the AFDC program, they are impressed enough to stop criticizing the Welfare Department, and me."

Probation Department: What Are We Doing?

The complaints of the Welfare Department notwithstanding, other agencies in the SSIS system are even lower in priority. The Probation Department was the last agency in the system to develop computer applications.

Presently the Probation file carries client's name, social security number, agency number, probation worker number, status of case (open or closed), and types of referrals in the past. Besides daily use by probation workers when new clients are taken on, the system serves in making primitive surveys of the population—location of cases in the county, types of referrals, clearance type, and rate of dismissals.

All the functions performed by the computer were previously done by hand. No new functions were added, and the utility of the computer for performing traditional counting and accounting functions is coming increasingly under question. As one high-level manager remarked:

> Occasionally we use Central Index to see if a client is on welfare, but very infrequently. What we hope to do in the future are some management studies.
>
> What we have to do is sit down and figure out what we are doing and what are our goals. Then we have to find out how much our programs are contributing toward these goals. I know this sounds simple, but things are very primitive around here. We are starting from scratch.
>
> We don't know, for instance, why our cases are "dismissed." Did the man die? Was he sent to [an] "advanced correctional institutions" like San Quentin? That's not what I call success, but according to the traditional criteria, the department is judged according to how many dismissals we generate in a month.
>
> Thus we don't know how our programs contribute, damage, or just have no effect on our cases. Bluntly put, Probation is flying by the seat of its pants, just as it always has, blind!

Interviews with the manager just quoted and with others in the Probation Department indicated clearly that the department did not have ultimate control over the kinds of information the computer files stored. Although the department could make suggestions, and did so on the Advisory Committee established by the Data Center in 1964, the last word was with the Data Center.

Welfare information that happens to be about Probation Department clients will not necessarily be used by caseworkers. Indeed, in the above-mentioned manager's view, volumes of unusable and inadequate information are collected and stored on the computer. Attempts to gather new kinds of information are resisted both by the caseworkers and the Data Center. A systems analyst in Probation expressed a commonly cited complaint about the type of information gathered by the Central Index:

> We have a number of ideas for management studies and review of case decisions. In order to accomplish these, however, we will need a complete revision of information procedures, or just a change in the kinds of information collected.
>
> Look at the case decisions around here. Now this is treason for a Probation Department officer to say, but we should look at

case decisions. Why are people kept or dismissed? We found out recently that in the Adult Division a number of case-workers were holding on to clients just because they liked their personalities!! So maybe that explains why clients are dismissed or kept.

But the claim of the caseworkers is that their decisions are "rational" and decided upon in disinterested fashion. All right, if that is so, then we can instruct the computer about the rules which the caseworker uses, tell the computer how to apply them, and let the computer make the decision or at least suggest a decision.

As I said, that's treason around here, especially with our professional staff. But then I say either their decisions are rational or not. If not rational, then why have a so-called professional staff to make irrational decisions? A person out there (pointing to street) could do that. Are we managers or not, I ask myself. If we're managers then we should try to be rational, right?

But the resistance of caseworkers to close supervision by computers is not the only source of "persisting ignorance" in the department. The resistance of professional workers to the SSIS project in Probation is based on the belief that it has little relevance for their clients. And essentially they are correct, according to the systems analyst cited earlier:

So far I've talked about the problems of changing our organi-zation around. You can't blame the professional for doubting and criticizing this whole computer project. See, he doesn't get anything out of it for himself or his client. All he gets back from the machine is simple little bits of information which he could, if he wanted, get for himself. Whether or not his client has a probation history, status with county agencies, name, address, et cetera. That's a beginning, but it has to provide more than that to be considered a useful tool.

Things like contingency tables for probation programs in [this county] would be a good start. It would tell the case-worker the past distribution of success for various probation programs and for various types of clients. That would help us managers evaluate both the caseworker decisions and the program of the department.

Now our progress in these newer directions is minimal. We started later than Welfare, but they aren't better from what I hear. We are having the same kinds of difficulties with the

> Data Center to do anything more sophisticated than count heads.
>
> We do a monthly compilation of cases, but that's pretty primitive. Even that took a monumental fight with the Data Center telling us that we didn't need something like that, and that they did not have the time to do it. We won that fight, but it was like pulling teeth.
>
> When we get to more sophisticated programs—management studies and program studies—I am sure the old conflict will start again, with us having to justify to someone in the Data Center, who does not understand our needs, just what we want to do.
>
> And they have it over us because they have the machines. They decide priorities. Right now, I'd say we're pretty low.

Although computer applications in Probation are much more recent than in Welfare or Health, it is worthwhile to note the similarity of complaints against the SSIS system. First, there is the general criticism that the centralized SSIS system does not satisfy agency-perceived needs. Related to this charge is the more specific complaint that much information stored by the Central Index is not useful for agency purposes, but instead serves the purposes of the Data Center or the Board of Supervisors (e.g., accounting information, numbers of referrals and dismissals, number of cases).

Second, resistance from "professional" caseworkers develops not only because the computer is seen as a threat to professional discretion or because it implies closer supervision, but largely because the SSIS system is not perceived as helping the clients. Insofar as the "professionals" in Probation believe in professional goals,—for example, "helping people"—the computer is seen either as irrelevant or as a waste of time and money. A former county probation officer said:

> When I see them spend $100,000 to hire a computer and some fancy-named specialists to run it, I get dizzy. Our men [Probation Department clients] need jobs, and $100,000 would be enough to hire job placement specialists to get jobs. So who are they kidding?

HEALTH AND AUTOMATIC IMMUNIZATION

The county Health Department is responsible for administering county mental health, dental, public school, and disease control and monitoring programs; in 1970 it had a budget of $5 million. In addition to county health programs, which are funded by the Board of Supervisors, the Health Department reports that it holds grants from the U.S. Public Health Service and the Office of Economic Opportunity for various poverty health projects, the Vaccination Health Project, and the Disease Control Register Automation Project.

The Disease Control Register and Immunization/Vaccination projects are of particular interest to us because they show how the use of computers can radically alter the production functions of formal organizations, and social service agencies in particular. Moreover, these projects did not receive support from the Board of Supervisors but are funded through federal grants to the state and county health departments.

Response to Centralization. The Health Department has undergone many of the same problems experienced by Probation and Welfare departments following centralization of computers. Interviews with the management and caseworkers of Health indicated an intense resentment of the Data Center personnel for their lack of commitment to agency needs, as well as frustration with the Center's priorities. In the words of the Health Department director:

> Our biggest problem is getting the right kind of information services from the Data Center and getting it on time. There are tremendous delays in receiving our work. In fact, we have considered having some of our work done outside by commercial firms, and we have received permission from the Board of Supervisors occasionally.
>
> The major cause of the entire problem is the lack of trained programmers at DPC. We received a grant from a foundation a few years ago to help us train computer programmers for the Health Department. The grant was for $60,000 and we trained ten programmers. We never got a penny's worth out of those people because they left the Data Center and went elsewhere. We wasted $60,000!

The high rate of programmer turnover is partly endemic to the field of data processing, but the Health management attributes a good deal of the turnover to the failure of the Data Center to display commitment to public health goals. A systems analyst for the Health Department commented:

> A part of the problem is the scarcity of programmers, but the Data Center has not helped. First, there is a general lack of commitment at the Data Center to help out the departments which it likes to call its "clients." The computer is in the

county auditor's and controller's offices, and we can't do a hell of a lot about that. They determine how and when we'll receive our stuff—sometimes we will get bumped off a schedule by the Tax or Highway departments.

Second, they have no leadership, no cohesion. You can't expect a programmer or other valuable computer personnel over there at the Data Center to be committed to the goals of Health or Welfare when their bosses themselves are not.

Once the Data Center trains people to program for us, they stay because the position or money is to their liking, not because of any commitment to us. They [the programmers at the Data Center] are very different from our caseworkers or public health nurses who have gone through a long training process and who are really committed to helping people in need.

And it isn't just that nurses are different from programmers. When we employed our own programmers, when we had the computers in our own department, we were able to keep programmers because we spent a lot of time indoctrinating them in the goals of public health—they felt they were doing something valuable, not just punching numbers into a machine.

Every day, as a participant in the SSIS system, the Health Department submits to the Data Center the names and addresses of clients it services. The largest category of clients are those who receive Medicare services. The medical histories and other medical information files are maintained in a separate, confidential Health Department file to which other agencies do not have access. The Central Index file is seen by the management of Health as irrelevant to Health goals and restrictive of departmental flexibility. The director is now more than skeptical about the purposes of the system:

You have to understand that the Data Center was the wet dream of the auditor and the then director of the Data Center, along with the county administrative officer. Presumably, it was designed to be big enough to handle everybody's needs, but it has worked out in practice this is impossible.

The Central Index was designed to reduce fraud and error largely in Welfare. We don't use it very often although Welfare certainly does use it a good deal, especially for Medicare eligibility. I think Central Index has improved information flow between Health and Welfare.

But also the Data Center resources are overly committed to the goals of the auditor and CAO. The Administrative Services package of the CAO, the tax program of the auditor, and other accounting programs take a big chunk of computer resources, which means we have less access.

Around budget time is when you see how relations between the Board of Supervisors, Health, and the CAO have changed as a result. We now have monthly budget reviews, expenditure justifications, and so forth. Before I could shift money from one project to another, where it was needed, whereas now I have to go to the CAO with surplus funds and try and justify a shift to another project.

In addition, we can't get funds from the Board of Supervisors, and we can't get the programs written by the Data Center which would support an evaluation of Health Programs in the County. The Data Center claims it doesn't have the time or resources for such a project, and the Board of Supervisors tends to listen to them more than they do to me. Health is just too low on the priorities right now, and as a result we don't receive funding from the Board of Supervisors, nor support from the Data Center on health projects we believe are vital.

The last county health survey (the Vaccination Assistance Project immunization survey) was completed in 1965 by the Health Department through a special grant from the U.S. Public Health Service. The results of the survey were instrumental in securing subsequent grants from the Public Health Service for two computer-supported projects in Western County: the Automatic Immunization Program and the Disease Control Register Automation Project.

Disease Control and Immunization. County health departments are charged with protecting the health of their communities, and historically this has involved immunizing the population against common, communicable diseases and recording the incidence of particularly dangerous diseases, such as venereal disease and tuberculosis.

Disease prevention and immunization are complicated tasks with a large population because of the intensive follow-up procedures required. Newborn infants are of course immunized against a number of diseases at the hospital where they are born. However, follow-up booster shots are required for many diseases, and the return to the hospital is left to the initiative and understanding of the parents. Frequently the parents do not understand the function of follow-up visits, cannot afford the return, or simply forget. Especially among lower socioeconomic groups in the county, the level of immunization to disease is comparatively low. The 1965 surveys revaled that only one-fifth of the county population was adequately immunized against all diseases on which information was gathered (polio, smallpox, diphtheria, tetanus, and for children, measles). The survey found considerable variability in adequacy of immunization among the various ethnic groups within the county: compared with white groups, 10–25% fewer Negro and Latin American children under age 5 had adequate immunity to the diseases mentioned.

Among the adult population, the recording and monitoring of the spread of communicable diseases, particularly VD and tuberculosis, is also highly complicated. Before the institution of SSIS, information about the incidence of new cases frequently was not transferred from its point of collection in a hospital to the county Health Department. The mobility of the population made record keeping highly inaccurate. New case data were not detailed enough or timely enough to permit the Health Department to isolate "high-incidence areas" and to launch preventive programs suited to specific groups within the population. Caseworkers said that venereal disease preventive programs initiated by the department in 1960 and 1961 were more successful among middle-class groups than in ghetto and working-class white districts.

Computer Centralization and the Disease Control Register.   The centralization of computers in the Data Center allowed the purchase of larger and more sophisticated computer equipment. Besides participating in the SSIS Central Index by submitting lists of clients with w'1om Health had contact, the Health Department initiated the computerization of its Disease Control Register in 1965.

Automation of the Register was intended to improve both the monitoring of incidence and the effectiveness of intervention in the community. It appears that both goals have been attained.

Presently, all hospital and mobile unit contacts with TB- or VD-infected people are recorded on IBM cards and submitted daily to the Health Department. The information includes the client's name and address, his census tract, race, and previous addresses.

Information collected at point of contact is checked against the Central Index files for accuracy. Changes in address for a client who has moved are made automatically by the computer. Monthly and if necessary weekly printouts are run to present a countywide picture of incidence.

In addition to improving the accuracy and timeliness of information collection and retrieval, the Automated Health Register has greatly raised the preventive capacities of the Health Department. According to the Department's statistician:

> One impact of the information system is more intensive and coordinated follow-up procedures involving other departments, principally Welfare. For instance, using census tract or other units such as school districts, we can identify the regions and socioeconomic makeup of areas where the incidence of VD is high. We then send out social workers—some from Health and some from Welfare, who know the district—into those areas to conduct further research, information campaigns, and in some cases to establish intensive prevention units.

In the case of the Automatic Register, a new type of service is being produced: area- and socioeconomic-specific disease prevention services.

Immunization Project.   A more striking example of how a new technology can stimulate the production of new services is provided by the Automatic Immunization Project (AIP). The AIP was designed to remove the following barriers to the immunization of children: ignorance, lack of information, and absentmindedness.

Under the AIP, all new births within the county are recorded daily by the computer, and immunization notices are sent out to parents automatically. The computer records all immunizations done by doctors in the county and sends out reminder notices to parents who fail to bring their newborns to a doctor for immunization within a specified period. In addition, when booster shots are required, the computer sends out booster and 18-month follow-up notices to parents every month until compliance is recorded.

Here too, as in the case of the Disease Register, the new computer technology has changed both the means and the ends of production in Health. The AIP represents an addition to the services provided by the Health Department, and the means of providing these services is very different from previous techniques.

Why Resistance Is Lower in the Health Agency

The Health Department's experience with the Data Center, the SSIS system, the county auditor, and the CAO is similar in many respects to that of the Welfare and Probation departments. The lack of commitment to agency goals, the increasingly intensive budgetary reviews conducted by the

CAO and the Board of Supervisors, and the failure of the Data Center to be responsive to agency needs, are.the oft-cited factors that create resentment of the Data Center on the part of Health management and caseworkers.

Yet despite resentment towards the Data Center and county elites, the attitude of Health Department personnel regarding the utility of the computer in achieving agency goals is more positive than in either Welfare or Probation. In the latter departments, the Data Center and SSIS Central Index are seen as no more than marginally beneficial to clients or to the agency. Instead, the Data Center is perceived as a sort of "foreign power" intervening in the department, and the Central Index appears as a type of regulatory or police power.

Although the Health Department faces similar political problems with the Data Center and county elites, it is markedly different in one respect: it has been able to go outside the county for funds to support innovative programs involving the computer facilities of the Data Center. That is, both the Immunization and Disease Control Projects are funded by federal grants.

As a result of finding outside support for innovative computer projects, and their ultimate success in achieving public health goals with the computer, the attitudes of Health personnel toward the SSIS project are more sanguine. A high-level manager in Health, himself an M.D., cites with obvious pride what has been accomplished:

> Our most advanced program is the Automatic Immunization Program. Our other programs are just information-storing ones—traditional activities of the Health Department that are now mechanized. But Immunization is something we are very proud of because it is the only truly automatic program we have and approaches the utopian ideas of what a computer should be able to do.

> From the beginning we had visions of the computer doing more than just accounting and record keeping. We wanted it to do our job better. Our goals were twofold: first we wanted to build a lifetime cumulative health history of everyone here in the county. Second, we wanted the computer to do some of the field work for us.

> With the Immunization and Disease Control Projects we have attained some of these goals. We are working on a family planning project: the computer has a way of picking out which births in the county are illegitimate, and from this information we will set up special programs in certain areas of the county, aimed at certain age groups, where illegitimacy is high.

We have had our own headaches with the computer—and a goodly number come from the Data Center. Our own professional nurses resist filling out computer forms, and as a result we have the greatest rate of computer kickbacks of all the agencies. The nurses apparently fail to see the relation between filling out computer forms and helping sick persons. That is our own organizational problem, something we can change through education.

But it took four years to put together the immunization project, in part because of the Data Center itself. Equipment changes, personnel turnover, the fact they are overcommitted to a variety of diverse agencies—these things drive me crazy. We used to be able to have some of our work done by private firms, but the county won't allow this any more. They want us to use the Data Center despite its shortcomings. In short, we could have done much more, gone faster and farther with our own computer center right here in Health.

Interviews with Health Department personnel lend the impression that despite the shortcomings of the Data Center, Health has been able to utilize the county computers to increase the effectiveness of its agency, and to do this by obtaining funds from federal agencies for innovative changes in its programs. In Welfare and Probation, the county computers have not functioned to increase the effectiveness of agency programs; therefore, a good deal more resentment is evident in those departments.

WESTERN COUNTY IN PERSPECTIVE: CENTRALIZATION AND RESISTANCE

Our observations of Western County suggest strongly that the use of sophisticated information technology has led to an increase in administrative centralization in the county government. Most informed observers in the county point to the central administration's control over and use of the Administrative Services Package, and to the SSIS system as evidence of this. Although there has been no change in the formal authority of the county administrative officer, his almost instant access to agency budgets, through a computerized budgeting system, has led to closer scrutiny and supervision of line agencies. In turn the central administration's control over the SSIS system has in effect vested in it the power to determine what kinds of information social service agencies will systematically collect, for what purposes, and the processing priorities. Here we summarize some of the conditions that account for this centralization.

One important factor suggested in our case study is the power of the CAO. Possessing the formal authority to determine budgeting procedures for all agencies, the CAO does not merely carry out the wishes of the elected Board of Supervisors; instead, he plays a crucial role in formulating the wishes and policies of the supervisors. Perhaps more important, the CAO and the county auditor were both very well informed about the uses and potentials of computer technology. The same could not be said of the supervisors, who knew almost nothing about budgeting techniques or about the administrative consequences of one technique versus another.

The advantage of the CAO's superior knowledge was of course aided by the principal computer vendor firm. The vendor was influential in reducing the costs of training programmers, supplying pamphlets and information free of cost to supervisors and the press, and trumpeting the advantages of computers to local government. The promises of great savings in administrative costs, reduction in social service fraud, and increased effectiveness of social services were sufficient to gain for the CAO and the county auditor almost a blank check in the design and implementation of the technology. Centralization has occurred in the county by design, not because of any ineluctable quality of the technology.

A second source of centralization was the lack of meaningful opposition to the central administration in the initial stages of designing the technology. But why was there no initial resistance? A number of reasons suggest themselves. First, the ignorance of the user agencies and their professional employees played a central role. Faced with the centralized SSIS design of the CAO and the auditor, the user agencies did not understand its potential consequences for their own agencies, nor were they able to suggest a viable alternative.

If the social service agencies had been allotted the funds to hire their own computer consultant or vendor firm, perhaps they might have been able to devise an information system that effectively transferred information among them but would not have caused them to lose control over that information. This is obviously speculative. In any event, the alternative was not politically feasible. The legitimacy of the social service agencies with the Board of Supervisors and the larger political public declined with each revelation in the local press of yet another scandal, diminishing in direct proportion to increases in social service budgets. Thus a second reason for the weak initial resistance to the SSIS design was the fact that the user agencies had very little political influence in the county. It is doubtful that the supervisors would have allotted them the funds to design their own systems.

A third source of centralization, we have suggested, was the process of designing and constructing the system. Once the mandate to construct the information system was given by the Board of Supervisors to the CAO and the auditor, the user agencies became involved only to implement plans decided on by these two offices. In addition, key personnel from the user agencies were hired away, so to speak, to become full-time members of the new information system. This process of formal selection of a system elite serves two functions. First, the selected elite is used to encourage acceptance of the project by their former colleagues. Second, the selected elite members lend their competence and expertise to the reform project. This method of legitimating a reform project, which we have called a Reputational Elite model, minimizes the influence of participating groups and maximizes the access of reform initiators to the constitutents.

One result of a Reputational Elite reform is that participants are left with very little influence over the project; in the case of Western County, the method of reform utilized ensured that the user agencies would have almost no voice in determining the uses to which the new technology would be put. The interests of those who initiated the reform prevailed.

Resistance to the construction and use of the information system in Western County by the user agencies is linked to its political consequence (i.e., strengthening the central administration) and to the political process of building the system.

We have suggested that one source of resistance by the social service agencies was their fear that shared information would be used by Probation and by the police to locate wanted persons. Perhaps this fear would have existed regardless of who controlled the information data bank. But it was compounded by the awareness that neither the Health nor the Welfare department had sufficient influence with the Data Center to prevent such misuse of client information.

Two other sources of resistance to the information system are more clearly related to the political process of its construction. The user agencies have lost the ability to determine what information will be systematically collected, and for what purposes or values. The user agencies have failed in their attempts to have the Data Center collect information about client histories, caseworker decisions, or jobs available for parolees. Priority is given to the processing of budgetary information and the prevention of fraud.

If one sentiment could capture the origins of resistance to the information system by user agencies, it would be this: the social service agencies perceive the information system to be pursuing goals that are irrelevant at best to the welfare of their clients and the professional interests of their own caseworkers.

It could be argued that social service agencies such as health, welfare, and probation agencies in local governments, have no clear idea of how to aid their clients and that the goals of such organizations are diffuse and not specifiable. However, each user agency we investigated had specific suggestions and plans for making the county computers more relevant to its clients' interests, as we have described. The problem lay not with the specifiability of social service goals, but rather with the inability of the social service agencies to convince the central administration to accept the worth of these goals.

1972—A Sequel

A return to Western County in middle in [1972] confirms our prediction that the use of advanced computer equipment was a prelude to a more comprehensive realignment of bureaucratic authority in which the county administrative officer was both the initiator and beneficiary.

In late 1971 the following article appeared in the *Western Herald*:

WESTERN COUNTY SUPERAGENCY

> Three Western County departments—Welfare, Probation, and Human Relations—were combined in a sweeping reorganization by the Board of Supervisors yesterday.
>
> The Board . . . merged the three into a Human Relations Agency with a combined budget exceeding $200 million. Named to head the superagency was . . . an administrator virtually unknown to the county's citizenry. [He] was senior analyst in the County Administrator's Office for 15 years.
>
> . . . The restructuring was recommended by the County Administrator . . . following an eight-month study by a welfare task force.

NOTES

1. 1960 Census, *State Economic Area,* Department of Commerce, Bureau of the Census.

2. *Vaccination Assistance Project Immunization Survey,* Western County Health Department, 1965.

3. *Ibid.*

4. 1960 Census, *op. cit.*; for the Spanish-surname group, I relied on data collected by Milton E. Ortega.

5. For a discussion of politics and government in nonpartisan jurisdictions, see Eugene C. Lee, *The Politics of Non-Partisanship,* Berkeley: University of California Press, 1960, Chapters 1–2; see also Edward C. Banfield and James Q. Wilson, *City Politics,* New York: Random House, 1963, pp. 163–167.

6. On the impact of purported "urban renewal" programs, see Herbert J. Gans, "The Failure of Urban Renewal," in Herbert J. Gans (ed.), *People and Plans,* New York: Basic Books, 1968, pp. 260–278; see also Martin Anderson, *The Federal Bulldozer,* M.I.T. Press, Cambridge, Mass.: 1964.

7. Data of Milton E. Ortega.

8. James Q. Wilson, *Varieties of Police Behavior,* Cambridge, Mass.: Harvard Press, 1968, p. 196.

9. The local newspaper (October 19–21, 1966) gave accounts of Brighton High School riots and of a boycott of the city schools organized by civil rights groups. From the neighborhoods in which these disturbances, occurred the Black Panther party later recruited its members.

10. Mayor's State of the City address, previously quoted.

11. *County Grand Jury Report of 1959.*

12. *Ibid.*

13. Estimates of cost-savings due to the installation of computers are next to impossible to obtain because of the changing requirements of government programs and the increasing levels of government service. Interviews with computer center directors in other counties indicated that there had been no study by state or local governments of the relative cost impact of computers once those computers had been installed. Projected cost-savings are of course commonplace in feasibility studies, where, as one director remarked, "everything but the kitchen sink is considered a saving."

Agency directors in Western County report no change, perhaps an increase, in employment of clerical personnel which the computer was supposed to check. The Welfare Department of Western County was assured that so many clerical people would be displaced by the computer that a large number of professional case workers could be hired to give more personal service to clients. A brief analysis of the Salary and Employment Ordinance for the fiscal years 1958–59, 1963–64, and 1968–69, supports agency management views that clerical employment has certainly not declined, probably increased, at the expense of fewer professional caseworkers.

Western County Department of Welfare Increases in Personnel and Clients

	1958–59	1963–64	1968–69
Managers–Supervisors	08%(71)	08%(79)	11%(196)
Clerical workers	32%(287)	35%(359)	36%(661)
Professional workers	60%(539)	57%(614)	54%(995)
Total Employment	897	1052	1852
Number of clients	35,000	46,000	71,000
Ratio of clerical to professional	.53	.61	.67
Ratio of clerical to client	.0082	.0078	.0093
Total personnel to client	.023	.011	.026

Agency management in Welfare says that the computerization of their records has required hiring more clerical personnel to feed and correct computer inputs. However, increases in federal government funding for "package" programs such as Aid to Families with Dependent Children have increased demand for clerical "eligibility technicians" whose sole function is to verify eligibility of clients for payments. In any event, the lack of concern by county officials with the cost-effectiveness of their expensive computers suggests that the installation of the machines served other functions, as we discuss later.

14. Harold L. Wilensky and Charles N. Lebeaux, *Industrial Society and Social Welfare,* New York: Free Press, 1968, Chapters 6 and 7, and pp. 265–272.

15. *County newspaper reports,* March 12, 1961, and June 4, 1961.

16. Welfare Citizens' Committee Report, *County Grand Jury Final Report, 1961.*

17. *Ibid.*

18. *Ibid.*

19. *Ibid.*

20. Wilensky and Lebeaux, *op. cit.,* p. vi.

21. See *ibid.,* pp. 251–264, for a discussion of interagency specialization and the resultant problems of coordination.

22. *Ibid.,* Chapter 7.

23. *Ibid.,* p. 270. See also Floyd Hunter, *Community Power Structure,* Garden City, N.Y.: Doubleday, 1953, pp. 207–210.

24. See V. O. Key, *Southern Politics in State and Nation,* New York, Knopf, 1949, pp. 27–30. Since 1965, the Western County Grand Jury has recommended, indeed, pleaded, that the state take over the administration costs of local welfare (*Grand Jury Reports,* 1965–1969).

25. A. D. Green, "The Professional Social Worker in the Bureaucracy," *Social Service Review,* **40,** No. 1 (1967), pp. 71–83. Green points out that the greater the intervention by political bodies, and campaigns for public accountability, the less agency workers, especially professional workers, feel loyal to the agency, and the more difficult it becomes for employees to derive satisfaction from their work.

26. Political interference and close public scrutiny seem to multiply the tensions existing between the requisites of bureaucracy and professional norms. As Corwin suggests, one of the mechanisms used to reduce conflict between professionals and administrators is organizational segregation. However, when managers of public agencies come under intense political pressure, they are forced to intervene directly into matters of professional concern, and mechanisms of segregation are not operative. Intense alienation, often rebellion, is one kind of outcome. See R. G. Corwin, "Professional Employee: A Study of Conflict in Nursing Roles," *American Journal of Sociology,* **66** (1967), pp. 604–615. See also Richard Hall, "Professionals in Bureaucracy: Alienation Among Industrial Scientists," *American Sociological Review,* **32** (1967), pp. 755.

27. County Budget Message, 1970–1971.

28. Banfield and Wilson, *op. cit.,* Chapter 13.

29. Richard Hofstadter, *The Age of Reform,* New York: Random House: 1955, pp. 174–214.

30. *Ibid.,* pp. 257–271.

31. Banfield and Wilson, *op. cit.,* pp. 140–150.

32. National Municipal League, *The County Manager Plan,* New York: 1945, pp. 15–30.

33. John C. Bollens, "Administrative Integration in California Counties," *Public Administration Review,* **11** (1951), pp. 26–43. See also, Bollens, *American County Government,* Beverly Hills, Calif.: Sage, 1969.

34. Edward W. Weidner, "Review of the Controversy over County Executives," *Public Administration Review,* **8** (1948), pp. 90–110. On city managers, see Harold Stone, Don K. Price, and Kathryn Stone, *City Manager Government in the United States,* Chicago: Public Administration Service, 1940.

35. Wilensky and Lebeaux, *op. cit.,* p. 225.

36. Wilensky and Lebeaux, *op. cit.,* pp. 319–325; see also A. D. Green, *op. cit.*

37. County Administrative Officer, *County Budget Message 1970–1971,* 1970.

38. Rue Bucher and Anselm Strauss, "Professions in Process: An Emergent Approach," *American Journal of Sociology,* **66** (1967), pp. 325–334.

39. *Ibid.,* see also W. J. Goode, "Encroachment, Charlatanism, and the Emerging Profession: Psychology, Sociology and Medicine," *American Sociological Review,* **25** (1960), pp. 902–914; Martin Greenburger, "The Uses of Computers in Organizations," *Scientific American,* September 1966.

40. George L. Bergst and Robert Donati, "County Aspects of the State Information Study," Lockheed Missiles and Space Company, Sunnyvale, Calif.: 1965, pp. 2–3.

41. California State Data Processing Association, "History of the State Data Processing Association," State Data Processing Association, 1969 (mimeo), p. 5.

42. *Ibid.,* p. 7.

43. In the mid-1950s and early 1960s computers were seen by those who used them as relevant to special problem-solving applications in business and government and as an adjunct to operations research. See Russell Ackoff and Patrick Rivett, *A Manager's Guide to Operations Research,* New York: Wiley, 1963. With the development of cheaper, yet larger machines in the early 1960s, less modest, even radical, proposals for the use of computers emerged within the data processing profession. Espousing the "total systems approach" to computer technology, the more euphoric writers foresaw that computers eventually would replace managers. See, for example, the series by Gilbert Burck, "Management Will Never Be the Same Again," and "Will the Computer Outwit Man " in *Fortune,* July–October, 1964. Less radical but equally ambitious uses for the computer in business are outlined by J. A. Beckett, "The Total Systems Concept: Its Implications for Management," in C. A. Myers (ed.), *The Impact of Computers on Management,* Cambridge, Mass.: M.I.T. Press, 1967.

For a critical review of the "total systems" approach and an appraisal of some actual uses of computers in large businesses, see Tom Alexander, "Computers Can't Solve Everything," *Fortune,* October 1969.

44. Edward F. Hearle and R. J. Mason, *A Data Processing System for State and Local Government,* Englewood Cliffs, N.J.: Prentice-Hall, 1962.

45. *Ibid.,* pp. 50–51.

46. California Association of County Data Processors, Minutes of the Meeting—Fall Conference, 1964 (mimeo).

47. Chapters 8 and 9 furnish a discussion of internal integration in criminal justice agencies and the relation of this quality to information sharing.

48. See "The Administration of Complaints by Civilians Against the Police," *Harvard Law Review,* **77** (January 1964), pp. 499–519.

49. "Real Time Information Retrieval—Social Service Files," demonstration and report at the California Association of County Data Processors, fall 1965.

50. On the functions of organizational privacy, see Alan F. Westin, *Privacy and Freedom,* New York: Atheneum, 1967, pp. 41–51.

APPENDIX

Design Specifications

The SSIS system is one part of the Data Processing Center's activities. The DPC serves all major county departments, and the SSIS system is one of four on-line, real-time systems that it operates. The SSIS system was developed by a staff of more than twenty programmers to fulfill the needs of four agencies (Welfare, Health, Institutions, and Probation) for real-time systems, as well as to provide a central index at which selected information about clients of each agency could be obtained by the other agencies.

The hardware requirements include computer main frame processors capable of nearly a billion characters of on line storage, terminal equipment for line operators with visual display input/output, and key-driven input devices capable of receiving and preparing hard copy output.

Software requirements include a system capable of processing inquiries from remote terminals in real time, high-order language compilers, and an executive control system capable of simultaneous remote terminal operation, as well as batch-type processing. Dedicated phone lines are used for teleprocessing.

SSIS Data Base

The data bases of the agency-specific, real-time files are more comprehensive than the Central Index, which is intended to serve the social service agencies' need to know whether a potential client is involved with other agencies. The Central Index contains the following information:

Name and address of client
Sex, age, date of birth
Welfare case number

Welfare caseworker number
Status of case—open or closed
Medical assistance eligibility
Year of status change
Census tract residence
Other agency contacts: case numbers
Other persons related to case
Accounts receivable (medical institutions)

This information is utilized by the Welfare, Health, and Probation departments through remote terminals. Software is arranged to allow several different kinds of argument to be made. Thus knowing a person's address and age, or his date of birth, first name, and sex, may be sufficient to elicit all the other information.

Hardware

The Data Processing Center operates two leased IBM computers as listed below:

Description	Quantity
Basic processors: IBM 360-50 and 360-40	2
Univac 9300 computer (for tape input)	1
CDC 8092 teleprogrammer computer	1
CDC 915 optical scanner tape drive (1600 bpi)	5
Univac 1701 keypunch-keyverifiers	8

The Data Processing Center operates seventy-eight remote terminals, mostly IBM 1050 and 2740 units.

Software

The Data Processing Center has more than 1700 programs, mostly in COBOL for batch processing jobs. The real-time systems are operated by modified IBM FASTER programs.

Systems Flow Chart

Figure 3 represents the flow chart for SSIS.

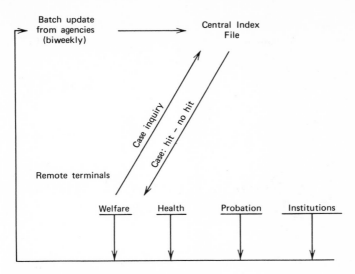

Figure 3. SSIS systems flow chart.

EIGHT

A Police Regional Information System

A SUMMARY HISTORY

PRIS is a regional police information network located in a western county. It was established in 1965 by the county Board of Supervisors and county law enforcement leaders to serve the county's thirteen separate police departments. Since 1965 PRIS has expanded to include more than ninety-five police departments in a seven-county region.

PRIS has served as a prototype for other regional systems in Western State. These regional systems were connected in 1971 to the Criminal Information Network (CIN) of Western State (see Chapter 10). Thus they now can exchange information among themselves and with state and federal criminal offender files.

PRIS is unique among the information systems we have investigated in that it is supportive of a highly decentralized administration of police agencies. Although the information system does redistribute a critical resource, information, the manner in which PRIS was organized assures that the administration of the police agencies remains decentralized. If anything, the PRIS system contributes to the persistence of a decentralized administration.

There has been no resistance to the PRIS system from user agencies. Both the decentralized character of the system and the lack of resistance to its initiation are related to the social conditions of its initiation and the political process of its construction.

COPS AND ROBBERS IN WESTERN COUNTY: MULTIPLE JURISDICTIONS

Law enforcement or police functions in Western County are performed within three overlapping jurisdictions: county sheriff, city police, and town police. The sheriff is the only elected law enforcement official in the county. In addition to his law enforcement powers, the sheriff serves papers for the civil courts and is custodian in charge of administering county jail facilities (the county jail and the rehabilitation center).[1]

The sheriff is the ultimate police power in the county, and his formal authority extends over all cities and unincorporated areas. A vestige of feudal England, the office of sheriff includes the authority of *"posse comitatus"*—the power to command any and all male citizens to aid the sheriff in emergencies. In practice, the sheriff's primary law enforcement activity is performed in the unincorporated suburban and rural areas of the county.[2]

There are seven city police agencies and six town police agencies in Western County. The largest and most prestigious city agencies are those of Brighton and Athens. The city and town police are responsible to city boards of supervisors and town mayors, and their chiefs are appointed to office by elected officials.

The effects of multiple jurisdictions on interagency relations are similar, though less severe, than those in Eastern State. In Eastern State (see Chapter 9) we found that the low homogeneity of criminal justice units, their jurisdictional integration, and gross differences in rural versus urban working environments, created competitive, hostile, and uncooperative relations among criminal justice agencies involved in the CIS project.

All participants in the PRIS system were originally police agencies; among them, homogeneity is higher and jurisdictional integration lower. All police agencies of the county are ultimately responsible to the sheriff and are subject to the standards of a review by the state Department of Justice. (These factors are discussed below.)

Local officials argue that despite multiple jurisdictions, relations between county police agencies have always been amicable and are improving over time. A police chief of a large suburban town in the county remarked:

> I know what Eastern State is like and Illinois, too, but in this state and here in the county, we have little bickering and hostility among the police. I don't know why that is; maybe we realize we're all in the same boat. I would say that since the early 1960s we've all come a lot closer. We serve on riot duty in Brighton and Athens together, we've come closer

just fighting students at Athens—a rock can't choose between
hitting a sheriff's deputy and one of our men.

Despite denials of hostility by officials, police officers in the town take a
cynical view of the county sheriff given his reported propensity for pub-
licity seeking and attempting to acquire an image as a "heavy" law enforcement type. As one patrolman in a large town commented:

> The sheriff is the headline grabber here—if it's student com-
> munists, Black Panthers, or drug raids, there you'll find the
> sheriff coming in to take over or direct the operation. But
> you gotta understand he's an elected official, and this way
> he gets his name on all the important cases.

The smaller geographical dispersal of the Western county agencies, and the
higher frequency of interaction at all levels from patrolmen to chiefs, minimize existing differences of political jurisdiction and homogeneity.

The factors that diminish the impact of multiple jurisdictions within the
county declined in significance as the PRIS system expanded from 1965 to
1970 to include other counties. Two large neighboring counties as of 1972
have already withdrawn from PRIS as they developed similar systems in
their own counties and regions. These counties are more urbanized, wealthier, and more prestigious in many respects than Western County. County
and law enforcement officials claimed they had unique problems and information needs that only they could service by establishing their "own computer system." Both counties do in fact represent different ecological and
demographic regions. Despite the withdrawals of these two large counties
from PRIS, the "balkanizing" effect of multiple jurisdictions is mitigated by
the growth of the state Criminal Information Network (CIN–Chapter 10),
which links the regional systems together.

The Historical Impact of Multiple Jurisdictions
on Police Administration

Multiple jurisdictions in Western County have not led to the intense political problems evident in Eastern State, yet they have created problems of
similar scale for the administration of criminal justice. For example, in
Western County each of the thirteen original police agencies, and the
county sheriff, maintained its own records and criminal files before the
advent of PRIS. When a citizen failed to appear in court or committed a

crime, a warrant was issued for his arrest by the local police. If the offender resided in the same jurisdiction, he was served with the warrant. However, if the offender lived elsewhere in the county, the warrant-issuing agency had no jurisdictional power, and the police in the other locality were relied on to serve the warrant.

In the past, warrants for out-of-jurisdiction offenders were not typically served except in the case of major felons. The warrant-issuing agency often did not feel it worth the expense and time to call up or write to the twelve other county police agencies, especially for minor offenders. As a result, local agencies often arrested a person for a minor violation and released him without knowing that he was wanted in another jurisdiction for a more serious crime. In addition, a local agency received no "credit" for serving a warrant issued in another jurisdiction.[3] Each jurisdiction would serve its own warrants first, then consider warrants from outside.

The growth of multiple political jurisdictions has occurred in a haphazard fashion, the biggest batch of new jurisdictions appearing after World War II when suburban townships were established in formerly rural areas. The introduction of new freeways and other means of mass transportation, and the continued growth of the suburbs, have increased the likelihood of criminals crossing jurisdictional boundaries to commit crimes or to escape apprehension. The utility of separate political and police jurisdictions decreased over this period, in fact becoming a hindrance to law enforcement agencies. Law enforcement agencies have experienced a decline in the capacity to serve warrants for arrest.

High Initial Homogeneity: The PRIS Agencies

In comparison with the other information systems we studied, the PRIS system units exhibited a high degree of homogeneity before and during computerization. However, this high initial homogeneity has declined somewhat as PRIS expands to include agencies in different functional and jurisdictional areas.

The thirteen agencies comprising the initial PRIS system were all police agencies, performing essentially similar tasks and facing similar problems of law enforcement. Attitudes and values that arose within different agencies but emerged from the performance of police functions, were remarkably similar, as others have documented.[4] A number of police associations in the county, regional, and state levels of government serve as a forum where "police values" are promulgated, reaffirmed, and defended. Western

County, the third largest in the state, has provided many police leaders to the state Peace Officers' Association and the Regional Police Chiefs' Association.

Specific norms of behavior differ among police departments because the law enforcement agencies serve in different types of communities or jurisdictions. Brighton police are nationally known as "tough, professional cops," ideally suited to urban environments. In Athens, college degrees are required for all police personnel, who have a local reputation for "cooling out" student dissenters (among Athens students, Brighton police are considered "heavies," and whenever real trouble breaks out it is usually the Brighton police who are called in to break up student disturbances). The police of Dorisville, a blue-collar urban area, are known locally for their corruption and toleration of organized gambling and prostitution.[5] The sheriff, in turn, is the prima donna of county police agencies, and his department is considered by locals to be the harshest law enforcement agency in the county. (The last sheriff was retired from office in 1970. The county grand jury had indicted him for "excessive brutality" in handling a student protest in Athens during which one student was shotgunned to death.)

Despite these differences in specific norms and reputations, there are overriding similarities in values toward "the crime problem," criminal offenders and the public:

> The patrolman's conception of the police role will vary to some extent with the character of the community and with the duty assignment of the officer, but the general features of the patrol problem—coping with disorder by exercising wide discretion over vital matters in an apprehensive environment—tend to impart to the police department as a whole its special character. Perhaps . . . the police organization develops its special ethos: defensiveness, a sense of not being supported by the community and a distrust of outsiders.[6]

Stratification among police agencies, our second dimension of homogeneity, is low in Western County compared with Eastern State (see Chapter 9). No single police agency or group of agencies is markedly higher in prestige than other agencies, and there are only small differences in political influence among the agencies. As an elected official, the sheriff possesses the most political influence in the county, with Brighton police close behind. Either can veto projects initiated by the lesser agencies. Without the support of the lesser agencies in smaller communities, however, neither Brighton nor the sheriff could implement countywide police programs such as PRIS.

Procedures for recruitment of personnel are also quite similar across county agencies. With the exception of Athens, which has higher standards, county police agencies recruit personnel according to standards established by the state Department of Justice. They generally recruit persons from similar social, economic, and educational backgrounds.[7]

The comparatively high homogeneity of PRIS agencies undoubtedly contributes to what local officials describe as "cooperative" attitudes and behavior prevalent among police agencies in the county. In turn, high homogeneity has aided efforts to increase information exchanges among these agencies as envisioned by the PRIS system.

Moderate Internal Integration: Effects of Propinquity

We have hypothesized that the higher the internal integration of a set of social units, the more difficult and the less frequent is communication among those units. We have used three dimensions to measure internal integration: degree of control exercised by internal elites over members, degree to which the unit is the predominant force of members' occupational and political identification, and degree to which units or members of units interact with other units. As we observe in the next chapter criminal justice agencies in general, and police in particular, exhibit very high degrees of integration when compared with other types of government agency.

On two of our dimensions of integration, PRIS resembles closely the CIS agencies of Chapter 9. Internal elites—police leaders—virtually monopolize control over unit members. Rewards and discipline of policemen rest solely with jurisdictional police chiefs. Pensions are not transferable from one jurisdiction to another. There has been no civilian interference with police procedures in Western County—no citizen review boards or grand jury investigations have occurred in the last 20 years, except for the indictment proceedings against the sheriff in 1970, mentioned previously. In this respect, the PRIS agencies differ greatly from the county social service agencies, which frequently undergo intensive public scrutiny.[8]

Second, as discussed in connection with homogeneity, the police agency becomes a predominant focus of occupational, social, and political identity for individual members. Low mobility to other government or private economy positions, and the nontransferability of pensions among police agencies, ensure that members will conform to agency expectations regarding their performance on the job. Social and political attitudes and values unique to policemen are attributable to their work situation.[9]

In terms of our third dimension, interaction patterns, internal integration of the PRIS agencies is not extremely intense. In Western County, the increase in "mutual aid" situations—student protests or urban riots requiring cooperation from several police agencies—has caused an increase in interaction among agencies in the last decade. The overlapping character of police jurisdictions in the county, and their physical propinquity, also increase interactions among police agencies. Finally, interviews with county policemen indicated that police within the county interact with police from different jurisdictions frequently through police associations and fraternal orders.[10]

The high homogeneity and low internal integration of the PRIS agencies have made for relatively low resistance to the establishment of a computerized information network among county agencies.

High and Increasing Interdependence: The Regional

We have said that the more interdependent social units become, the more communication between them is required to continue performance of their tasks. Moreover, we have argued that successful formal information systems, such as PRIS, must structure themselves to take account of this interdependence. In Western County, and in a seven-county region, marked changes in demographic and other social characteristics have significantly increased the interdependence of police agencies.

The western state, and the Western County region in particular, experienced rates of population growth far in excess of national figures. In the 1950s the county's population expanded 35%, the region's by 50%. In the decade of the 1960s, increases were 40 and 51% respectively. Vehicle registration in Western County increased 250% between 1950 and 1970.

Population increases, and even larger increases in age groups with high age-specific crime rates, have caused major crimes to climb 150% between 1950 and 1970, but increases in population mobility due to higher automobile use and freeway growth have enhanced the likelihood of criminals crossing police jurisdictions to commit crimes. Thus in 1960 it was necessary to transfer 40% of Western County's warrants and 60% of the region's warrants to other police agencies for service. PRIS officials estimate that in 1950 fewer than 20% of county warrants and 30% of regional warrants had to be transferred.[11]

Changes in population and social characteristics of the population and increased mobility have made law enforcement in one community dependent on police agencies in other communities. The thirteen county police agencies issued 70,000 warrants in 1964, but they had a backlog of 70,000 outstanding (unserved) warrants. The ninety-five police agencies in the region issued 300,000 warrants in 1964, but they also had a backlog of 500,000 unserved warrants. The great majority of unserved warrants in both county and region were for traffic offenses—"scofflaws" accounted for about 80% of the unserved warrants. The remaining warrants were largely for minor felonies (e.g., burglary, theft, auto theft, prostitution).

The backlog of unserved warrants, and their increase over time, indicated to local police chiefs the failure of a law enforcement system based on autonomous jurisdictions:

> The continuing growth of the county and the several cities which are a part of it is a mixed blessing. The responsibility of public officials to preserve peace and to enforce the law is becoming more complex and more difficult with each addition to the population. Crime is on the increase, traffic fatalities mount, congestion stifles movement. . . . These problems were at one time the sole concern of the several local jurisdictions. Today this is no longer true. The thief who preys on the citizens of the community may well live in another. The motorist who is delayed or inconvenienced in one jurisdiction may have started his trip in another, and seeking to travel to still a third. Our myriad problems can no longer be succcessfully resolved by independent civic action because of these relationships.[12]

By 1964 the uncomfortable fact that criminals were no longer committing crimes in their own backyard had begun to challenge the traditional structure of law enforcement in the region, as well as the ideology of "local civic action" on which that structure was based. Nurtured by the aggressive salesmanship of major computer firms, there began to appear in the middle 1960s a new ideology of law enforcement in which the "cop" is pictured as a professional, scientific manager (interchangeable with managers from any large corporation), and the centralized information system replaces the sheriff's posse.

Precomputer Characteristics: A Summary

The precomputer characteristics of the PRIS agencies boded well for the establishment of a formal, centralized information system. The high homogeneity and moderate internal integration of the agencies increased the likelihood that these agencies would cooperate in their own interests. Sharing tasks and functions, the agencies required similar kinds of information from one another to perform their tasks adequately. Moderate internal integration and high homogeneity also reduced hostility and competition among the agencies.

The effect of multiple jurisdictions on relations between PRIS agencies was lessened by high homogeneity and moderate internal integration. However, the existence of multiple jurisdictions lowered the effectiveness of law enforcement in the region and county, especially as interdependence was increasing. Besides decreasing the capacity of county police to serve warrants, the growth of interdependence resulted in a significant revenue loss for local political jurisdictions: the 240,000 outstanding traffic warrants in the region represented $5–$7 million in unpaid fines—a fact that was not lost on county boards of supervisors or city and town mayors when considering participation in the PRIS system.

CENTRALIZING LAW ENFORCEMENT INFORMATION: ELITES, PARTICIPATION, AND CONSENSUS

The initiation of the PRIS system follows a very different path from the other systems we investigated. First, it is initiated by a group of internal elites—local law enforcement officials—and is encouraged by external elites—the county executive officer and the county Board of Supervisors. Among the initiating elites there is a very low degree of elitism, no one police unit dominating the PRIS system. Third, participating agencies maintain control over the system through an authentic consensus mechanism, the Policy Committee. External elites, county elected officials, and town mayors and councils, exercise virtually no control over PRIS. As we discuss later, PRIS developed as a low-control, highly responsive information system.

Internal Elites: The Western County Chiefs of Police

The initial realization that interagency information transfer problems existed, and the PRIS idea as a solution, emerged from informal meetings of the county's police chiefs which had been occurring since the late 1950s. A Brighton official said:

> The chiefs of the police forces are really quite close to one another, and since the late fifties they had been meeting weekly

to discuss ways to overcome line and management problems that they have in common. I guess you could say they were "led" by [the Brighton chief then], but the sheriff was favorable to these meetings, too. Anyway, [the chief] and others in Brighton, mainly people from Brighton's computer center, were well ahead of their time in terms of electronic data processing techniques for police work. They began selling the idea of EDP to the chiefs, and it was seen that this was really a regional problem, not just the county. So a regional committee was set up to explore ways of building a useful police information system.

Formal meetings of the county chiefs took place in 1961, and in 1962 they established the Regional EDP (Electronic Data Processing) Advisory Committee, which was to conduct an investigation and to report its findings. Recognition by the state Peace Officers' Association was desired by the county chiefs to convince their colleagues in a neighboring county that a regional system was being planned, not simply a county system.

The Regional EDP Advisory Committee began to study regional information flows and requirements in November 1963. The committee persuaded the Director of the Hilltown Police Bureau of Identification that a regional information system was called for, and this official joined the committee, campaigning actively to win support from Hilltown County police chiefs. At this stage the Regional Committee had the support of the three most powerful and prestigious police departments in the region.

The Regional Committee in turn was wooed by three large computer firms—Burroughs, National Cash Register, and IBM. IBM promised to aid the chiefs in investigating police information problems and to build a pilot information system free of cost. The pattern of IBM penetration of government computer markets is well illustrated by the PRIS experience. Free fringe benefits (e.g., expert advice, help with studies and pilot projects) are offered in the early feasibility study period; at the end of this period, IBM is the only company with the contacts and experience to implement the project that is chosen.

Together with IBM's technical staff based at an IBM "Education Center," the Regional Committee began its 1963 study of law enforcement information needs. From responses to a questionnaire sent to all regional agencies, asking police chiefs to list their twenty most important information files, the study concluded in 1965 that warrant files were the most important and the least difficult to automate.

Publication of the study, "Regional Law Enforcement Information Control" in June 1964 and a series of flashy, well-illustrated pamphlets was designed to kick off a coordinated public relations and political campaign to win support for the PRIS warrant control system.

A prepublication conference was held at the IBM Education Center for the regional police chiefs in plush carpeted rooms the chiefs were exposed to the findings of the study and a demonstration of a pilot simulation:

> In June 1964 the committee met with the Regional Chiefs of Police and Sheriffs to discuss the warrant research findings and the committee recommendations. The meeting was held at the IBM Education Center in order to provide an actual demonstration of an automation concept for the consideration of the police officials. As a result of this meeting, the recommendations were approved and the committee was directed to take additional steps preliminary to implementation of an actual program. The critical recommendations upon which the system design evolved were: (a) that the law enforcement agencies develop and utilize a central warrant file or index rather than attempt to continue maintenance of independent files, (b) that the law enforcement agencies support the principle of employing modern data automation technology for warrant control in view of the inadequacy of present manual processes, and (c) that law enforcement agencies consider utilizing the services of an existing government data service center for the operation of the initial warrant control program rather than become involved in the establishment of an independent law enforcement data center.[13]

A participant's-eye view of the same conference is more revealing:

> IBM really had a slick operation going, well-oiled. They could have sold the chiefs on automated motherhood and they would have bought it. There was a sort of euphoria at the meeting. IBM treated the chiefs like they were chiefs of conquering armies—and that's quite a change from the reception the chief of police usually gets from the public. The leaders were on the rostrum telling us how much warrants automation would end our problems, technicians were wiring up this demonstration, and secretaries were filling coffee cups. It was a pretty effective snow job.

Having won the support of the regional chiefs, the Regional Advisory Committee's next task was to gain financial backing from the Western County Board of Supervisors. A presentation to the board was planned for July 1964.

Members of the Board of Supervisors were sent a multicolored, IBM pamphlet describing the virtues of the proposed PRIS system. In their pamphlet, IBM and the chiefs pointed out that PRIS might become self-supporting, given the backlog in traffic fines. In any event, it was in the interests of law and order:

> Warrants of arrest, both fugitive and traffic, represents a key aspect in the administration of criminal justice. The apprehension of criminals is seriously jeopardized by the multiplicity of police agencies in our county. All too often a wanted person is stopped and questioned by an officer only to be released because of inadequate information. Our proposal will provide the officer with instant access to the information he needs to arrest this suspect.
>
> Less serious but equally vexing are the 10–15% of all traffic violators who are cited in our county, violators who fail to satisfy the requirement of judicial appearance. The bail on some 50,000 outstanding traffic warrants approximates $1 million.
>
> We propose that the superb electronic data processing facilities of Western County be brought to bear on these and similar problems.[14]

At the July 30, 1964, meeting of the Board of Supervisors, Western County police notables presented their case. Press coverage of the affair was more than complimentary: the PRIS system would "put Western County on the map." A large, conservative paper reported the meeting on the day it was held:

> COUNTY PLAN FOR ELECTRONIC INFORMATION SYSTEM BACKED
>
> Western County could become the regional center for an electronic police information system that might serve as a national model.
>
> Such is the consensus of backers of a plan to introduce information from police records into the county's Data Processing Center.
>
> Virtually instantaneous, 24-hour service could be provided to officers in the street.
> Projected costs would be $215,444 for 1965–1966, $378,079 for 1966–1967, and $466,136 for 1967–1968. . . .
>
> The [Western County] sheriff, who headed the presentation of the plan to the Supervisors, said a centralized record system

is the prime police need in combating crime in a growing and mobile population.

The Brighton police chief said chiefs of all the county's other 11 departments favor the proposed program.

He called the present records system "antiquated, inefficient, and costly," and predicted that if the electronic plan is adopted, police agencies from all over the United States would send representatives to inspect it. The system would pay for itself.

A Brighton police captain said the electronic proposal would be a model system for a U.S. urban area.

SOUND APPROACH

The Director of the County Data Processing Center agreed, and said the plan was technically feasible and found it is an "orderly, progressive approach."

The PRIS project was well received by the Data Center, for it provided the funds and the excuse for buying the latest IBM 360-40 computers. The Board of Supervisors was itself being pressured by its county grand jury to "do somehting about law and order" in 1963 and 1964:

> Grand Jury Recommendation 38: The County and the various agencies within the County should continue their efforts to centralize certain law enforcement functions, such as the establishment of a consolidated identification bureau. As has been recommended by past grand juries, certain law enforcement functions can be economically and efficiently combined on a county-wide basis, which would improve the quality of service without affecting the autonomy of local police departments.[15]

Thus in late 1964 the Board of Supervisors agreed to fund PRIS as a voluntary automated warrant information system. Participating agencies would pay a fee, based on levels of use, for access to PRIS, thereby covering costs of operation.

Consensus Mechanisms: The Policy Committee

The county enabling legislation left the operation of PRIS entirely in the hands of local police officials. The Regional Advisory Committee was changed to the PRIS Policy Committee, with representatives from five of the participating county police agencies; membership rotates annually among the police agencies.

PRIS became operational in June 1965, and since that time has taken on six regional counties. Membership in the Policy Committee has expanded to eleven as new counties are brought "on-line." In any one year at least one police official from each of the counties in the region serves on the committee.

In 1970 the system was expanded to include other criminal justice agencies, such as the Western County District Attorney's office. As new functional areas are brought into the system, representatives from these areas join the Policy Committee.

With the expansion of PRIS, the function of the Policy Committee has changed. Originally designed to implement and monitor PRIS, the Policy Committee now decides on new applications of computer resources in the criminal justice area. A county police chief describes how the Policy Committee works:

> The Policy Committee is a quasi-governmental body which controls PRIS. We established it in 1965 to ensure police would control it [PRIS] and not civilians. After all, we were paying for a lot of it and we were using it, so we should control it. When I worked with it, we were just setting up PRIS, but now they review and decide upon new applications. For instance, we need more than warrant information here in Suburb City. We need a lot of management information— like what our cops are doing with their time. So right now we have an application in to the Policy Committee to help us set up a real-time resource deployment system. If they have the computer resources, they can help us out there. It looks encouraging. In the future, we want to do some crime frequency studies and personnel records studies, and here PRIS can be of help.

Since 1965, the Policy Committee has approved a number of computer applications from individual departments in Brighton, Athens, and Suburb City. These projects have all involved the weekly publication of computerized crime trend (time, location, type of offense) reports.

A Voluntary System: Basis of Participation

Participation in the PRIS system is voluntary, allowing each agency and jurisdiction to withdraw from the system at will. Two counties withdrew in

1971 when they established their own county-regional systems. Since 1965, however, there have been no withdrawals due to dissatisfaction with the system. On the contrary, oversubscription to PRIS by agencies in outlying counties has presented over load problems to the PRIS management and some delays in service. (According to a PRIS official, inquiry-response time rose from the original 3 seconds in 1965 to more than 30 seconds in 1970 in peak demand periods.) PRIS offers important material incentives to participating agencies and jurisdictions, and agencies have been eager to join.

For the participating police agencies, PRIS has increased the probability of issued warrants being served. One of the measures used by police and civilian elites (boards of supervisors and town mayors) to evaluate the effectiveness of their police agencies is the ratio of issued to served warrants.[16] PRIS serves directly to increase the self-perceived effectiveness of local police agencies, as reported by the police chief of a large suburban town in the county:

> PRIS wasn't designed to bring about changes in police operations but to increase our effectiveness. It is an effective crime prevention tool: our view is, "the best prevention is the sure promise of swift apprehension." Now in the first month operation back in 1965, the number of warrants we served went up 92%. The more people we can convince that they won't get away with a crime, the more crime we prevent, as far as I'm concerned. Another benefit is that it has saved police lives. PRIS has reported since 1968 on the "violence potential" of a wanted person. If he's a Black Panther or some other nut, our men want to know that before they get out of their cars to make an arrest.

Police support for PRIS arises from the belief that the system aids them in their day-to-day operations and makes a material, visible contribution to their effectiveness.

The PRIS network does not alter the traditional political boundaries within the county—each jurisdiction maintains control over its own police. The costs are ultimately borne by these jurisdictions, which must pay the Western County Data Center monthly for the use of its computers. In the words of one Data Center manager, "There is money in warrants for everyone," and this accounts for the support PRIS receives from the participating jurisdictions. Local jurisdictions, especially the small townships and cities, rely on traffic fines to defray part of the costs of area law enforcement, and PRIS contributes materially to their budgets by increasing the amount of traffic fines collected.

A second benefit to local jurisdictions and county political leaders is the political capital that can be gained by supporting local police—a popular theme among politicians at all levels in the County. The Athens student unrest of the early 1960s, the Brighton riots of 1965 and 1966, and the growth of the Black Panther party in Brighton have contributed to a conservative law-and-order reaction among elected officials in Western County and in other regional counties. Urged by successive grand juries, who represent the more conservative elements of the region, and by two large, conservative area newspapers to "do something" about rising crime, local political leaders of the mid 1960s took a hard line on law and order. On March 31, 1965, one of these journals published the following:

COMPUTERS JOIN THE WAR ON CRIME

Computers will soon start helping police catch law-breakers. Enthusiasts here predict they are building the prototype of a nationwide network of criminal hunting electronic equipment.

Growing disrespect of the law is costing counties millions of dollars. More than 5 million, possibly 7 million dollars in 500,000 unserved warrants in seven regional counties, exist, says [a Metropolis Police Department spokesman].

Crime is up over the last decade by 100% [he says]. Western County's rushing new Data Center had the facilities, the brain-power, and was willing to operate PRIS. Western County Supervisors agreed to a proposal and said any other county could join on a cost-sharing basis.

Low and Declining Elitism

From its inception in 1962, PRIS was dominated by chiefs and sheriffs from the most prestigious and politically powerful counties in the region— Hilltown and Western. Since the expansion of PRIS after 1966 to other counties and in 1969 to other functions, the leadership has broadened considerably.

Since 1966 Suburb City and other small towns have seen their chiefs elected chairmen of the Policy Committee. County sheriffs from smaller counties have also been chosen for this post.

To date no participating nonpolice agency has elected a chairman to the Policy Committee, although such agencies are represented on the committee. In this respect PRIS has remained largely a police operation with little guidance or interference from civilian officials or from other government agencies.

The Reform Process: The Collegial Model

The PRIS system stands in marked contrast to the SSIS and CIS systems (Chapters 7 and 9) insofar as it was originated and is currently operated by a group of internal elites. Although PRIS received the active support of external elites—the Data Center, the county auditor, and the Board of Supervisors of Western County—it is not in any way controlled by this group. The mechanisms of legitimation utilized by the PRIS initiating elites correspond in our typology to the Collegial model of reform.

In the Collegial model a typically small group of internal elites initiates the reform project through the establishment of an advisory committee. This committee differs from that employed in the Notables, Reputational Elite, and Pluralist models in several respects. First, the advisory committee is composed solely of internal elites or their representatives, whereas in the three other models external elites play a large role. Second, unlike the Notable and Reputational Elite models, the personnel of the Collegial advisory committee are formal representatives of participating groups, selected by those groups to protect their interests. Members maintain multiple affiliations, alternating between full-time reform project administration and full-time duties for the constituent organizations. The burden of leadership in the reform project tends to be organized by yearly rotation of leaders, the constituent groups "loaning" one of their members—sometimes on a part-time basis—to the reform project for a year. Such an arrangement differs from the Pluralist model, in which constituent representatives serve occasionally on policy committees of the reform, but have no administrative responsibilities, and from the Reputational Elite model, in which selected notables become full-time members of the reform project.

The Collegial model alone functions to maximize constituent control of the reform project and to minimize the likelihood of the reform project taking on a life of its own, independent of the constituent organizations.

The PRIS Advisory Committee, as noted earlier, was initiated by a small group of county law officers; but it quickly expanded in 1962 to include law enforcement officials from other regional police forces. The functions of the committee were twofold: first, to establish a consensus on the kinds and methods of information exchange among the agencies, and second, to recruit and train the experts required to operate the project.

It should be noted here that the PRIS project involved a relatively small number of homogeneous police agencies (thirteen initially), making it more likely that consensus could be reached among them on the nature of information sharing. Moreover, the project was small in scope—that is, it did not involve recruiting and training large numbers of personnel, nor did it require extensive computer equipment. The small amount of resources called for made the project less dependent on external groups.

We have said that the decision to exchange warrant information was based on responses to a simple questionnaire sent to all regional police agencies. Implementation of the project required the support of some external groups. The training of computer personnel and the supply of computer equipment were beyond the abilities of the PRIS agencies. However, a number of options for external support presented themselves.

A very few police officers, fifteen originally, were trained to operate computer terminals in the local agencies. As one official explained, the idea of hiring civilians to run computers in local agencies is "abhorrent to the rank and file." One full-time systems designer was needed, along with an initially large staff of programmers and designers. Computer firms offered to design the system free of cost, and other local time-sharing concerns offered to train police officers in return for a contract to supply the equipment. It would have been more convenient for the PRIS project to use county data processing facilities, but the project was clearly not dependent on the county.

Had the project involved the retraining of many policemen and large investments in computer equipment, the county government might well have exercised more control over PRIS. In the event, however, this was neither politically feasible (the police could always go elsewhere if they chose not to make concessions) nor technically required.

Besides maintaining its control over the personnel who operate the computers in local agencies, the PRIS committee was successful in convincing the Data Processing Center to hire a former Hilltown police official to act as liaison between the Center and the Policy Committee. Unlike Western's SSIS and Eastern State's CIS, the PRIS constituent agencies retained full control over the design and implementation of the project; moreover, the technical personnel who operate the system were either chosen by the police agencies or made directly responsible to them.

Participation in ongoing decision making (e.g., daily operations, priority setting, and new applications) is ensured to local agencies through the Policy Committee. Unlike "advisory committees" of other systems, the Policy Committee appears to operate as an authentic consensus mechanism. Complaints, suggestions for improvement, and new applications are discussed by the committee every week; membership rotates annually among participating agencies, and the committee has the power to act on members' suggestions.

The internal guidance and the voluntary and participatory characteristics of the PRIS system have contributed to its acceptance by members as an effective tool for transferring warrant and other criminal offender information among local agencies and jurisdictions. Paradoxically, the very success of PRIS is partly responsible for its change; so many warrants are now being served that other criminal justice agencies are "breaking down," the district attorneys and the courts experiencing sharp, unplanned increases in workloads. The latter agencies are now seeking to broaden the scope of PRIS from a purely police operation to one involving all the criminal justice agencies.

A Model of the PRIS System

Before the implementation of PRIS in 1965, the transfer of warrant/wanted information among the thirteen police agencies in Western County was initiated by a telephone call from an inquiring agency to the other twelve agencies. This method of information transfer required a total of seventy-eight telephone lines and up to 8 hours (if the first few agencies called did not have outstanding warrants). Following confirmation of an outstanding warrant, a photocopy of the warrant was mailed from the issue agency to the serving agency. This usually required one to two days.

The PRIS system has reduced the number of telephone lines required to transfer warrants from seventy-eight to thirteen. Each of the original thirteen county police agencies had a remote computer terminal connected to the central computer at the Data Center by a dedicated telephone line. Requests for warrant/wanted information from the field (patrolmen) were keyed into the computer from these remote terminals. Response time was reduced from 6–8 hours down to 3–20 seconds, depending on demand levels. A positive response results in a hard copy printout of a legally valid warrant.

As of 1970 the PRIS system stored more than a million outstanding warrants on real-time, random access programs. In 1971–1972, on the completion of the State Law Enforcement Transmission System (SLETS), PRIS began to interface directly with the state's Criminal Identification Network (see Chapter 10). PRIS now provides regional police agencies (and DAs, courts, prisons, and probation departments) with summary criminal history, fingerprint, and name-alias information. Through SLETS, the PRIS system also interfaces with the state Department of Motor Vehicles computer file of stolen cars and the FBI's National Crime Information Center in Washington. Figure 4 is a graphic model of the PRIS system.

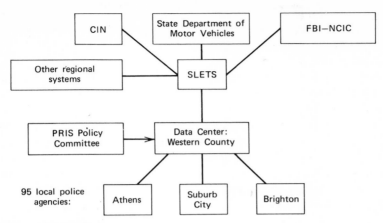

Figure 4. The PRIS system.

CONTROL, RESPONSIVENESS, AND COMMITMENT: THE FIRST FIVE YEARS

The PRIS system has been able to generate high and increasing commitment among participating agencies. Initial commitment was good due to the factors in the initiation period discussed previously: internal elite guidance, effective consensus mechanisms, and high initial benefits to participating agencies and jurisdictions. However, the initiation of PRIS has had a "pump-priming" effect. Returns on the initial investment have been reinvested, so to speak, producing additional benefits for agencies and bringing an increase in commitment.

Police agencies receive from PRIS two kinds of benefit: (1) an increase in the effectiveness of traditional police programs (e.g., better warrant service, increases in stolen auto arrests, better protection of patrolmen from "violence-prone" persons, and more rapid retrieval of information on criminal offenders), and (2) an increased capacity of police agencies to influence budget allocations of county elites (boards of supervisors and town mayors).

Responsive System: Expansion in Scope and Function

Since its inception in 1965 the PRIS system has expanded its scope of operations from thirteen agencies in one county to ninety-five agencies in seven counties. The utility of the system to participating agencies is a function of the number of interagency exchanges the system can maintain. In this sense its utility to participating agencies has increased markedly in the area of warrant exchanges alone.

In large part due to influence of internal elites on PRIS, the information system itself has been highly responsive to police-perceived needs. However, we have construed "responsiveness" to have a more general meaning—namely, it characterizes relations between nonelite agencies and elite political decision makers. Here, too, PRIS has an effect. Besides providing for specific operational information needs of police agencies, PRIS is now being used to generate information and knowledge about police needs which can be used to influence political decision makers.

For example, the very success of PRIS has been useful in changing and increasing budget allocations to police departments in one major city. A PRIS official commented on the impact of the project on police manpower utilization:

> The PRIS system has put manpower strains on the police departments as more warrants are now served than ever before. The intensity of warrant service has gone up, in other words, as the different police departments communicate with one another more effectively. This means that the cop on the beat spends more time bringing people in to be booked and less time on the beat. Where before a cop would make two rounds of his beat every hour, now he makes only one and spends the rest of the time at the station house booking people, or in court. The mayor and council like to hear this sort of thing—it's the first time police have been able to show politicians that a real increase in service has taken place. In Brighton the police have been very successful in finding new money to hire additional personnel to keep up with the new pace. They've even hired cops specially trained in systems development work to do special studies of police deployment and crime patterns. A couple of years ago few politicians would have supported this kind of police work. To them, and to a lot of police, they could only think of police as "cops on a beat" or in terms of more patrol cars, more bodies. Now they seem more amenable to letting the police decide on where the money should go.

This experience in Brighton is an indirect consequence of the PRIS system, but a more direct use of its flexible computer resources to change budgetary allocations is seen in the police department of Suburb City—a rapidly growing suburban town in Western County.

Where Are the Police?

Contrary to widely held beliefs, and notwithstanding the pronouncements of police departments, the deployment of police manpower and equipment in large urban areas is only marginally related to the real needs for police services. With the exception of "crisis" law enforcement events (e.g., urban riots, natural disasters, and serious crimes of high public visibility), the day-to-day allocation of police resources within a city and within individual precincts is subject to the influence of factors that have little or nothing to do with the occurrence of crime. Crime patterns and frequencies are variable although not unpredictable. The time of day or night, the season, the type of building structure, population movement patterns, traffic patterns, and police patrol patterns themselves have all been found to have significant effects on criminal activity.[17]

In his study of the Boston Police Department in the nineteenth century, Roger Lane suggests that the allocation of police to divisions of the city was largely a function of direct political intervention by central business district interests and community leaders of the wealthier suburbs. As a consequence, crime was tolerated in the poor districts and the law under-enforced.[18] Niederhoffer, a veteran New York City police officer turned sociologist, and Dodson, a student of police–community relations in New York, both suggest that the direct political intervention by politically organized groups is a significant influence on allocation of police resources.[19]

Others attribute prevailing patterns of police resource allocation to the indirect influence of the community's political culture:

> Thus, police work is carried out under the influence of a political culture, though not necessarily under day-to-day political direction. By political culture is meant those widely shared expectations as to how issues will be raised, governmental objectives determined, and power for their attainment assembled; it is an understanding of what makes a government legitimate . . . the political culture can only be inferred from the general behavior of political institutions. Nor does the word "culture" imply that everyone in the community supports and approves of the way things are done; it only suggests that most people would expect, for better or worse, things to be done that way.[20]

In this view, police agencies adopt policies and "styles of behavior" in accordance with their perceptions of the political and social character of the community within which they work. Accordingly, cities and districts within cities receive the kind of police service that police believe is desired.[21]

Police administrators attribute the disjunction between need for and distribution of services to failure of police management, lack of skilled, professional administrators, and the influence of tradition. Such early commentators on police administration as Raymond Fosdick and Bruce Smith criticized police managers for not taking into account the predictable yet variable frequency of crime.[22] These studies showed that police patrol practices did not adjust according to time of day or night, season, type of building, size of population, or frequency of citizen complaints. Police resources were assigned equally to three 8-hour patrol shifts. Frank E. Walton, Commander of the Los Angeles Patrol Bureau, Los Angeles Police Department, confirms the view that contemporary police practices have not changed:

> Now then, as Chief of Police of a city containing twenty-six radio car districts, you have learned over the years that most of the crimes, most of the demand for service, most of your police problems, occur in districts K, P, and X. As an alert police administrator, do you spread your patrol force equally over these twenty-six radio car districts? Of course not! Just like the fisherman who drops his line into pools which past experience shows will produce the most trout, so do you concentrate your patrol strength in the districts which will be most productive in terms of reduced crime, criminals captured, calls answered, and community service. . . . You might, but don't bet on others. As a matter of fact, the assignment of police manpower in relation to police problems, in terms of day of week, time of day, and area . . . is by no means wide spread.[23]

The professional police administrator looks to the "scientific approach" to police allocation problems as one way of overcoming the influence of tradition within the police department and as a potent weapon against groups outside the department who press their specialized demands for police service.

> By studying past experiences, the scientist can predict future occurrences. So, too, can the alert police administrator anticipate the distribution of need for his patrol force on the basis

of the past distribution of the problem. This scientific approach
is not only efficient and intelligent; it is defensible! It is the
administrator's best defense against pressure groups in one area
who demand more police service, which would have to be
provided at the expense of another area.[24]

For the police professional, the "scientific model" serves to insulate the
police from political interference and to consolidate the administrator's
control over police policy.

According to a fourth and more provocative explanation of contemporary police allocation patterns, there is no such thing, in a practical sense,
as an "objective need" for police services if this means some measure of
crime frequency. Generally voiced in conjunction with the "political culture" argument, this view suggests that the important function of police is
not to maximize efficiency, effectiveness, or "rationality" in accordance
with universalistic criteria (e.g., arrests, property crimes prevented, or decreases in response time per unit of expenditure). The important function
of police is to satisfy specific citizen complaints (which predominantly
are not criminal). The citizen is interested in how police respond to his
report of a burglary, to his report of a prowler, or to his call for police
assistance in rescuing a cat from a tree.

The elected officials of a community are likewise most concerned with
particular events involving the police, not the day-to-day operations of
police. The town mayor or the county board of supervisors want to know
why a black citizen was beaten by police subsequent to arrest, why the
police failed to apprehend a bank robber, or what the cost of riot equipment will be next year.

In this view, the manner in which police allocate their resources is beyond the understanding, and, more importantly, beyond the interest, of
citizen and political decision maker alike. That police resources are not
allocated according to universal criteria points out the irrelevance of those
criteria to the practical situation of the police:

> . . . the police administrator acquires . . . a particularistic
> concern for the behavior of his men. That is to say, what
> preoccupies him—other than the overall level of crime—is
> not how the patrolmen generally behave but how they behave
> in a particular case. Police Chiefs do not as a rule lose their
> jobs because crime rates go up; indeed, rising crime rates
> may make it easier for them to get more money and manpower
> from city councils. But they often get into trouble and some-
> times lose their jobs because a particular officer takes a bribe,

steals from a store, associates with a gangster, or abuses a citizen who is capable of doing something about it.[25]

If some communities with high crime rates receive less police service than others within the same city, it is because of the lack of citizen complaints from the affected communities, and, implicitly, because of higher community tolerance for crime. In the rare event that community group complaints of police negligence attain political importance, police respond—typically with much fanfare—by temporarily assigning a specialized "crime fighting unit" to the area. In any event, police policy with regard to the allocation of its resources is characterized by "unarticulated improvisation" designed to answer particularistic complaints or demands for service and to prevent political brushfires from spreading.[26]

The Standard Formula

Regardless of which explanation of poor allocation of police resources one accepts, most commentators on the debate agree that there is a growing gap between the need for police services and the location and availability of police resources. Typically, urban ghetto areas with the highest crime rates but the least political influence receive poor police protection. Central business districts and wealthy neighborhoods receive a disproportionate amount of police service.

The maintenance of this pattern of allocation of police resources is encouraged by the inability of both the larger community and its elected officials to observe police strategic decision making. In the annual budget hearings where one might expect that police policy and proposals with regard to the use of public funds would be examined, the traditional line-item budget effectively conceals the ultimate use of public funds. Focusing on the costs of gasoline, supplies, building maintenance, and wages instead of on the man-years of patrol, average investigation costs per case, or patrol-miles per year by region or area of the city, allows the police themselves to remain ignorant of their actual policy.[27]

A director of police training has commented that the traditional police budgetary procedure is revealed in the formula $OSQ + CI = MPP;$ that is Operational Status Quo + Crime Increase = More Police Personnel.[28] A student of the Hartford, Connecticut, Police Department describes the annual budget procedure:

> The annual cycle begins in November, when the Chief of Police and the captains in charge of the various divisions of

the police . . . discuss the Department's needs for the coming year. In these hearings last year each division captain gave a brief speech describing the pressures on his division and stating that even barely adequate service for the coming year would require more men. The budget officer had special knowledge of police operations, which enabled him to ask intelligent questions about police policy and efficiency. But the police officials parried questions about policy with assertions that their present practices were clearly "the most efficient." The police rarely offered factual support for these claims, but on most questions the budget official had no facts with which to refute them. Thus questions of policy remained typically shrouded by the myth that the only police policy was "full enforcement" of the criminal law. In one illustrative exchange during November 1966 hearings at Hartford a budget official managed to put together information from two lists and a map on the wall and formulated the question: "Why are your beats of equal size when there are fourteen times as many complaints about crime coming from one as from the other? He was told that the present force distribution was the most effective one possible and the issue was dropped.[29]

For police officials, as well as for directors of other kinds of agencies, budgetary hearings represent an opportunity to convey the impression of a dedicated, overworked, and undermanned agency. The inability of budget officers to probe systematically into the use of public funds assures the police a virtual monopoly over the formation of its broad policies of resource allocation.

The Unholy Alliance: Community Groups and Professional Police

During the 1960s two factors emerged which tended to upset the tradi-tional patterns of police management: organized groups from poor com-munities began to question the adequacy of police service, and professional, college-trained managers assumed positions of leadership within police agencies.

In contradiction to the assumption of some scholars of police–com-munity relations, the residents of ghettos and poor districts of major Amer-ican cities do not believe that police activity is about as good as can be expected.[30] The President's Commission on Violence found that ghetto resi-dents were suspicious and cynical about police performance, but desirous of more police protection.[31] The wish for improved protection is hardly surprising, since the ghetto poor are more likely than others to be the victims of urban crime.[32]

In some cities during the 1960s Community Action Projects with the assistance of Legal Aid Societies began to express publicly the desires of poor city residents for more police protection. City officials and police administrators in these cities became painfully aware that supposedly "high-crime-tolerance" communities desired greater police attention. The response of police departments to these newly organized demands for their services varied from indifference to well-publicized but temporary crime suppression campaigns, depending largely on the political strength and importance of the complaining groups.[33]

Quite unexpectedly, the demands of some community groups for greater police service served to strengthen the case of police professionals operating within departments. Positions in the police department were once monopolized by members of the lower class. However, from the end of the depression in the late 1930s to as late as 1950, college-educated men were a large part, sometimes a majority, of the recruits of police departments of major American cities. In 1940, for example, more than half the police recruits in New York City held college degrees; Los Angeles, San Francisco, St. Louis, and other cities were comparable. In periods of economic uncertainty, police work offered security and salaries in excess of those paid to young lawyers. In recent years, however, men with college degrees rarely exceed 5% of the average recruit class.[34]

The brief influx of middle-class, college-educated men into police departments introduced a new set of conflicts:

> These middle-class college men formed the nucleus of the future elite group; before long they began to try to raise the prestige of the police occupation to match their own middle-class ideologies and attainments; to transform it into a profession.

> But within the ranks many of the less educated, tradition-directed members of the force continue to fight to preserve their hegemony. Dissension has reached serious proportions, verging on internecine class conflict between the lower-class conservatives and the upwardly-mobile middle-class radicals . . . many patrolmen are willing to drift along doing as little as possible. These members of the force feel threatened by the proposed changes. In self-defense they join the opposition to professionalism and become part of the subculture of cynicism.[35]

Despite internal resistance to police professionalism, the "new cop" quickly advanced through the ranks from patrolman, detective, captain, to the higher administrative ranks such as inspector or division director. By the late 1960s it was not unusual to find the posts of police commissioner and police chief, as well as most of the headquarters staff in major cities, in the hands of the professionals.

The police professionals, like other aspiring professionals, stress autonomy from "lay review" (although for reasons entirely different from those cited by the average patrolman), high admission standards, the development of a special body of knowledge called "police science," licensing of members, dedication to service ideals, and the "scientific administration" of police resources.[36]

Telecommunications, radar, radio, computers, crime labs, photo labs, office machines, aircraft, complex intelligence gathering devices, and training schools are the tools of the professional. The "billy club," prominent in the precinct, is rarely seen at headquarters, and the Smith and Wesson .38 is worn inconspicuously. Whatever one may think about the utility of the so-called gadget craze of American police, the panoply of technological devices and the organizational specialization required for their use, have served to increase the number of occupational positions open to rising professionals and to stabilize the political position of such individuals within police departments.

The professional cop has generally been a friend of the "good government" reformers in local politics who seek to deny influence over law enforcement to political machines and other outside groups. The professional police administrator favors the development of a "legalistic" or bureaucratic style of police behavior, founded on a set of universally applicable rules, administered fairly.[37] Besides appealing to the professional's ideals of fairness, equity, and rationality, the "bureaucratic style" can be defended to a frequently hostile public.[38]

During the most visible phase of the antipoverty reform movements of the 1960s, at various times and places, two unlikely political bedfellows—protesting community groups from poor urban areas and police professionals—unintentionally formed a rarely public alliance. The community groups raised embarrassing questions in public hearings about the poor distribution of police resources in general and the quality of service in particular. They wanted an equitable proportion of police services to remedy the former, and civilian review boards to help obtain the latter.

With two notable exceptions (New York and Philadelphia), the professionals publicly joined rank-and-file patrolmen in rejecting civilian review boards, for they had little faith in the ability of "civilians" to review adequately police behavior. Citing the dangers of political interference with the police function, they also questioned the propriety of such boards. Where the professionals were ambivalent toward or supportive of civilian review boards, rank-and-file rebellions led by patrolmen's benevolent associations resulted. In New York City the professionals lost a number of top administrative posts, as well as political influences over police policies, as a result of their initial support for a review board.[39]

The professional response to charges of misallocation of resources was muted agreement. Many administrators found that they could not answer charges of inefficiency and ineffectiveness simply because they did not know where or how their own men were allocated. Information about arrests, offenses, and clearances was plentiful, but there were no data on calls for service, hourly and geographical crime rates and trends, police response rate to requests, and the distribution of men and cars. Until very recently not a police department in the United States could account for the daily whereabouts and activities of its on-duty force. At any given moment in the average precinct or division, information about the location and availability of patrol cars and the identity of men in court could not be obtained by the police themselves. As one New York City police administrator remarked, "About all we knew was that somewhere out there under the smog we had only 10,000 on-duty men—eating, testifying, walking, patrolling, and sleeping."

Phasing Out the Sheriff's Posse: Real-Time Resource Allocation

Although hampered by political opposition from outside their departments and resistance from traditional officers within, many police administrators addressed themselves to the issue of resource allocation. New York City established its Tactical Patrol Force (TPF) in 1964—a flexible, elite corps of officers who could be transferred quickly to "high-crime" areas. However, the TPF is too small (400 officers) and resistance from precinct patrolmen too great to effect major changes in crime patterns.[40]

Besides the political difficulties inherent in any large-scale change in police allocation procedures, the lack of timely and accurate information on changing crime patterns has inhibited reallocation of police resources. Los Angeles has begun an experimental program in which men are assigned to patrol divisions according to a formula that weights such factors as previous year's crimes, radio calls, and population. Although this system can cope with long-term (i.e., over a year or more) changes in crime patterns, it is useless for short-term tactical deployment, and there has been no attempt to measure the effect or costs of selective distribution schemes.[41]

An example of the importance of timely information to effective tactical deployment of police resources is provided by the results of an experiment conducted by the New York City Transit Authority. Responding to public complaints of a rising "crime wave" on the subways during the night, the Transit Authority reversed its police deployment tactics from two-thirds day shift, one-third night shift (8 P.M. to 4 A.M.) to one-third day and two-thirds night. The experiment began in October 1968 and was evaluated one year later, after crime frequency had been manually tabulated. The results probably came as no surprise to criminal offenders, who changed their own tactics:

> Because of a sharp increase in crime committed during daylight hours, subway crimes reported to police are running 29 percent above last year.

> The Transit Authority said night time police saturation had brought a 15.4 percent drop in crime on the subways between 8 P.M. and 4 A.M. But that has been more than offset by increases in criminal activity the rest of the time. "When you put out a massive police program to cover the high-crime hours, the shifty criminal element shifts to other hours," explained Daniel T. McCannell, an executive officer of the Authority.

> Between the hours of 4 A.M. and 8 P.M. reported subway crime is running 39.9 percent over last year.[42]

Keeping track of "the shifty criminal element" obviously calls for more rapid information retrieval and analysis. Monthly, weekly, even daily crime frequency and pattern information is required. In Suburb City, the PRIS system is currently being used to change both short-and long-term allocations of police resources.

Suburb City

In 1969 the PRIS system began weekly delivery of crime frequency, type, and location information to the Suburb City Police Department. According to the police chief, in 1970 the department initiated changes in police patrol patterns and resource mix—the variable proportion of patrol cars, foot patrolmen, detectives, and plainclothes police. The results of the experiment, which are not fully tabulated, have nevertheless been impressive, as the following remarks by the police chief indicate.

> The President's Commission on Law Enforcement showed the direction of the future really by pointing out the relation between time of apprehension and solving the crime: the quicker we can arrive on the scene, the more likely it is we make an arrest of the criminal. In the past we thought we were doing just that. But it was all seats of the pants; what the last chief did, a sort of tradition. We had a lot of our men during the night downtown, where the business district is, mostly in patrol cars. Now we see that isn't the best policy. Since the 1960s the town's expanded, the business district is spread all over—gas stations, grocery stores, new shopping centers. In these outlying areas we needed more mobility: more cars and fewer men, while downtown we needed fewer cars and more men on foot.

> In the last council meeting we presented our findings. We were successful in getting more cars and explained our new policy.

> In the next few years when we get better at this, we'll be able to say to the mayor and council that if we can have X more cars we can prevent X amount of a certain kind of crime. Of course we don't believe we can stop all kinds of crimes, but we can increase the likelihood of an arrest in most types of common crimes—burglary, traffic offense, theft, et cetera. When we get a little more experience with this real-time resource system we should be able to predict when and where crimes of a certain type will take place. That's a hell of a lot better than just doing more of what we've done in the past, which is the usual police policy.

Suburb City is the only police department in Western County now developing a real-time resource allocation program. The expense of this type of program is large—on the order of $10,000 per year—and the total cost of the program may be far greater. With more apprehensions, the total costs of law enforcement (arrest, booking, court, and prison) rise very rapidly.

The Political Functions of PRIS: Increasing Responsiveness

Utilization of the PRIS system for evaluating and changing police resource allocations is limited to the prototype Suburb City experiment, despite the system's great potential in this area. In other agencies PRIS functions only as a means of exchanging warrant and stolen automobile information.[43] The political functions of PRIS and its impact on relations between political decision makers and police agencies have tended to make the former more responsive to police requests for additional resources, while at the same time minimizing the capacity of political decision makers to control the use of these resources within police agencies. In this respect PRIS differs markedly from the SSIS and CIS projects (Chapters 7 and 9) which have functioned to expand political decision makers' control over agencies.

Two consequences of the PRIS project support the view that political decision makers have become more responsive to police agencies in the PRIS network. First, the effectiveness of PRIS has led to increases in the number of arrests, in turn, new arrest statistics have been used effectively by police officials in budget hearings as evidence of the need for additional manpower and other resources.[44] Second, the PRIS project has been useful to participating agencies as a convenient "backstop" in public pronouncements. PRIS serves as a public relations tool to enhance the reputation of police agencies as efficient but overworked, progressive but understaffed.

The PRIS project does not constitute a new trend in relations between police, political decision makers, and the community; rather, it stands as the extension and maintenance of an ongoing trend. That is, it functions to preserve the tendency to keep the public in the dark regarding police resource allocation decisions of direct interest to them; moreover, it functions to extend the commonplace police monopoly over the information that would be needed in any systematic evaluation of their operations.[45]

Both these trends began long before the invention of modern, high-speed computers, and they are linked more directly with the growth of police professionalism and "good government" reform movements that have attempted to reduce civilian interference with police operations.[46] The questions are, Do projects such as PRIS alter or maintain these trends, and what are the consequences for the society at large? These matters are discussed below.

RUNNING FASTER, STAYING IN PLACE: CHANGE IN A LOW-CONTROL SYSTEM

PRIS can be described as a "low-control" system: one that has not expanded the capacity of elites to guide and/or monitor the behavior of nonelites. The relation between county elites (mayors, councilmen, boards of supervisors, and county administrative officers) and PRIS nonelite units is mediated by the PRIS Policy Committee and local police departments. Any evaluations of police resource allocation are designed and conducted by the police themselves, using PRIS resources. The knowledge and information produced by the system tends to filter up to elites only if it supports police policy or changes in policy desired by police.

The kinds of changes that have occurred in police procedures and effectiveness because of PRIS largely reflect the traditional police view of their social role. In this traditional view, the police function is largely one of apprehending and dealing with violators of the law. The new professionalism among police officers has not changed this tradition. Indeed, the efforts to "professionalize" police often lead to large increase in arrests for minor violations.[47]

This "traditional view" receives support from the structure of rewards, both within police departments and in the larger society. Intradepartmental rewards and distinctions are distributed according to the effectiveness and efficiency with which members "process" criminals (i.e., generate arrests and clearances).[48] In turn, police departments are rewarded by the society for apprehending and processing more and more criminals.[49] Police department budgets expand to the extent that spokesmen can convince public officials that the demand for police services is rising faster than the supply.[50]

Only a cynic would claim that police have a vested interest in generating arrests or increasing criminal behavior; nevertheless, the rewards offered policemen and police departments encourage them to take a very narrow, and expensive, view of the "crime problem" and means for its amelioration. This position was expressed most clearly by a Western County chief of police who remarked that "the best prevention of crime is the promise of sure, swift apprehension."

Under police management, the PRIS system has led to elaborations, albeit innovative, within the traditional police conception of their role. The use of computers to transfer warrant/wanted information among the agencies has increased the efficiency and effectiveness of warrant service dramatically. Suburb City reported a 92% increase in warrants served in the first month of operation. Brighton Police and the county sheriff reported similar results. The allocation studies have increased effectiveness (although not necessarily efficiency) measured by arrests within certain jurisdictions through altering the resources mix. Interfaces with the state Department of Motor Vehicles Stolen Auto Computer File have increased the rate of stolen auto arrests, according to local officials.

Without discounting the value of these changes, it should be noted that some recent research indicates that the pursuit of effective law enforcement by increasing police efficiency and effectiveness is relatively more costly than other alternatives and may lead to a deterioration in the quality of criminal justice by infringing on the civil rights of citizens.

For example, the great bulk of police arrests in the United States are for nonserious, "peace-keeping" offenses. About 80% of all arrests in 1967 were for non-Crime Index offenses (Index offenses are murder, forcible rape, robbery, aggravated assault, burglary, larceny, and auto theft).[51] About one-half of all arrests were for drunkenness, vagrancy, or gambling, with drunkenness the largest component—about one-third of total arrests.[52] It is estimated that the cost per case of an arrest for drunkenness is $50 and that the national bill in criminal justice systems costs is $100 million.[53]

Thus a great deal of police effort, time, and other resources goes into arresting people for relatively minor infractions of the law. It has been suggested that the police be relieved of the responsibility of arresting and processing drunks, vagrants, and gamblers. Lower costs, reduced manpower, and more humane treatment of minor violators are cited as reasons for this change. Federal money is presently supporting a pilot program in Buffalo, New York, in which drunks are taken to detoxification centers by low-skill hospital adies. In the "de-tox centers" drunks are given counseling and offered help instead of mere confinement. Local police, who resisted this change initially, now are able to spend more time on serious offenders.[54]

According to local district attorneys, the PRIS system has resulted in a surge of nonserious offender cases that must be processed through the DA's office and courts:

> For us the biggest impact of PRIS is the case load increase. The police are scoring more "hits" every time they stop a car on the streets. They find the guy has a warrant for a scofflaw in another jurisdiction, and he must appear in court. We have to process all these cases. So the courts are more jammed up than ever, case processing has increased, but we have less time to prepare cases, and as a result the quality of our work has gone down, I'm afraid.

Approximately 80% of the warrants in the PRIS system are for traffic offenses. And one of the consequences of PRIS has been to drain police manpower from serious offense cases to lesser offenses such as traffic violations. By all tradtional indicators of police performance, PRIS has produced notable achievements: more arrests, more warrants served. Clearly, however, this does not result in the best use of expensive resources such as trained police. Some cities, including New York, are contemplating the removal of traffic offenses from police responsibility altogether. Traffic offenses would be handled by a Traffic Bureau without the intervention or costs of the courts, police, or detention facilities.[55]

A second benefit claimed for PRIS is an increase in the number of arrests for stolen automobiles. The interface between PRIS and the stolen auto file in the state capital had increased the probability of an arrest by patrol cars routinely checking suspicious drivers.[56] Auto theft is considered to be a serious Crime Index offense by the FBI, and in 1967 this act accounted for approximately 15% of the serious offense arrests. Auto theft is a young person's crime: 90% of auto thefts are committed by people under 25 years of age, and the predominant reason for theft is "joyriding." According to the FBI, 75 percent of stolen autos are "borrowed" and returned to the owners within 72 hours, unharmed.[57] In large urban areas of the United States, auto theft is inversely related to the availability of public transportation.[58]

Although one eastern state is preparing to spend $10 million on a complex license-plate scanning system, and the PRIS system agencies spend a sizable but indeterminate amount of resources checking, apprehending, and processing auto theft cases, others have suggested far less expensive non-police alternatives to reduce auto theft.

Since only 25% of all stolen cars are taken for resale or parts, it is likely that minor changes in ignition technology would yield major reductions in the rate of auto theft. Simple devices such as those required by law on the 1970 models would suffice: a buzzer rings whenever the car is stopped and the key left in the ignition, and the steering wheel locks when the key is removed. It is argued that these simple technological devices would reduce auto theft by 70%, obviating the need for complex computer systems designed to apprehend thieves.[59]

Structure and Strategy: The Need for Higher Control

Defining the appropriate political and administrative relations between local police, politicians, and the community has always constituted a dilemma in American politics. Since the inception of police agencies in the early nineteenth century, when a citizen had to pay the local constable for apprehending a criminal, the notion that police should be responsible to and controlled by the local community was dear to the American experience.[60]

As much as any tax-supported public agency, it was thought that the police should be controlled by the citizens and/or their representatives who payed for the service. Moreover, the capacity of the police to use legitimate force against the community was thought to be a special reason for ensuring local control of police. Yet local control presented the potential, and eventually created the reality, of police who were most responsive to those members of the community with more money, political power, or prestige. Thus arose the dilemma of organizing the police to ensure broad political control by the larger community while at the same time insulating the police from particularistic control by special interest groups.

The late nineteenth and early twentieth centuries saw a number of attempts by external (i.e., nonpolice) elites to exert greater administrative control over local police, yet to insulate them from partisan politics. "Blue ribbon" police commissions in the cities composed of prestigious civilians and sponsored by urban reformers, and in some states a state police commission with control over local appointment and promotion, were typical solutions. These bodies failed to remove the police from partisan politics; moreover, their efforts served to make the police less accountable to local communities and incurred the resistance of police officers who were suspicious of any civilian interference in their operations. Such forms of external civilian control through "administrative reorganizaton" have fallen into disuse.[61]

In some localities—by and large the suburban townships and smaller states—civilians continue to exercise strong administrative control over their local police, and elsewhere vestigial political machines exert a powerful influence, but the larger majority of urban police agencies fall into neither pattern.[62] What has emerged instead is a "hands-off" pattern of police–politician–community relations, the police being left alone to determine their strategy and tactics of law enforcement. There is no lack of ideological commitment to the notion of local control of police. In the words of the President's Commission, however, "The actual means for exerting control (over police agencies) have become quite obscure."[63]

Although legislative, judicial, and executive decisions presumably exert heavy control over the broad strategies of police agencies (e.g., by defining illegal acts, prescribing procedures of evidence, and funding police agencies), in fact local police retain considerable discretion to enforce specific laws, to seek out specific types of offenders, and to allocate public funds to specific programs.[64] Moreover, whereas constitutional protections and judicial decisions are designated to restrict and control the law enforcement tactics of police agencies (e.g., by enumerating citizen rights vis-à-vis government and defining rules of due process), it is also true that local police exercise considerable discretion in deciding when or whether to initiate actions against citizen offenders, and how such action will be carried out.[65]

Recent attempts to exert greater political control and better defined ad-

ministrative control over specific police strategies and tactics were successfully and vigorously opposed by the police themselves. In addition, failure
has greeted most efforts to remove from the books—thus from police
authority—laws regarding such behavior as the possession of small amounts
of marijuana, prostitution, and homosexuality.[66] There have also been unsuccessful attempts to introduce citizen review boards and civilian om-
budsmen to consider formally specific police actions and to provide the
citizen with prompt civil remedy for illegal police acts. But the political
opposition organized by police unions and professional associations was
not the only cause of such failures—they result in part from the impossi-
bility of defining beforehand how police officers should behave in myriad
situations.[67]

The contemporary trend in which police agencies escape civilian review
at any level—strategic or tactical—is attributed to several causes. Some
suggest that the rise of urban "good government" reform movements has
inhibited elected officials, to say nothing of the community, from critically
reviewing their police agencies for fear of being charged with "playing
partisan politics with the police."[68] Others have argued that the growth of
professionalism among the police, especially the officers, serves to legitimate and strengthen police autonomy from "lay" review.[69] Third, the
growth in the political strength of police unions in some cities has clearly
increased the costs of intervention into police affairs by elected officials.
Yet a fourth factor, especially relevant here, which partially accounts for
police autonomy from civilian review is that there simply is no body of
knowledge or systematic information about the relative costs and benefits
of police strategies and tactics.[70]

Whatever its causes, the consequences of the contemporary autonomy of
police agencies from civilian review at any level is that police agencies,
unlike other local government agencies, select the strategies and tactics to
be used in the performance of their duties without the knowledge of outsiders. Regardless of whether this process of selection is a conscious, rational, organizational process, or a process of "inarticulate improvisation,"
the resultant quality of police strategic decision making exhibits two features.[71] First, selection of police strategies is often detrimental to the operation of other criminal justice agencies, and results in expanding police
agencies—in personnel and other resources—at very high cost to the
society as a whole. Second, the process of selecting police strategies is
structured to prevent the community and its representatives from obtaining the information and knowledge necessary to evaluate the relative costs
and benefits of those strategies.

The PRIS project illustrates these two features of police strategy selection both as a process and in terms of its consequences. Its autonomy from external elites assured that PRIS would not be used to evaluate police allocation decisions or to inform the public. Instead it is used to maximize the production of arrests by increasing warrant service and the probability of apprehending stolen automobiles. This in turn results in other criminal justice agencies becoming overloaded with nonserious offenders (e.g., traffic scofflaws and joyriders).

We are arguing that the maximization of police production functions, isolated from other criminal justice agencies and other governmental agencies, does not maximize the criminal justice system as a whole and is more costly to society than any one of a number of alternatives. Indeed, one of the great faults of the PRIS system, and others like it, is that police agencies will be allowed to maximize their output with little regard to the consequences for other criminal justice agencies or the society. The overcrowded court dockets and penal institutions of Western County and other urban areas in the United States bear witness to this situation.

Clearly, there is some doubt about the wisdom of the view that the best prevention is the promise of sure, swift apprehension. Chronic drunks, narcotics users, gamblers, vagrants, scofflaws, and youthful joyriders have not been deterred by traditional police policies of apprehension, nor are they likely to be deterred in the future.[72]

One suggested alternative is to simply remove a number of laws from the books, such as drug, drinking, and "morality" laws—laws relating to crimes without victims. Taken alone, this policy would ignore the need for police to adopt new man–machine mixes, new technologies that would enable them to increase their effectiveness in dealing with serious crimes, as well as their other peace-keeping functions (i.e., patrol, mediating in family quarrels, stopping professional auto theft, etc.).

There is a real need for systems like PRIS which, properly used, would permit police to rationally allocate resources and to evaluate their own effectiveness. One possibility would be to enlarge the structure of PRIS to include representatives from external elite groups—such as the County Administrative Offices or other persons who are responsible to central budget elites and who are technically competent to work with information systems. A larger structure that included external elites would provide the structural basis for evaluating the allocation of strategic resources to police and other agencies, leaving the tactical allocation of police resources to the police themselves.

For example, let us consider the problem of auto theft. The Western

County police have argued that auto theft could be significantly reduced by increasing rates of apprehension; rates of apprehension could be increased, according to them, by a computerized information system, accessible to patrol cars by radio, in which information on stolen autos is stored. As more thieves are apprehended (predominantly joyriders), more men and more patrol cars are necessary because more resources are required to "process" the offenders. In addition, the DAs, courts, and penal institutions of the county would need additional resources to handle the larger number of offenders.[73]

Up to now, Western County officials, and others in Eastern State, have accepted this rationale. Backed by cost-benefit studies, police have been able to convince elites that the best police method of reducing auto theft is the establishment of complex, expensive information systems.[74] The question of the relative cost of police methods versus non police methods in reducing auto theft is seldom asked.

One purpose of including external elites in the PRIS system, or systems like it, would be to compare a number of nonpolice alternatives with the police alternative. Thus the cost-benefit ratios of improved ignition and steering-wheel lock devices, proximity alarms, and so on, would be set against the cost-benefit ratios of police alternatives: an information system, more men, and more cars.

Once a strategy to deal with a specific crime problem had been adopted, and strategic allocations of resources have been made, police can maximize the tactical utilization of their resources. In the case of stolen autos, assuming simple devices were adopted as a strategy to prevent youthful joyriding, police might decide to concentrate on professional thieves who would not be deterred or thwarted by simple devices. (Since professional thieves typically alter or disassemble a car almost immediately after theft, police information systems coupled with patrol cars usually will not be effective against professionals, either.[75])

Other types of problems heretofore defined as "crime" would be considered in a similar format—for example, "de-tox centers" as opposed to increased police manpower in skid row areas, Methadone treatment versus increased narcotics and detective squad allocations, and noncriminal Traffic Bureaus as opposed to traffic police.[76]

Our proposal to broaden the structure of decision making about strategic resource allocations to police by including external political elites or their representatives within the PRIS information system may well meet with initial opposition from police. County or other elites, such as city mayors, would be exercising greater control over the police and evaluating the comparative costs of their policies. A good many types of behavior labeled criminal by present laws no longer be within the province of the police (e.g., drunkenness, traffic offenses, drug addiction). Many of these responsibilities are considered to be bothersome "mickey mouse" details anyway, work that forces policemen to spend a good deal of time in booking rooms, night courts, and prisons.[77]

In the long run, opposition to a broadened structure would decline, as long as police are given control over tactical resource allocation problems and over such other information needs as summary criminal histories, rap sheets, and fingerprint retrieval services. That is, police opposition would be minimized as long as the information system functioned to make external elites responsive to police departments' self-perceived needs. Furthermore, opposition would drop because police would no longer be spending most of their time on nonserious offenses but could begin to concentrate on serious crimes and their prevention. Greater training and a new degree of professionalism would be required of police for these tasks, which would serve to raise the status of police and most likely their salaries. In short, the "new cop" would be very different from his predecessors. The image of the cop as the unsophisticated and heavily armed "human tank" would be replaced by that of a white-collared, civil servant type of "sleuth" on the model of U.S. Treasury Agents or the Secret Service men.

To be sure, such changes will not come about overnight. However, there is growing pressure from various quarters to remove certain behavior from criminal codes—addiction to drugs or alcohol, gambling, homosexuality, prostitution, and other crimes without victims.[78] Since approximately 80% of all arrests are for these and other minor types of infraction (non-Index offenses), urban governments face the prospect of hiring more and more police, and spending ever greater sums of money, simply to apprehend, process, and confine minor offenders. Systems such as PRIS, as presently constructed, will perhaps allow the police to perform their functions in the traditional manner, yet more effectively (greater arrests) and more efficiently (lower cost per arrest). Unless major transformations in police behavior and the societal conception of the police role are forthcoming, however, the possibility that the police and other criminal justice agencies will simply be running faster but staying in place is very real. The police may succeed in doing with the utmost efficiency that which should not be done at all. A responsive information system like PRIS, which would enable police to respond more effectively to their environment *and* would expand the control and guidance capacities of external political elites and the larger community over police, could contribute toward a transformation in police practices, besides reducing the societal costs of the police function.

PRIS IN PERSPECTIVE

The PRIS system illustrates one of the principal findings of our study: a centralized information system is fully compatible with a highly decentralized administrative structure. In this case more than ninety independent police agencies from various political jurisdictions cooperatively pool information and permit its exchange for common benefit. The result has not altered in the least the political and administrative relationships between elected officials and central executives, on the one hand, and police agencies on the other. As we have suggested, the police agencies may have become more independent from the supervision of elected officials and central administrations as a result of PRIS. That is, PRIS sustains the traditional police monopoly over important information that is useful to the public evaluation of their activities.

Another noteworthy feature of the PRIS system is the total lack of resistance from user agencies. Without exception, the user agencies were highly supportive of PRIS, as were the employees who were interviewed.

It appeared to me that the lack of resistance to PRIS was related to the initial conditions of the user agencies. The agencies involved were all local police agencies performing identical tasks in different jurisdictions. The high homogeneity of the user agencies made agreement over the kinds of information to pooled and exchanged more likely. In the PRIS example, a survey of the user agencies was used to determine that warrant information was the data that could be of maximum benefit to all participants.

Also conducive to the acceptance of the PRIS system were preexisting traditional social ties among the agencies. Most of the agencies in the system—all the initial county agencies—were active members of a regional police association; in recent years urban and university disturbances in the area had provided occasions for these agencies to cooperate closely. Moreover, the increased mobility of the population and the greater number of autos in the region, made the entire process of warrant service dependent on the cooperation of autonomous police agencies.

These initial factors, we suggest, were conducive to an initial consensus about the need for a system like PRIS and were at least partly responsible for the low level of resistance to construction. But other factors related to manner in which PRIS was constructed were important to the low resistance, as well as to the decentralized character of the system.

The PRIS system is unique among our case studies in terms of the extent to which user agencies control the design and implementation of the information system. In the very early stages the police agencies themselves, with the aid of a major computer firm, established what kinds of information could be exchanged most usefully. At no point in the design stage did nonpolice considerations enter into the selection of the kinds of information to centralize or the purpose for which each was chosen.

The implementation of the system was also unique. Although one result of PRIS is the centralization of warrant information in a common county data bank, this information is never out of the hands of fellow police officers. The PRIS Policy Committee, the directing committee composed of representatives from user agencies, administers the day-to-day operation of the system; the county Data Center hired a former police official to administer the actual processing of information at the data bank.

Initiated, controlled, and operated by police for police, the PRIS system is suggestive of the kind of reform we have called a Collegial model. In that model, no single constituent exercises a disproportionate control over the reform, and each constituent possesses a veto.

We have cited the egalitarian nature of the PRIS system and the high degree to which it reflects constituent desires as being among the reasons for the very low resistance among user agencies. At the same time, these features of PRIS present problems for other agencies in the criminal justice field, and they raise questions about the proper utilization of this new technology.

The PRIS system develops with little or no consideration given to its effects on other criminal justice agencies, such as the district attorneys, the courts, and the prisons. One consequence is an increase in the prosecution and conviction of minor criminal offenders. Other agencies become overburdened with the processing of such offenders, and the whole question of whether minor offenders should be the principal object of police innovations is forgotten.

This raises another question: Why was there no attempt by civilians (e.g., elected officials, scholars or concerned citizens), to criticize the rationale of the PRIS system? Put another way, Was it proper for a major computer firm, in cooperation with local police, to design the uses of this new technology with little or no public review?

The answer to the first question is easier. Public ignorance of the consequences of a complex technology partly explains their apparent lack of concern. Yet another explanation might be the desire of politicians to avoid "interference" with police operations. The development of this new technology by the police and for the police can then be seen as the continuance of a tradition in which the police escape public review and scrutiny.

Yet few would argue that the abdication of police review by politicians and concerned civilian groups, and a total reliance on police professional norms, is proper in our society. Clearly, as the discussion of PRIS illustrates, such a course may result in the police doing most effectively what they perhaps need not be doing in the first place.

NOTES

1. For an historical discussion of the development of the urban sheriff, see Roger Land, *Policing the City—Boston—1822-1885,* Cambridge, Mass.: Harvard University Press, 1967, pp. 6-12.

2. County Board of Supervisors, *County Government,* 1970.

3. Interviews with PRIS officials. For a discussion of the impact of quota systems and clearance rates on police behavior, see Jerome Skolnick, *Justice Without Trial,* New York: Wiley, 1967, Chapter 8. See also, for a discussion of traffic quota systems, James Q. Wilson, *Varieties of Police Behavior,* Cambridge, Mass.: Harvard University Press, 1968, p. 97.

4. On the development of a police "working personality" and "police culture," see Skolnick, *op. cit.,* Chapter 3. On the emergence of distinctive police department "styles," which are related to the larger political culture of localities, see Wilson, *op. cit.,* Chapter 8.

5. Interviews with Athens patrolmen.

6. Wilson, *op. cit.,* pp. 48-49. Some have said that police think of themselves as a minority group and that this consciousness arises from the danger of their work and the perceived lack of community support. See Michael Banton, *The Policeman and the Community,* London: Tavistock, 1964, and William A. Westley, *Violence and the Police,* Cambridge, Mass.: M.I.T. Press, 1971. See also Westley's "Secrecy and the Police," *Social Forces,* **34** (1956), pp. 254-257. For a discussion of the development of work associated police values among black patrolmen in New York City see Nicholas Alex, *Black in Blue—A Study of the Negro Patrolmen,* New York: Appleton-Century-Crofts, 1969, pp. 86-89, 171-174.

7. Police agencies throughout the United States recruit primarily from the working class. Police recruits in both Los Angeles and New York are 85% from working-class families, less than 4% having college experience. See Arthur Niederhoffer, *Behind the Shield,* Garden City, N.Y.: Doubleday, 1969, Chapter 2. Niederhoffer finds "security of job" a principal reason for joining a police force. See Joseph D. Matarazzo et al., "Characteristics of Successful Policeman and Firemen Applicants," *Journal of Applied Psychology,* **40** (1964), pp. 123-133.

8. On the reward and penalty structure of police bureaucracies, see Niederhoffer, *op. cit.,* Chapter 3, especially pp. 58-94, and Skolnick, *op. cit.,* Chapter 8. On the ability of police departments to prevent civilian review boards from being established in their towns, see *The New York Times,* February 10, 1966, p. 1. See also, for a general discussion of civilian review boards, "The Administration of Complaints by Civilians Against the Police," *Harvard Law Review,* **77** (January 1964), pp. 499-519. As discussed in Chapter 7, the social service agencies of Western County are the subject of frequent investigations by public and private groups.

9. Skolnick describes the dominant political and emotional persuasion of the police officers he studied as "that of a Goldwater type of conservatism" (*op. cit.*, p. 61). See also James Q. Wilson, "The Police and Their Problems: A Theory," *Public Policy,* **12** (1963), pp. 189–216. That policemen as an occupational group exhibit unusually high degrees of social solidarity is well documented. Only 16% of those Skolnick interviewed had failed to attend a single police banquet or dinner in the past year (*op. cit.*, p. 52). The high social solidarity among policemen is attributed by most to their isolation from the rest of society. See, for the English case, Ben Whitaker, *The Police,* Middlesex, England: Penguin, 1964, pp. 128–140.

10. See Skolnick, *op. cit.*, for similar findings.

11. "Regional Law Enforcement Information Control Study Committee Report," 1965, Brighton Police Department.

12. *Ibid.*

13. From "History of the Regional Study Committee," Peace Officers' Association of Western State, undated; probably autumn 1964.

14. From "Centralized Electronic Information System—The Key to Effective Law Enforcement," Brighton Police Department and IBM, July 1964.

15. *County Grand Jury Report, 1964.*

16. This criterion has become especially popular since the initiation of PRIS in 1965, and it furnishes a useful and simple number to distribute to the public and elected officals during budgetary hearings.

17. President's Commission on Law Enforcement and Administration of Justice, *Task Force Report: Science and Technology,* Washington, D.C.: Government Printing Office, Chapter 2. See also Bruce Smith, *Police Systems in the United States,* 2nd ed., New York: Harper & Row, 1960, pp. 31–50.

18. Lane, *op. cit.*, pp. 174–179.

19. Niederhoffer, *op. cit.*, p. 12. See also Daniel Dodson, *Proceedings of the Institute of Police–Community Relations,* East Lansing: School of Police Administration and Public Safety, Michigan State University, 1956, p. 75.

20. Wilson, *Varieties of Police Behavior, op. cit.*, p. 233.

21. Michael Banton, in *Policeman and the Community,* arrives at a similar conclusion: *op. cit.*, Chapter 8.

22. Smith, *Police Systems in the United States, op. cit.*, pp. 122, 116–118, 208–242. See also Raymond B. Fosdick, *American Police Systems,* New York: Century, 1920, pp. 300–315.

23. Frank E. Walton, "Selective Distribution of Police Patrol Force," *Journal of Law, Criminology and Police Science,* **49** (1958), p. 165.

24. *Idem.*

25. Wilson, *Varieties of Police Behavior, op. cit.*, p. 65.

26. The view that police allocation and other policies are ad hoc adjustments to specific situations and that general patterns of police allocation of resources are the largely unintended result of numerous independent and improvised decisions is that of the President's Commission of Law Enforcement and Administration of Justice, *Task Force Report: The Police,* Washington, D.C.: Government Printing Office, *op. cit.*, Chapters 1 and 2.

27. For a general discussion of the problems of defining police goals and relating them to specific operations, see President's Commission on Law Enforcement and Administration of Justice, *Task Force Report: Science and Technology, op. cit.,* Chapters 1 and 2. See also Walton, *op. cit.,* pp. 165–171; and Carl Shoup, "Standards for Distributing a Free Government Service: Crime Prevention," *Public Finance,* **19,** No. 4 (1964).

28. Harold Klimkowski, "The Police Budget: The Mistake of Using the $OSQ +$ $CI = MPP$ Formula," *The Police Yearbook,* **50** (1966).

29. "Program Budgeting for Police Departments," *Yale Law Journal,* **76** (March 1967), p. 823.

30. See Wilson, *Varieties of Police Behavior, op. cit.,* p. 233.

31. See *The Challenge of Crime in a Free Society,* President's Commission on Law Enforcement and Administration of Justice, Washington, D.C.: Government Printing Office, 1968, pp. 135–142, 160, 162, 164, 255–257.

32. *Ibid.,* p. 255.

33. See James Cahn, "The War on Poverty: A Civilian Perspective," *Yale Law Journal,* **73** (1964), and "Comment, The Right to Nondiscriminatory Enforcement of State Penal Laws," *Columbia Law Review,* 1961. Notable incidents of community group objections to lack of police service have occurred in San Francisco, Los Angeles, Chicago, New York, and Detroit.

34. Arthur Niederhoffer, *op. cit.,* p. 17.

35. *Ibid.,* pp. 18–27.

36. *Ibid.,* p. 19.

37. Wilson, *Varieties of Police Behavior, op. cit.,* Chapter 8, especially p. 259. On "good government" reform movements and their implications for professional management of city agencies, see Edward C. Banfield and James Q. Wilson, *City Politics,* New York: Random House, 1963, pp. 115–187.

38. Next to pursuit of professional goals, the belief that a more rational allocation of police resources will result in greater public support is the most frequently cited reason for adopting new allocation procedures. See Walton, *op. cit.,* p. 171, and O. W. Wilson, "Selective Distribution of Police Patrol Force," *Journal of Criminal Law Criminology and Police Science* (1958), p. 379.

39. For New York City's experience, see Niederhoffer, *op. cit.,* pp. 182–198. For the Philadelphia experience, see *The New York Times,* July 24, 1964, p. 9.

40. For a review of the Tactical Patrol Force of New York City and the conflicts it has generated within the police department, see *New York Times,* October 12, 1969.

41. See President's Commission of Law Enforcement and Administration of Justice, *Task Force Report: Science and Technology, op. cit.,* p. 18.

42. *The New York Times,* October 30, 1969.

43. Personal communication, Director of Operations, Brighton Police Department, June 1971.

44. See Wilson, *Varieties of Police Behavior, op. cit.,* p. 98, who suggests that organizational specialization within police departments typically results in higher arrest rates.

45. *Ibid.,* p. 259. See also "Program Budgeting for Police Departments," *op. cit.,* pp. 822–838, and President's Commission·on Law Enforcement and the Administration of Justice, *Task Force Report: The Police, op. cit.,* Chapter 2.

46. Wilson, *op. cit.,* Chapter 8, *Task Force Report: The Police, op. cit.,* Chapter 2, and Niederhoffer, *op. cit.,* Chapter 2.

47. The FBI rates the prevention of crime above the apprehension of criminals in its list of police functions; but as Klimkowski, *op. cit.,* suggests, apprehensions, arrests, and clearances are the basis of evaluation of police officers and departments. See J. Edgar Hoover, *Should You Go Into Law Enforcement?* New York: New York Life Insurance Company, 1961, p. 7. Wilson, *Varieties of Police Behavior, op. cit.,* suggests that "legalistic" police departments encourage their officers to utilize formal procedures in response to observed violations of the law—even minor violations.

48. See Skolnick, *op. cit.,* pp. 164–181, and Aaron Cicourel, *The Social Organization of Juvenile Justice,* New York: Wiley, 1968, Chapters 2–3.

49. It has been argued that securing favorable statistics for use at annual budget hearings is one of the principal functions of police efforts to gather arrest and other information on organizational activity; Wilson, *Varieties of Police Behavior, op. cit.,* p. 185, and Walton, *op. cit.,* p. 168, suggest that frequently the surveys of the planning division have no impact whatsoever on police operations but are instead used to give a favorable impression of the department.

50. On budgetary tactics of government agencies in general, see Aaron Wildavsky, *The Politics of the Budgetary Process,* Boston: Little, Brown, 1964.

51. U.S. Department of Justice, Federal Bureau of Investigation, *Crime in the United States—Uniform Crime Reports 1967,* Washington, D.C.: Government Printing Office, 1968.

52. *Ibid.*

53. See Orval Morris and Morris Hawkins, *The Honest Politician's Guide to Crime Control,* Chicago: University of Chicago Press, 1969, Chapter 6.

54. See President's Commission, "The Challenge of Crime in a Free Society, *op. cit.,* pp. 540–542, and Morris and Hawkins, *op. cit.*

55. *The New York Times,* September 14, 1969.

56. It has proved impossible to document adequately the claims made for the PRIS system because the effects of the information system cannot be separated from the effects of changes in patrol procedure, changes in the number of stolen autos, and increases in the size of police forces, which all contribute to higher arrest rates for warrant service and stolen atuo offenses. Police officers and administrators using the system however, indicate, that they are convinced it has led to much higher arrest rates for scofflaws and auto theft. The county district attorney, who must handle many of the cases, arrived at the same conclusion. Furthermore, we are not interested in whether police efficiency or effectiveness increases by 5% or 10% but in how the policemen perceive the information system in relation to their goals.

57. Morris and Hawkins, *op. cit.*

58. IIT Research Institute, *A Socio-Economic Valuation Study for the Automatic License Plate Scanning System,* Annapolis, Md.: 1969, p. A-13-1.

59. Morris and Hawkins, *op. cit.,* Chapter 7.

60. Lane, *op.cit.*, Chapters 1 and 2.

61. For a description of the various reform efforts aimed at the police see Smith, *op. cit.*, Chapter 5.

62. Wilson, *Varieties of Police Behavior, op. cit.*, p. 276.

63. President's Commission, *Task Force Report: The Police, op. cit.*, p. 30.

64. The decision to arrest and process large numbers of vagrant drunks in Oakland is an example of police discretion over enforcement strategy, as well as the use of quota systems for traffic police. See Wilson, *op. cit., Varieties of Police Behavior*, p. 97, and pp. 118–135.

65. See Skolnick, *op. cit.*, Chapter 8.

66. See Kaplan, *Marijuana—The New Prohibition*, New York, World, 1970; and E. M. Schur, *Crimes Without Victims*, Englewood Cliffs, N. J.: Prentice-Hall, 1965.

67. See Wilson, *Varieties of Police Behavior, op. cit.*, Chapter 1 and Niederhoffer, *op. cit.*, Chapter 7.

68. Wilson, *op. cit.*, pp. 160–195, 276.

69. *Ibid.*, and Niederhoffer, *op. cit.*

70. Wilson, *op. cit.*, pp. 49–69.

71. See President's Commission on Law Enforcement and Administration of Justice, *Task Force Report: The Police, op. cit.*, p. 18.

72. Kaplan, *Ibid.* See also Morris and Hawkins, *op. cit.*, Chapter 9, and E. M. Schur, *Narcotic Addiction in the U.S. and Britain*, Bloomington: Indiana University Press, 1962.

73. One author describes the Brighton traffic ticket procedure as a positive feedback system: the more cars one stops and tickets for minor infractions, the greater the chance of catching a real criminal. If you catch a real criminal, you make yourself look good; thus you have an even greater incentive to stop and ticket cars. See Wilson, *Varieties of Police Behavior, op. cit.*, p. 185.

74. In the case of CIS, three research and development firms concluded that the proposed Automatic License Plate Scanning System was not a wise investment. Finally a fourth firm was found which arrived at the desired conclusion, namely, that ALPS was cost-beneficial. This study is widely circulated by CIS (see Chapter 9).

75. IIT Research Institute, *op. cit.*, p. A-37.

76. See the recommendations with regard to "de-tox centers" in *The Challenge of Crime in a Free Society, op. cit.*, pp. 533–537.

77. Niederhoffer, *op. cit.*, p. 75. Police frequently try to underenforce the law with regard to minor offenders, and they resent efforts of police management to have minor offenders arrested. Niederhoffer concludes in his study of police cynicism that patrolmen feel it is useless to arrest drunks, prostitutes, and gamblers because they are let out of prison early or, frequently, not even sentenced to a prison term. The "good pinch" is one that involves a shooting, an armed robbery, or other "important" crime perpetrator.

78. See President's Commission, *Task Force Report: The Police, op. cit.*, pp. 533–537. For a recent local government report criticizing the police emphasis on enforcing "morality crimes," see *The San Francisco Chronicle*, June 7, 1971; this article summarizes the recommendations of the San Francisco Crime Commission. See also Kaplan, *op. cit.*, and Morris and Hawkins, *op. cit.*

APPENDIX

PRIS Design Specifications

The PRIS system was developed in conjunction with the Data Processing Center of Western County (see the Appendix to Chapter 7 for a description of that system's hardware and software). The PRIS system relies on the Center's IBM 360-40 computer, in conjunction with an IBM FASTER real-time program. An overview of the PRIS system is presented in Figure 5.

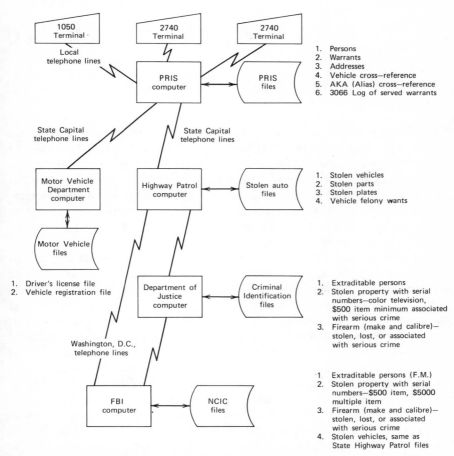

Figure 5. Police information available through PRIS.

NINE

An Emerging State Department of Justice

The Eastern State Criminal Identification System (CIS) was created by act of the state legislature in 1965. Located in the state capital, CIS was the first statewide computerized criminal justice information system in the country; today it is the largest such system in existence. Other states, notably California and Michigan, are usng CIS as a model for similar systems being constructed there. In addition, the FBI has recently implemented its own National Crime Information Center (NCIC) based in part on the experience and techniques of CIS.

In contrast to criminal justice information systems in other states, CIS has been operational since 1965 as an independent, autonomous state agency. Eastern State, unlike California and Michigan, has never had a state Department of Justice with broad authority and responsibility over criminal justice functions such as administering police, correctional institutions, or courts. Since the time of Andrew Jackson politics and government in Eastern State have been more "balkanized" than in the "newer" Western states. CIS can be seen as an attempt by the state executive, the governor, to gain greater control over criminal justice agencies operating in the state.

Thus in 1965 it was necessary to create a new agency responsible solely for criminal justice information; merely extending or enlarging the functions of an established agency would not do. This is an important distinction to bear in mind, because the creation of a new agency presents the possibility of a host of problems created by such questions as: Who will be represented by the agency? Who will participate in its formation? Who will pay its costs? What relation will it bear to established local agencies? And whose political interests will be affected, and how? When an established state agency extends its functions and jurisdictions within the state, many of these problems do not arise, or at least not with the same potency.[1]

GOALS AND MISSIONS: RAP SHEETS AND FINGERPRINTS

The announced mission of CIS is to provide a central, computerized criminal identification file to criminal justice agencies in city, county, and state government. In 1967 there were more than 3600 such agencies in Eastern State—police, district attorneys, courts, and probation, correction, and parole agencies.

The task of identifying criminals had been the responsibility of the Bureau of Criminal Identification (BCI) within the Department of Corrections. In the BCI of years past, a mechanical file was maintained. Local city and county agencies kept their own files on criminals sentenced to local correctional institutions, augmenting local police files on arrested persons. Local and regional courts, district attorneys, and probation departments also maintained criminal identification files.

CIS was intended to centralize the local criminal identification files, to assure quick and easy access to the central file by local agencies, and to expand the amount of usuable information retained on all arrested criminals.

The identification of criminals and criminal suspects traditionally involves "searching" three different files: name files, fingerprint indexed files, and summary criminal history files. Before the development of third generation computers, these files were searched manually.

Presently, according to CIS data, the system stores more than 7 million sets of fingerprints; of these, more than 2 million are stored on computer. The name file (a manual file) contains more than 6 million names of arrested criminals, and the summary criminal history file (on computer) duplicates the "rap sheets" of approximately 500,000 persons.

Besides computerizing the identification files, CIS developed a program that can connect all three files automatically, thereby expanding their usefulness. Having only one piece of information—say, a name, or fingerprints—it is now possible to search all three files at one time. CIS is also responsible for a facsimile transmission network that connects local agencies to CIS and through which fingerprints, names, and other identification can be transmitted. The process of identifying criminals or arrested persons is illustrated in Figure 6.

Limitations in software programming technology have prevented auto-

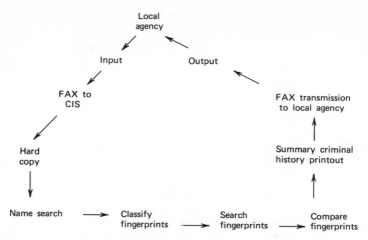

Figure 6. Steps in the CIS identification process.

mation of the classification of fingerprints. Fingerprint comparison involves checking latent fingerprints developed at the scene of a crime (partial sets of fingerprints) against both the fingerprint and summary criminal history files. Despite intensive efforts at CIS and in federal agencies, large-scale, automated latent fingerprint analysis is several years away, sanguine hopes and predictions to the contrary notwithstanding.[2]

In 1972, the latest year for which data are available, CIS reported that it had received one million sets of fingerprints, 1.5 million name search requests, and had transmitted approximately 600,000 summary criminal histories to local agencies, primarily police agencies and district attorney's offices.

Of the one million prints sets submitted to CIS, more than 45% resulted in identification of known former criminals and output of their respective summary criminal histories. The use of computerized files in fingerprint identification has reduced the in-house time for processing received fingerprints into transmitted summary criminal histories from six days to three hours.[3]

EXTENSION OF IDENTIFICATION TASKS

CIS received in 1967 a federal grant of $180,000 to develop an Automated License Plate Scanning Project (ALPS). In the ALPS project, television scanning devices to be located at crucial intersections around the

state and would automatically feed license plate numbers to a CIS computer. The computer would search its file of stolen cars and cars connected
with other crimes, reporting back to a Highway Patrol car at the intersec-
tion. After three independent engineering and cost-benefit studies rejected
the idea as uneconomical, CIS was able to produce a study favorable to the
idea by a fourth independent research firm. Referred to derisively by some
local criminal justice agencies as the "Blue Sky–Clean Highway Project,"
the ALPS program is still in the planning stages, awaiting larger state
funding.

A second research and development project is the Automatic Personal
Appearance Data System (APADS); like ALPS, it is funded largely by
federal Law Enforcement Assistance Agency (LEAA) monies ($77,000).
Under the APADS project, studies are being conducted into systems of
classifying personal appearance data (hairline shape; face, lip, mouth
shapes, etc.) A third R & D project at CIS is the Fraudulent Check Module
being developed in connection with APADS. Personal appearance and
fraudulent check "trademarks" of writing style are being studied to determine whether a computer-based classification system can be developed.
Both APADS and FCM suffered from cutbacks in state funds as of 1972.

The largest CIS secondary identification project is the SEARCH program (System for Electronic Analysis and Retrieval of Criminal Histories),
which is funded entirely by LEAA with a budget of $300,000 to cover
Eastern State's participation. SEARCH is an attempt to create CIS-type
systems in six states (the others are California, Michigan, Pennsylvania,
Ohio, and Illinois) and to provide for the interstate transfer of criminal
histories through computer-to-computer interfaces.

Project SEARCH is the darling of state officials and politicians who are
seeking to maintain state control over criminal justice information, and it
is bitterly opposed by the FBI, which is developing its own system—
NCIC.[4]

The ancillary identification projects just described are largely in the research and development phases and will not be operational for perhaps
another five to ten years. They are an important part of the CIS story, however, for they are the basis of much criticism by local agencies. The local
criminal justice agencies are generally dissatisfied with the performance of
CIS's principal mission: summary criminal history and fingerprint identification. They charge CIS with major failures in delivery schedules and
quality of services, also citing a tendency to ignore the needs of local
agencies for computer services while promoting futuristic and apparently
irrelevant programs within the CIS system. Police agencies are less prone
to criticism of CIS (although dissatisfaction exists there too) than the

other criminal justice agencies, such as the courts and corrections departments, which feel largely ignored by CIS.

ORGANIZED CRIME INTELLIGENCE MODULE

The second public mission of CIS is the collection and centralization of intelligence on known and suspected members of organized crime syndicates in Eastern State. The automation of organized crime intelligence is the most technologically difficult and the most politically sensitive program in CIS's repertoire.

Intelligence on organized crime is traditionally collected and stored by local police and district attorney's offices. There are no standard information formats, and each police department or DA decides what kind of information is useful for its purposes. Intelligence files are thus more idiosyncratic than fingerprint, name, or summary criminal history files, and they are a good deal more difficult to standardize and automate. Many agencies do not even keep organized crime intelligence files, largely because of the lack of any commonly accepted definition of "organized crime."[5]

Second, intelligence on "organized criminals" raises a number of thorny political questions. Such intelligence involves the collection of hearsay and personal observation information on persons who are only suspected to be potential perpetrators of a crime. Frequently the pursuit of this kind of information leads to the harassment of individuals who have not committed any known crime. Organized crime intelligence thus raises certain civil liberty questions: on what grounds can police agencies invade the privacy of a citizen, what limits and criteria ought police agencies observe in collecting intelligence, and who shall review the police powers in this field?

The courts have not answered these questions definitively, although police agencies have been allowed to invade the privacy of certain individuals (using wire taps and other special intelligence measures) when they can convince a judge that the person(s) in question may commit a crime that would not be publicly observable.

More immediate political problems are raised by the Organized Crime Module (discussed below), problems that become apparent when one realizes the functions of criminal intelligence for local agencies. Not only does intelligence on members of a community have value in prosecuting criminals, it can be used as "chips" in the local political game.[6] Intelligence has political implications insofar as it can indicate where the "skeletons" are hid and how they may be revealed or buried deeper. Most organized crime intelligence is a matter of public record (e.g., a certain city commissioner is seen having lunch with a suspected member of an organized crime syndicate). Given the political sensitivity of such intelligence, however, and the potential for its abuse, local agencies are not enthusiastic about the prospect of turning over their intelligence files to a state agency. They are even less happy about "standardizing" and rationalizing this intelligence.

For example, suppose a police agency reports that no known crime syndicate personnel are operating within its jurisdiction, according to its intelligence reports. If state investigators subsequently arrive at the opposite conclusion, it will appear to some that the local police are covering for the criminals. This circumstantial evidence would not have been brought to light if there were no state intelligence agency, and if, as in the past, local agencies were not asked to submit their intelligence reports to a state agency, such as CIS.

In 1970 the Organized Crime Module was in a pilot stage, with intensive information being collected on 200 "known" members of organized crime. The pilot project has produced a series of intelligence summaries for twelve participating agencies and an Organized Crime Registry accessible to all CIS members. The Registry is a computerized name, history, and personal descriptor file on the 200 individuals. A "theory of penetration" is now being developed to explain how organized crime works its way into legitimate enterprises, and a model data collection plan is on the drawing board.

Progress on the Organized Crime Module has been very slow, since the nature of organized crime is typically associated with production and distribution of illicit goods or services (prostitution, gambling, drugs, loans, etc.). Moreover, it is politically sensitive, and its funding cannot be traced through the usual channels. Thus a full-scale version of the pilot program is still years away. Ironically, the need to service the Organized Crime Module was used as one of the original justifications for establishing CIS. In 1974 the organized crime module was dropped, due to opposition from local police agencies.

TECHNOLOGY AND POLITICAL REFORM

Aside from its public goal of coordinating information and intelligence flows among criminal justice agencies, CIS entails a change in the political relationships between the state executive branch (the governor, and his Division of the Budget, especially) and criminal justice agencies. There is very little quarrel among participants in CIS about the need for greater information exchange between criminal justice agencies, yet there is intense disagreement about what information is to be collected by the new state agency, who will have access to it, and the purposes for which it will be used. The real issue raised by the creation of CIS is political: to what extent will local criminal justice agencies be subject to the control and guidance of the state executive branch.

The initiators of CIS, members of the governor's staff, envisage it as the beginnings of a state Department of Justice with broad policy and budgetary authority over local police, district attorneys, courts, and correctional institutions. Political opposition by local agencies and their constituencies discouraged the state executive branch from making a direct attempt to establish a Department of Justice; instead, a state information agency (CIS) was created to centralize budgetary and other administrative information. Later, this information can be used as a basis for criticizing and ultimately reorganizing local criminal justice agencies under a Department of Justice.

Former Executive branch personnel believe that "home rule" sentiments of local politicians and the claims of local agency managers for autonomy from state "political interference" simply disguised the desire to maintain local patronage systems, corruption, and inefficiency. It is argued that since the state in the mid-nineteenth century abdicated its responsibility and authority over local agencies to control corrupt city politicians, local agencies have virtually monopolized the administration of criminal justice, accountable to no one except local politicians.[7] However, all local governments in Eastern State operate at the convenience of the state (there being no "home rule" cities); thus the state can legally recover control over these agencies.

Computer technology in this instance serves a group of reformers in state government and provides a base from which the reform movement can expand. The technology gives the state executive an opportunity to systematically collect, process, and analyze information about the performance of local agencies which heretofore would have been a technologically difficult, expensive task.

Since the technology is itself identified in the public mind with "efficiency" and "rationality," the technology serves to conceal the political changes envisaged. CIS—in the tradition of "good government" reforms—presents itself in public documents and announcements as an administrative tool to assist local agencies and to increase their efficiency and effectiveness.

To minimize initial opposition, CIS began operation with one group of agencies—the police—and established a seemingly innocuous computerized file on criminal offenders and members of organized crime syndicates.

From this police base it is hoped that CIS will be able to expand to collect information on the clients of the other criminal justice agencies—district attorneys' offices, courts, and probation, corrections, and parole departments. Progressively CIS will add budgetary information about local agencies, and finally information on the activities of personnel employed in these agencies (e.g., number and type of arrests by a narcotics squad; decisions of individual judges, especially with regard to organized crime figures; the productivity of a given group of judges, the average delay before trial in different cities, and suicide rates in various prison systems). As one experienced student of criminal justice in the state commented:

> There are thousands of embarrassing pieces of information about these agencies which no one—not the cities, state, or federal government—has ever collected. And under the cover of "home rule," "self-policing by professionals," or separation of judicial and executive branches, the grossest kinds of incompetence, corruption, and medieval inefficiency parade as virtues. Before CIS no one took responsibility for these agencies—each was left to do what it would. But who is responsible for an incompetent or drunken judge, a doddering sheriff, a corrupt narcotics squad, when the local agencies will not, or cannot, exercise control over their own members?

As envisaged by its proponents, the data base of CIS will be used by the Division of the Budget to monitor and investigate the operation of local agencies. According to the former member of the governor's staff just quoted:

> One day the Division of the Budget will release a report which might say, for instance, that the Metropolis City judicial district productivity is far out of line with others in the state; and "in the interest of efficiency" and judicial competence the state will be obliged to create and enforce certain standards of appointment, conduct, and results. Another report might find that for reasons of efficiency the state should take over city prison systems, or that organized crime investigations should be conducted by a special state agency because it is inefficient to have so many separate district attorneys pursuing the same people, et cetera. That is when it will happen: a state Department of Justice will be the logical repository for these new state responsibilities. CIS is obviously just the start of a long battle.

CIS is far from attaining the lofty dreams of its sponsors. Local agencies were quick to recognize the stakes involved in the creation of a state criminal justice information system. The awareness of local agencies and their political strength have impeded the development of CIS, as we document later.

One way for "good government" reform efforts of mayors, governors, and even presidents, to overcome initial opposition to their programs is through the cooptation of important interests into a meaningful policy relationship with the reform program.[8] Professional administrators within agencies have been a frequent and useful ally of state and local "reform" politicians.[9] In the process of organizing CIS, however, local agency professionals were not successfully included in the design or implementation of the reform. As a consequence, the local agency personnel joined with local political leaders in opposition to CIS, making for a future that is at best unstable.

CORPORATE PLANNING IN ORZANIZED CRIME: THE ORIGINS OF CIS

On a blustery autumn day in November 1957, a famous gambler was playing host to more than one hundred friends at his country mansion in Eastern State. This friendly conference was unusual because all those present were suspected "crime syndicate" leaders from the major cities of the United States and Canada and the Caribbean.

The meeting apparently caught federal and state intelligence agencies completely by surprise. In fact, many of the syndicate leaders were being followed individually by separate intelligence agencies from the Bureau of Narcotics and Dangerous Drugs to the Secret Service, and it was not until agents began literally running into one another that the size and importance of the syndicate meeting was recognized.

Dubbed the "Mountain Meeting," the conference touched off a series of investigations into the criminal backgrounds and histories of participants. Federal, state, and local law enforcement agencies began competing over the spoils almost immediately. On leaving the meeting, the syndicate leaders were arrested, fingerprinted, and released on bail. Competition between the various levels of law enforcement became so severe that it is still not known precisely how many attended the meeting, who they were, or what they were doing. According to a state official formerly connected with the investigation of the meeting, the agencies collecting such information continue to refuse to share it with others.

In 1958, following the Mountain Meeting, a state Commission of Investigation was formed to gather evidence about participants in the meeting and to provide the state Attorney General with information about major personages in attendance. After a two-year effort involving more than ten lawyers working full time, all the criminal information on individuals being investigated had not been gathered from state and local files. Federal files were largely unavailable, and local police and district attorneys' files were either difficult to obtain or were composed of irrelevant newspaper clippings and loose notes. A rather insignificant up-state syndicate leader was the subject of more than 200 separate official police files in a surrounding area of 300 miles from the Mountain meeting.

Only twenty prosecutions resulted from the Mountain Meeting, and all were dismissed on appeal. Syndicate chiefs could be arrested temporarily for suspicion of conspiring to commit crimes, but the charges had to be dropped for lack of evidence. A few syndicate leaders were wanted in various states and localities, but information about the charges was not available for up to three years after the Mountain Meeting. At best, the meeting simply provided more bulk for federal, state, and local intelligence files. Nevertheless the Mountain Meeting had the positive effect of illustrating publicly the dismal condition of law enforcement's store of criminal information. Subsequently, this situation was used to justify the political reorganization necessary to centralize criminal justice information in the state.

IN THE BEGINNING . . .

The "official" history of CIS reads like an allegory: evil is present and perceived; good men are aroused to find a way to slay the wrongdoer; a solution is indeed found, and, alas, the pursuit of evil is thrust aside while the good men return to their normal lives. Thus in 1961 the state's Republican governor appointed "John Williams," the former chief of the commission that investigated the Mountain Meeting as an Assistant Council for Law Enforcement. Responsible to the governor, Williams was charged with searching "for possible remedies to the problems presented by the Mountain investigation, as well as the deluge of papers and files inundating operating agencies concerned with the administration of criminal justice." Out of his inquiries into the application of electronic data processing techniques to criminal justice came CIS—the state Criminal Identification System project.

In early 1963, the governor, in concurrence with the state legislature, authorized the formation of a "broadly based" Advisory Committee and commissioned a feasibility study to determine the costs and benefits of CIS. Two years later the legislature gave the governor authority to establish CIS.

GATEKEEPERS, HURDLES, BATTLES, AND SCARS: THE POLITICAL PROCESS

Official histories, while almost never wrong, are almost always inaccurate, besides being boring and dull. Behind the bare facts of the official history of CIS lie a panorama of events and persons that not only illuminate the policy formation process in a large state but also reveal the specific compromises and decisions that shaped the development of a statewide criminal justice information system.

The Present as History

Eastern State's political and administrative map has been called a Populist utopia by some political commentators, and an administrator's nightmare by others. Both these metaphors refer to the same phenomenon: as a result of early nineteenth-century ideologies, movements, and reforms, the majority of administrative offices in state and local government became elective positions. In successive state constitutional conventions of 1821, 1826, and 1846, the governor was stripped of appointive powers over state civil servants, town and city mayors, the judiciary, and law enforcement officers. The extension of suffrage to landless farm workers and mill-town laborers was supported by a popular view that any citizen "was qualified to decide any matter of public importance" and driven home with the slogan "Keep the Power with the People"—coined, ironically, by the son of a wealthy family.[10]

In the Federalist heyday before 1821, when politics was a caucus of landed, country aristocrats and government—both civilian and military— was a playground for their wealthy and educated sons, the governor made 15,000 appointments through his Council of Appointment. The Populist reforms radically changed the nature of politics from a caucus of notables to a congeries of political machines based on the local organization of votes and directed by the local boss.

Whatever the consequences of these nineteenth-century reforms for the responsiveness of government to "the people," the democratizing of the state's political institutions did not make directly for financial purity or efficiency, or administrative ability. The decline of central political power signaled the rise of corrupt local bosses. The absence of central administrative authority to enforce standards of competence and integrity on state and local agencies led to a decline in the competence and quality of civil servants. Under the umbrella of democracy, gross disparities among local communities in the quality of justice, law enforcement, education, welfare, and transportation paraded as virtues.

Lacking either political or administrative integrative mechanisms, the state political system in the late 1800s contained a plethora of power centers and interest groups, each with sufficient power to veto programs not in its interest. The traditional divisions along rural–urban and social class lines multiplied into a hundred different cleavages: sheriffs versus local police, Big City versus Little City, justices of the peace versus district judges, district attorneys versus the state Attorney General, and so forth. Each center of power was strong enough to maintain the status quo, but none had the power to engineer needed changes in government structure. The road to becoming and remaining a successful governor lay in not offending key local interest groups (represented by municipal machines that controlled the vote). The condition of any action in the present was the full recognition and acceptance of the past.

Structure and Strategy: The Process of Change

Since the reforms of the early and middle nineteenth century, the structure of Eastern State government has not been conducive to internally self-initiated change. However, beginning with the demise of the political bosses in the late 1800s and extending through the present period, many of the more corrupt political organizations have fallen victim to their own venality. When large-scale corruption rose to public attention early in the twentieth century, different reform groups frequently were able to secure public support for plans to reorganize state government.

Thus between 1918 and 1935 Eastern State government experienced rapid centralization of administrative authority and political power. Scandals in the administration of state funds led to the return of gubernatorial appointment powers and central control over the state budget. Scandals in local welfare, education, and highway agencies led to state grant-in-aid programs and the growth of the state departments of Welfare, Education, and Highways.

Criminal justice agencies were largely immune to this second period of reorganization until the election in 1958 of yet another reform governor. In communities across the state the entire leadership of criminal justice agencies—sheriffs, district attorneys, judges, probation officers, and county correctional officers—were elected or appointed by local political machines. In other words, all the elements of law enforcement accessible to the citizen were accountable to no one but local political interests. A former member of the governor's staff noted:

> At that time [before 1958] in this state and in every other state, policemen could come in off the street, be sworn in, get a gun and an hour later be out with the uniform with full powers. No training whatsoever was required. Prosecutors had long ago, of course, been part of the state structure, but were now completely local, and locally elected as were the sheriffs.

Two important changes have occurred in this traditional pattern: the Police Training Council Act of 1959, and a similar act supporting local district attorneys. Let us consider how each bill works to bring about change. Through the police training act, the state approves and funds applications from local agencies for setting up training programs. Individual officers receive some remuneration for their participation. The state agency establishes standards and levels of competence.

Gradually, local agencies and personnel become dependent on state monies—or at least desirous of their continuance. Thus they are under pressure to maintain training programs and to increase their standards as the state demands over a period of time.

One informant (Williams), closely involved with the passage of the Police Training Act, describes the process:

> Because of the changing population [and] changing crime problems, increased mobility of the population—whether through major highways or trains or planes—led to a changing need and yet, government structure wasn't changed. . . . At the December 1958 policy meeting of the governor's staff I and others pushed for the first state law enforcement policy approach. His recommendation to the legislature later in 1959 to establish state standards for police officers was a great accomplishment in itself. It's just one of the holy of all holies [sic], you don't even talk about local police. Ultimately it was passed, the Police Training Council Act, . . . It was the first in the nation's history, and we slowly built up the number of required hours in the course and training structure, setting new and higher standards year by year, educating the police community like mad, constantly.

> I was sent from the Executive Chamber [of the governor] to
> attend every convention they had anywhere in the state. . . .
> I knew every major police chief and sheriff in this state on
> a first-name basis by the time I was done lobbying for the
> bill.

> Once, of course, you get state money involved, ultimately
> you'll be able to get some kind of state control, then you'll
> be able to get "standard setting," then you'll be able to get
> other things. But the first step is to get the financial hooks
> into them.

> . . . not to take over local police departments. That would be
> politically impossible, I believe, within my lifetime, and per-
> haps not even desirable. But using the model of the state
> system of education where administrative control is left in
> local hands but state financing gives an absolute lever to state
> standard setting—thereby you provide a means of getting be-
> yond the little red school house, where a miscellaneous group
> of whomever in a particular community might be well moti-
> vated to run their own school, but who would do it in a
> disastrous fashion.

State-initiated efforts to increase accountability, professional standards, and
the quality of local criminal justice agencies in Eastern State have continued since the passage of the Police Training Act. The largest and most
controversial of these programs has been the CIS project, which is a product of the same group of men close to the governor.

BEYOND THE LITTLE RED SCHOOLHOUSE, OR
SYSTEMS ANALYSIS OF A NONSYSTEM

> Unitary Concept of Criminal Justice

> It is in the public interest that, to the greatest extent possible,
> government agencies concerned with the detection, apprehen-
> sion, prosecution, sentencing, confinement, and rehabilitation
> of criminal offenders share among themselves available infor-
> mation relating to such offenders.

> From *Crime '68: The CIS Response*

The CIS project was, and still is, one of the most ambitious attempts made
by Eastern State government to increase accountability, professionalization,

and quality of criminal justice agencies, if only because the system is ahead of its time both technologically and in its political ramifications.

Its primary task is to standardize the collection and reporting of the following information on criminal offenders: name, criminal history, and fingerprints, and to create an automated information network through which all this information can flow instantaneously from collection point to point of need. Second, it is intended to provide the executive branch with budgetary and management information about criminal justice agencies. There is no automatic way to "read" fingerprints by machine—this must still be done manually by methods developed at the turn of the century.

The techological impediments to full and rapid development of CIS are formidable and persistent. Some of the roadblocks, such as latent fingerprint analysis and the criminal history retrieval problems, are lessened by the infusion of federal monies through the LEAA. Others require that a good deal more time and money be spent in the area of crime technology. Meanwhile, the technological difficulties become grist for the political critics of CIS both within the state and federal government.

In a political sense, too, CIS is far ahead of its time; more important, the idea of CIS exceeds the authority and political resources of the CIS agency. Computer experts, systems analysts, and technological zealots of one kind or other, are all wont to speak of the need to modernize "the criminal justice system"—referring of course to the various agencies of government that administer programs having to do with that area.[11]

But it is the grossest reification to refer to the "criminal justice system" as if to imply a closely interwoven and coordinated subsystem of government composed of police, attorneys, courts and prisons. Nowhere in the United States today is there a "criminal justice system" in the strict sense. Indeed, the Constitution argues for strict separation of police, executive, legislative, and judicial powers.[12] Although this in itself would not prevent cooperation among agencies, historically, as pointed out with regard to Eastern State, virtually every agency involved with criminal justice was created and developed in a context of political and organizational autonomy. The CIS enabling act contains the following provisions.

SERVICE AGENCY ONLY

To establish, through electronic data processing, and related procedures, a central data facility . . . serving qualified agencies concerned with the administration of criminal justice . . .

VOLUNTARY PARTICIPATION

. . . so that they may, upon such terms and conditions as the director and the appropriate officials . . . shall agree, contribute information and have access to information contained in the central data facility.

HOW MUCH, HOW MANY, AND WHERE?

It is said that the mother of invention is necessity, and its father is frustration. Frustration results when reasonable men are asked to cope with an unreasonable situation. Surely it does not appear unreasonable to ask professional lawyers and investigators to collect relevant background information on a hundred well-known leaders of organized crime. But in the framework of the contemporary criminal justice apparatus of Eastern State, surrounding states, and even the federal government, such an end is unattainable. The former Chief Counsel of the Mountain Meeting Commission of Investigation describes his experience after two years of effort:

> At first we said there were 65, [participants in the Mountain Meeting] but there were well over 100, an unbelievable event as circumstances have established beyond doubt. . . . I found myself with the specific assignment of finding out as quickly as possible everything we could about the meeting and everybody who was there. This proved to be impossible and was one of the most frustrating things I ever did in my life, because the people who were there were really significant in organized crime.

> Insofar as Eastern State was concerned, it was as important as the Warren investigation of the Kennedy assassination. As a political event it was maybe more important, and we could not do what seemed obvious and elementary. Nobody could really believe things were as bad as they were. This took me into the files of a lot of police departments, district attorneys throughout the state, in other states, into the federal government files. I was just stunned.

> Inaccessibility of information, the fragmentation of the structure, of file systems—there simply was no index cards, file systems, no nothing.

As we have already noted, despite lack of substantive success in prosecuting participants of the organized crime meeting, the former Chief Counsel was appointed Special Assistant Counsel for Law Enforcement to the governor in 1961.

His first task was to collect some basic facts in the field of crime and criminal justice for use in the governor's policy address to the legislature in

1962. In the event, even the most general sort of information was unavailable. The former counsel comments on this Kafkaesque period:

> One of the governor's attributes as a person is that he runs around asking all kinds of questions about the basic functions of government . . . for the basic facts, that's all; and he has this way of forcing staff people to put them on charts. So whether it was a conscious thing or not, his habit of being half chart-crazy was teriffic.
>
> He asked for facts on crime, innocent questions, but no one could answer. The fact that they couldn't— that the simplest kind of information wasn't available in this area—was a great alarm builder.
>
> No one could tell how much it cost to run the criminal justice administration in the state, how many people were processed, how many people were employed and what their payroll was, what are the capital involvements each year, and all the budget making and policy facts were not there. More important, there was nobody who was even supposed to collect them.

Recourse to the research director of the state Department of Corrections, where by historical accident state criminal statistics were stored, proved to be of no avail. The Department of Corrections, despite steadfast lobbying for improvements by the research director, stored information only on offenders incarcerated in state prisons—half the total prison population of the state; this figure accounted for fewer than 20% of all criminal offenders in a single year.

Turning to the courts for basic information on cases, acquitals, convictions, and so forth, the Special Counsel found an even worse state of affairs. The state's judicial system is divided into eleven administrative divisions, and each division is responsible for administering the courts in its region. The Counsel learned that none of the divisions had kept any statistical records on caseloads. The Judicial Conference, created under pressure from the governor in 1960 and designed to coordinate court activities from the state level, had little formal power; nor did its members display much desire to renovate the court record-keeping system.

On his journey through the state criminal justice bureaucracy the Special Counsel fortuitously met others facing the same problems; but few had either solutions or the political power to effect change. An important exception to this rule was "Robert Dorn," a high official in the state Division of the Budget. He had broad authority within the executive branch to collect statistics on departmental budgets, as well as authority to investigate discrepancies. In addition, he was charged with introducing new technological developments into the state bureaucracy where appropriate (e.g., automatic copying equipment, business machines, and computers). With the Special Council, who had expertise in the criminal justice bureaucracy, he attempted to improve the state of criminal justice statistics.

MOVING THE LEVIATHAN: PUSH AND SHOVE

The first attempt of the two officials to improve criminal justice statistics involved convincing the Judicial Conference that it needed a small computer to handle its information problems. However, neither would-be reformer had the authority to do more than "urge" the Judicial Conference leaders, all lawyers, to improve their statistics. In the words of the Special Council:

> This was sensitive as hell because the Judicial Conference is the third party of government. You know the old traditional legislative, executive, judicial stuff? Here we were the executive trying to get the judicial to be more efficient in a way that would coincide with executive purposes but which would also burn a lot of rear-ends in the judiciary.

> We went through hell, went through all kinds of studies and wonderful reports. Brains were racked and bodies were broken over it, finally we wound up thinking we ought to, had to, get a computer in the Judicial Conference. We had to get the courts to put more clerical manpower in reporting dispositions, then force definitions of what data was, et cetera. And so, all the really ultimate questions in the mechanical side of CIS I went through with [the budget official] back in the 61–62–63 period in this Judicial Conference Project.

The Judicial Conference never made substantial use of the computers to automate its information functions, for the Conference itself had no authority to compel the Judicial Divisions to submit standard reports.

Two very important studies by Dorn and Williams did emerge from this early trial-and-error period. The first study was prepared for the governor's Chief Counsel and was essentially a road map to the state's criminal justice apparatus. This was the first such report in the state's history, and the most difficult task was reportedly finding and listing the names of all the agencies that had something to do with criminal justice in the state. As it turned out, there were more than 3600 such agencies.

The second study, completed in late 1962, was more directly related to finding a solution to the amazing lack of criminal justice information. Using Rockland, a middle-size industrial town in the state, as a base for intensive study, Williams and Dorn tracked twenty-five criminal offenders through the entire criminal justice apparatus:

> We checked these guys from arrest right through to prison and parole. And there was almost total duplication of records. In fact, if you took the label off the top, say the Parole Identification sheet, it would have been a Police Identification sheet, and that was the clincher so far as I was concerned.
>
> It should have been obvious all along that all of these agencies were using the same information. It's like most really good ideas—simple. The police need to know who the guy is and what he did, basically, and so did every other agency in the fragmented system of criminal justice, to perform their separate functions even though [the system is] administered autonomously. CIS, as a concrete idea, really emerged from that study.

Thus the concept of a centralized state repository for the basic information about criminal offenders emerges from conversations and from studies by a small staff group around the governor's office. The real work of making it a political reality remains.

THE GOVERNOR'S GATEKEEPERS

Like most political executives, governors surround themselves with a small group of trusted political and governmental advisors. These men carry out the governor's personal instructions and present him with useful ideas, insights, and information when a problem arises. Much of what a governor does while in office depends on the actions and competence of his personal staff. New ideas are rarely presented to the governor directly, for study and evaluation would waste much of his valuable time. Instead, new ideas and information must filter upward through his staff, and during this process they may be squelched, distorted, or simply forgotten about, depending on the sentiments of the staff members.

Fortunately, the concept of CIS appealed to the govenor's Chief Counsel and was presented in cabinet meetings during 1962. The political problems, some of them formidable, were identified, and strategies designed to deal with them were devised. As a test balloon, the CIS idea was mentioned in the governor's 1963 legislative address; it received mild applause but no real notice. It was still just an idea, and the opposition did not materialize until serious efforts were made to establish a central criminal justice information system.

ALL THE KING'S MEN AND THE SHERIFF'S POSSE: THE STUDY PERIOD

In spring of 1963, Williams, encouraged by the governor, organized an "Advisory Committee" as a "responsible way of providing a cutoff opportunity to kill it [CIS] if [such action] was thought to be the proper thing." Two points deserve emphasis in this stage of the development of CIS.

First, the transition from idea to reality is always difficult, especially in a political bureaucratic structure where personal careers and agency budgets may be jeopardized by innovations. As a rule, change initiated by insiders—by internal elite groups—is generally not structure changing but only "bit changing." Indeed, as we said in Chapter 3, the condition of an innovation being acceptable to internal elites is often the maintaining of the status quo.

Second, up until early 1963, CIS was the brainchild of external elites— the governor's staff—most of whom had very little professional expertise and only a modicum of political influence within the criminal justice community.

The generic problem at this stage of an innovation is to internalize elite guidance—to find internal elites within the criminal justice community who would be sympathetic to the CIS proposal or who could be convinced not to veto it. In Williams's words:

> The selection of the particular individuals on that Advisory Committee was crucial because [the project] would have turned off right there, and that's where the background that I had played its greatest role—in choosing the right people, knowing enough about the sheriffs to pick the right sheriff. . . . But we had to know ahead of time who would be best or accepted and who wouldn't be accepted.

Sheriffs, police chiefs from major cities, personnel from the State Police, district attorneys, judges, parole officers, and others were invited through their various associations to join the Advisory Committee. By "smoking out" the opposition in the Advisory Committee, the governor's staff hoped to be able to make sufficient compromises to quell any uprisings and yet retain the essential elements of the original CIS concept.

SHERIFFS, STATE POLICE, AND CITY POLICE

The most difficult opposition faced by CIS in the study period came from the police agencies. The State Police were absolutely convinced that criminal information was their function, and if anyone had a computer, it should be their agency. The sheriffs, in turn, were firmly opposed to the State Police having anything to do with the computer or CIS. The hostility between the sheriffs and the state police dates back more than half a century. The inability of a county sheriff's office to solve the murder of two women in 1917 indirectly led to the formation of the State Police as a law enforcement agency that could cope with the new mobility that criminals acquired, thanks to the automobile.

Since that earlier period, the sheriffs and the State Police, whose jurisdictions overlap, have been fighting over everything from newspaper credits to budgetary appropriations. The sheriffs, who are often heads of their county party organizations, have one of the strongest lobbies in the state capital and have blocked moves to expand the State Police for more than 30 years.

The opposition of the State Police to CIS was not particularly serious because this agency operated in relative political isolation. But the opposition of the sheriffs, given the strength of their legislative lobby, was indeed critical. Thus in the summer of 1963 a strange agreement had to be worked out to accommodate the sheriffs. First, it was agreed that CIS would not be associated with any functional, line agency in the criminal justice bureaucracy. That is CIS would not be connected to the State Police specifically and would be entirely independent. This may have pleased civil libertarians who shudder at the thought of police-controlled criminal information systems; in fact, however, the arrangement was a political necessity. In any event, since participation in CIS was to be on a voluntary basis, small-county sheriffs would not be required to join if they did not feel that CIS was necessary to their counties.

METROPOLIS CITY'S FINEST: THE MEN IN BLUE

Metropolis City, often called a state within a state, is the home of almost half of Eastern State's population. Traditionally, the city has been Democratic. Its demographic strength is not reflected in its political strength in state politics because of rural overrepresentation. Nevertheless, the city is generally capable of killing state legislation that might affect its historic independence from the state.

The city government has consistently fought attempts by the state to exert control over its bureaucracy. The city has its own police, prisons, courts, and probation and parole agencies, for instance. The Police Training Council Act mentioned earlier was passed by the legislature only because Metropolis City was exempted from the program. The police of the city see themselves as a professional organization, independent of and superior to other police agencies. The other agencies of criminal justice have developed similar attitudes with respect to state interference.[13]

Since the city would be the major contributor to and user of the proposed CIS system simply because of the size of its criminal population, it was essential to obtain support for CIS from the city, especially its police department. Efforts to interest the Democratic mayor in CIS did not meet with success. The mayor's office was neutral, and the mayor's staff were skeptical about the usefulness of CIS to the city. At the time, the mayor and the governor were at loggerheads over state aid to the city; in such an atmosphere, any project sponsored by the governor was destined to receive a cold shoulder from the mayor's office.

The police department was not enthusiastic about CIS largely for parochial reasons. Williams relates his experience:

> We were having great difficulties bringing along this extraordinarily conservative and complicated, difficult bureaucracy [the Metropolis City Police Department]. There was a lot of internal opposition within the professionals in the police department most concerned with the CIS area—namely, the Bureau of Identification of the city police department—the records people, and so on—for what I thought were the worst kinds of reasons: parochial, "this will affect my job," or the detectives who were sort of blockheads who thought that any change was wrong, they were just anti-change.

A simple solution was arrived at: CIS needed a director, and by hiring a well-known and respected member of the city's police department, the whole department might be brought along.

Thus in 1963 the director of the proposed CIS agency was chosen from the city's police: George Monti. Monti was a veteran police officer, having worked his way up the ranks in the best Metropolis City fashion. In addition, he was director of the Planning and Development Division of the city police, was especially aware of the need for innovations in criminal justice, and was favorably disposed to the idea of an automated state information system. More important, after twenty years on the force, Monti could pick up the phone and "get things done or turn off a low level revolt," according to a CIS staffer. Thus the city police department was not a major force against CIS, even though it was not a major force for it.

The appointment of Monti as Director of CIS changed the city police department's stance from active opposition to quiet sniping from the sidelines, especially in legislative circles. Despite agreements from numerous police commissioners to close out the city's Bureau of Criminal Identification, to this day the department maintains its own BCI and separate intelligence files.

THE WALLS ARE LISTENING: FEDERAL OPPOSITION

Somewhat surprisingly, relations between local governments, local police agencies, and the FBI are far from cordial. Through its National Police Academy, the FBI has attempted to become the sole agency for training police and to foreclose individual state efforts to establish training centers and to pass standard-setting legislation. According to a Metropolis City Police Academy official, the FBI has opposed the city's police academy, as well as state training centers for police, on the grounds that police training should be a national effort conducted by the FBI.

When the FBI is called in, or when it imposes itself, "to solve" nonfederal crimes, its agents frequently embarrass the local police, and they seek to control the public relations aspects of the case. They tend to restrict the access of local police to their files, grabbing the significant headlines, and receiving the credit for solving the crime.

The FBI counteracts much of the lower-level hostility to itself through a well-orchestrated public relations and political lobbying effort. FBI agents lecture frequently to police departments around the country on the latest crime fighting techniques; they also permit access to FBI laboratories in unusual crimes and train a very small proportion of local police officers. (My Metropolis City Police Academy source said that 2 out of 40,000 police officers in Eastern State receive FBI training each year.) In addition, the FBI tries to have former agents appointed to important and crucial positions within local police and other agencies. In some regions of the country, notably southern California and the Deep South states, many state and local police leaders were once with the FBI.[14]

Thus by maintaining a high public profile and by penetrating local governments, the FBI is able to significantly influence (some would say control) new developments in the criminal justice area. When Eastern State, for instance, passed its police training legislation, the FBI reportedly "went up like a roman candle." One informant reports the following:

> The FBI is a peculiar amalgam of not giving local government people what they really want, like operational assistance— not control—and information sharing. So he [Hoover] doesn't give them what they've got to have operationally, but gives them services with great public fanfare, and it's a marvelous sort of public relations gap he's got most of the local guys caught in.

The FBI succeeded in placing one or two men on the Advisory Board of the Police Training Academy of Eastern State. From this vantage they hoped to control the direction of the training academy and its course material. However, the state representatives would not tolerate FBI interference, and the agents were withdrawn. According to the governor's staff member just quoted:

> He [the FBI agent] was voting no when the others were all voting yes. They won't play any real role in anything they can't control, and by control, I mean really control. There can be six guys in the room, all from different agencies. One of them is an FBI man. The FBI sees that meeting as one that the FBI man should control. He may not sit at the head of the table, but everything happens that he wants, and nothing happens that he doesn't want. . . . It got to the point later on, where I know that Hoover sent hand-delivered letters to the governor blasting Mr. . . . . That's heat!

FBI reaction to the CIS proposal can only be described as visceral. Besides informing the governor that the Bureau considered information sharing among criminal justice agencies to be its responsibility, the FBI opposed CIS from within the state—principally through its contacts with former agents in the state and city police organizations. Failing to squash the CIS concept in the early stages, the FBI hoped to make it at least redundant by building the National Crime Information Center (NCIC) beginning in 1965. One informant close to CIS explained:

> He [FBI Director J. Edgar Hoover] and his local agent saw CIS as upsetting this delicate balance. Information sharing really threatened them. The very concept of information sharing was a deep threat to the entire way the FBI now

operates. You might say the FBI operates nationally on the premise that local agencies will not share information.

They don't even share information with the federal government. He doesn't give the federal Bureau of Narcotics information, or not until recently.

The proposed NCIC was originally conceived as a gargantuan network of city-based FBI agents and local police feeding information into three computer centers located in the western, midwestern, and northeastern United States. These computers would store all the basic criminal offender information: summary criminal histories, fingerprints, stolen car and personal property data, and so on. The need for state criminal justice information systems would be obviated.

THE STRONG ARM OF THE LAW

Sensing that an operational NCIC would kill any chance for developing state systems, especially CIS, those close to CIS in Eastern State decided to fight fire with fire. In 1965, after presenting a number of civil libertarian and other objections to NCIC before a group of liberal Republican congressmen, supporters of CIS prepared a report, signed by the congressmen, which was critical of NCIC and was designed to slow it down or kill it.

On the morning of publication, according to one of the originators of the report, FBI agents "forced their way" into the congressmen's offices and personally reprimanded them for opposing the FBI.

Although sufficiently intimidated not to publish the critical report, the congressmen were ultimately successful in reducing the budget appropriations for NCIC to a small fraction of the amount originally proposed.

The FBI has subsequently ignored the development of CIS and has worked on establishing its crime information center in Washington as a "backup" system to state-operated information systems.

BARNSTORMING THE BOONDOCKS: LEGISLATIVE PROCESS

After making the essential compromises with the sheriffs and other interest groups, and fighting off federal opposition, a permanent CIS Advisory Board was established in 1963. Its members were representatives from all the major branches of criminal justice—police, DA's, courts, parole, corrections, and probation. Along with providing a forum for interest groups affected by CIS, the Advisory Board prepared the ground for an extensive lobbying effort in local constituencies.

Williams and Monti, the proposed director of CIS, contacted virtually all the criminal justice administrators in the state, either personally or through association meetings, during the summer of 1963. They recall:

> The average legislator does not know much about CIS or other criminal justice reforms unless he's been in the criminal justice area—been a DA or a sheriff. So when a technical type of development like CIS comes along, their first reaction is to pick up the phone and to call in their constituency—three, six, people within the limited constituency of this special legislation—and say to them dead out, "What do you think? Are you for this Charlie?" They rarely inquire beyond that. If the answer is no, they may go along or may not. It depends.

> So part of the reason we have built this from the very beginning with the constituencies was so that when the phone call was made, the answer would be the right one, from the local area.

The CIS legislation was almost unanimously passed in early 1965, creating a voluntary criminal justice information system to provide computerized data on criminal offenders to all participating agencies. CIS undertook its initial development work with a $2.2-million budget. According to its own plan, the system would be operational in some areas by 1967 and fully operational by 1971. Neither deadline was met, and despite a nearly quadrupled budget by 1970 ($7.8 million) CIS has not solved persisting conceptual, political, and technological problems. The origins and the nature of these development problems are discussed below.

CIS: A TABULAR REPRESENTATION

The CIS information system is the most complex information system in our study in the sense that it attempts to combine in one computer network agencies that perform multiple functions within diverse autonomous political jurisdictions. A clearer picture of its structure is given by Table 8. The difficulty of coordinating information flows among the agencies charted is due partly to their shear number—3600. In addition, many of the agencies are responsible to different political constituencies and jurisdictions. These characteristics distinguish CIS from Western County's SSIS and PRIS systems, which involve only a few agencies, comparatively, and with far less diversity among agencies. CIS differs from our other systems in a number of other respects related to the size and diversity of the participant units.

Table 8   Structural Components of CIS

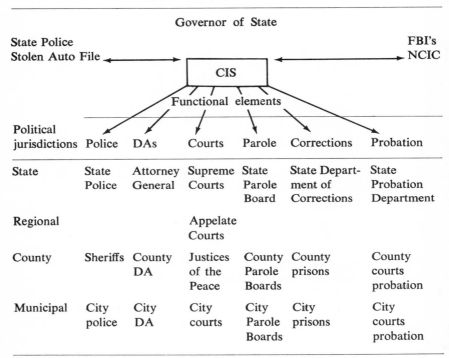

Political jurisdictions	Police	DAs	Courts	Parole	Corrections	Probation
State	State Police	Attorney General	Supreme Courts	State Parole Board	State Department of Corrections	State Probation Department
Regional			Appelate Courts			
County	Sheriffs	County DA	Justices of the Peace	County Parole Boards	County prisons	County courts probation
Municipal	City police	City DA	City courts	City Parole Boards	City prisons	City courts probation

CIS AGENCY CHARACTERISTICS

Low Aggregate Homogeneity

One of the social factors facilitating the flow of information among social units is the degree of homogeneity among the units. Three dimensions of homogeneity concern us here: (a) the extent to which units occupy similar positions in the division of labor, thus are homogeneous with regard to the tasks they perform; (b) the extent to which units occupy similar positions in a stratification hierarchy; and (c) the similarity of status recruitment procedures and role requirements among social units.

On all the foregoing dimensions of homogeneity, the CIS participant units are very low compared with member units of the other information systems we have investigated. On our first dimension of task homogeneity, we see that units perform similar tasks only within each functional area. For example, state, city, county, and regional police do perform similar tasks, and they do require similar kinds of information resources; however, across functional areas there is low task similarity—police, DAs and courts perform very different tasks. Looking at the entire group of criminal justice agencies, task similarity exists only within functions, not across them.

Second, the member units of CIS are highly stratified in terms of political power, budgetary resources, and occupational prestige. State agencies generally wield more political influence than county and municipal agencies, for example, and have more control over budgets. Within political jurisdictions, courts, DAs, and police, respectively, far outweigh corrections, parole, and probation agencies in prestige, influence, and resources.

The heterogeneity of tasks performed and the high degree of stratification among member units encourage very different recruitment and career patterns among the units. The man who spent eight years in the criminal justice bureaucracy as lawyer, investigator, Special Counsel, and researcher, describes the "typical" career pattern in criminal justice:

> I was becoming something I wasn't aware of myself—really sort of generalist on the criminal justice system. And there were very few of these—there should be many more.
>
> What we have instead in the criminal justice hierarchy are lawyers who get their start as prosecutors in a small jurisdiction. Eventually they work their way up the ladder and end up in some top policy level position in the criminal justice system—advisor to the governor, appelate judge, et cetera. This is the traditional route. Police don't come up that route, and you don't find people from Rehabilitation, Probation, or Parole. But these most influential men, by coming up as prosecutors, rarely know anything about police, corrections, probation, parole, even though they talk about knowing it. And their knowledge of the courts is that of prosecutor—they know next to nothing about the administration of a court, costs, or anything like that.

With the exception of lawyers, there is little interfunctional mobility among criminal justice agencies. Police are not encouraged to even change from one police department to another, since their pensions are not transferable.[15]

The social isolation of personnel in police, courts, corrections departments, and district attorney's agencies is also fostered by great differences
in educational experience and professional training. The dissimilarities in
education, training, and role requirements serve to effectively isolate individuals in the various criminal justice functional areas from one another.[16]

High Internal Integration

The level of internal integration within a social unit also affects the flow of
information among social units, having important consequences for any
attempt to increase the flow of information among social units.

The level of integration in a social unit can be calculated on three
dimensions: (a) the extent to which unit elites possess the resources to
control unit members and the means to utilize such resources effectively,
(b) the extent to which the social unit is the predominant focus of members' occupational and political identification, and (c) the extent to which
members interact predominantly with members of the same social unit.

Regarding these measures of integration, the individual participant agencies in CIS are very high, as is the case with most criminal justice agencies
throughout the country.[17]

The criminal justice agencies of the United States are reknowned for the
control they have preserved over internal operations and for their success
in preventing close public scrutiny. Desptie numerous large-scale efforts in
major cities, police citizen review boards have been repulsed or short-
lived.[18] An interesting comparison can be made between criminal justice
agencies in CIS and the SSIS agencies in Western County.

In Western County, it is commonplace to have at least one investigation
of the social service agencies per year, and in 1961–1962 there were three
simultaneous investigations of welfare by the Citizens' Welfare Commission, the county grand jury, and an area newspaper. Compare this with
Metropolis City, where despite a series of "suicides," "disturbances," and
riots in the jails during the early 1970s, the city's Department of Corrections successfully avoided an independent review of its internal operations.

Police agencies stand out as social units with extremely high levels of
internal integration. The pressures on young police officers to conform with
"departmental" values and norms stem from the lack of potential for
mobility to other police agencies, the in-bred character of elites who have
worked up the ranks, and the rookie's odd working hours and experiences,
which limit social contacts largely to other policemen.[19]

The strength of integration among police agencies is demonstrated in a recent work by William A. Westley. In his study of a small police department in a midwestern town with a population of 140,000, the author asked a small sample of policemen what they would say in court "if a punk had talked a policeman into accepting $500 and then brought charges for bribery." Four out of five said that they would perjure themselves in court to protect a brother officer. Westley comments:

> Secrecy among the police stands as a shield against the attacks of the outside world; against bad newspaper publicity, which would make the police lose respect; against public criticism, from which they feel they suffer too much; against the criminal . . . ; against the law, which they too frequently abrogate.[20]

Police are not very different from other agencies in criminal justice. The courts in Eastern State have effectively forestalled most legislative attempts to increase the efficiency of their operations. The courts supported a bill to create a Judicial Conference that would make a study and suggest ways to improve court efficiency. The Judicial Conference, as described earlier, is a powerless body of lawyers and judges with little inclination to lose any persuasive capacity they now possess. Thus, in the opinion of one Conference official, they do not act.

Given the high degree of internal integration within criminal justice units at all levels of government in Eastern State, secrecy, competition, and hostility characterize the relations among these agencies. Moreover, the attempt by CIS to increase and standardize the flow of information among the agencies is received with suspicion.

Low Aggregate, High Regional Interdependence

The need for communication among social units increases as a function of increasing interdependence.[21] "Interdependence" refers to the extent to which the activities of one social unit affect those of another. There are many different kinds of interdependence, and the structure of formal organizations functions to facilitate information flows among its interdependent units through a variety of mechanisms. The most important formal mechanisms are: (1) departmentalization—the grouping together of highly interdependent units, (2) standardization—the use of formal rules to guide and coordinate activities, and (3) hierarchy—the use of authority to guide and coordinate.[22]

The CIS information system is predicated on the assumption that a new formal organization is required at the state level to coordinate information flows among increasingly interdependent criminal justice agencies within the state. The system's development plan states:

> The problem of [information needs] is influenced by environmental factors. Local criminal justice agencies serve limited populations and geographic areas; but the population of the state is increasingly mobile. Although a large police agency may contain the criminal records of 1,000,000 individuals and a medium-sized agency may hold records of only 7,000, both records systems are victims of criminal mobility.
>
> To illustrate, in one large up-state city, almost 30% of the persons who have been arrested one or more times for fingerprintable offenses have arrest records in other jurisdictions within the state. The problem is even more acute for chronic offenders; in the same city approximately 55% of persons arrested two or more times have records in other in-state jurisdictions. For the state as a whole, the respective percentages for the "average" jurisdiction are 29% and 47%.

Since the "averages" show 29% of first and second offenders and 47% of second offenders and other recidivists, it would appear that a state criminal justice information system might be the most efficient form of achieving information exchanges among state criminal justice agencies. However, the statewide averages conceal the regional grouping of criminal arrests and the regional character of interdependence.

Fewer than 15% of the arrests made by Metropolis City police are of offenders with criminal records outside the metropolitan region, and police departments in other large cities report similar experiences. The regional character of criminal offender mobility suggests the need for greater coordination of information among police departments within a given region, not at the state level. An officer of the city police department's Bureau of Criminal Identification reports the following:

> We carry in our own BCI about 1.5 million criminal records, fingerprints, and names. For us CIS really isn't necessary and and we don't use it that much. Most of our requests for information result in the finding that the guy has a record in the same county or in surrounding cities.

Interdependence among criminal justice agencies is regionally high in a second respect. That is, interdependence is high at the local jurisdictional level, not between state, county, and city agencies. Thus in Metropolis City, persons arrested are tried in city courts, judged by the city Probation Department, sent to city prisons, and judged again by a city parole board: From the local agency view, therefore, the greatest need for coordination and information exchange is between local agencies in regional areas.

Precomputer Aggregate Characteristics

The precomputer characteristics of CIS participant agencies did not augur well for the success of the new system. Although the CIS computers can store large amounts of information, including criminal histories, fingerprints, and offender names, the low homogeneity of the participant units suggests that this information is not of the same utility for all agencies. In fact, as we see below, the principal complaint against CIS by the courts, parole, corrections, and probation agencies is that it does not store the information they need for day-to-day operations. This is partly due to the technological limitations of computers—none is large enough to store at the state level appropriate information for all the agencies.

Second, the high internal integration of CIS participants indicates that to be successful in coordinating and standardizing information flows among these agencies, CIS would need both political authority and legitimacy to change the prevailing patterns of information collection, exchange, and utilization. As a voluntary information system, CIS simply lacks authority to instigate the necessary changes. Moreover, it does not have the required legitimacy among participant units, largely because of its faulty consensus formation mechanisms, its elitist character, and its reliance on external elites. (These factors are discussed below.)

Third, the low aggregate but high regional interdependence of criminal justice agencies suggests the need for regional information systems, not state-level systems like CIS: regional systems could provide for a broader range of information storage and retrieval, and they would be far less expensive than state systems. In addition, their services would be more relevant to the operational needs of regional agencies.

THE EFFECTS OF MULTIPLE JURISDICTIONS

We have argued that individual criminal justice agencies differ from other government agencies with respect to their high levels of internal integration regardless of political jurisdiction or specific function. We said that any reform effort, such as CIS, must possess both the authority and the legitimacy to overcome the resistance to "outside interference"—in a sense, a certain amount of deintegration of these units would be necessary before they could be integrated into a broader, more encompassing control structure.

The structure of the political system itself has similar consequences for state-level reform efforts. That is, criminal justice agencies, like other agencies, are closely integrated into their respective political jurisdictions at the city, county, and state levels. The reasons for high levels of jurisdictional integration are obvious. First, of course, a criminal justice agency in Eastern State is subject to the direct authority and political power of jurisdictional elites—the mayor, the county sheriff–political leader, or the governor. Second, the predominant focus of political identification for agency members, beyond the agency, is toward the political unit within which the agency works.

The career patterns of civil servants support the formation of attitudes and values unique to each jurisdiction. Once recruited to work in a jurisdiction, civil servants rarely leave that jurisdiction. Thus not only is there comparatively low mobility between functional areas among American civil servants, there is also very low mobility between levels of government.[23]

The occupational structure of the civil service, besides supporting "localistic" attitudes and values, aids the formation of hostile attitudes toward agencies and civil servants at other levels of government. The civil servant class is highly stratified in terms of prestige, power, and money rewards. The ordering of ranks among the civil servants proceeds from the federal level, to state, county, and city levels. It is in the American cities generally that one finds the lowest paid, least trained, and least respected civil servants.[24]

The existence of multiple jurisdictions, and the resulting integration of criminal justice agencies and personnel into unique political units, presents another barrier to reform efforts initiated by external elites. In the case of CIS, given the strength of city and county jurisdictional interests, it was necessary to make concessions in the legislature—namely, creating a voluntary information system. By so doing, CIS lost any hope of changing the collection, exchange, and flow patterns of criminal offender information, to say nothing of obtaining the kinds of information desired by the state executive.[25] The ineffectiveness of CIS is ridiculed by county and city agencies with a "see, what did I tell you" or "those state people just don't know what goes on in our city" attitude. The net result of this self-fulfilling prophecy is a decrease in the legitimacy of CIS and an increase in the alienation of county and city agencies from CIS.

OVERCOMING INITIAL RESISTANCE: INTERNALIZATION

The initial characteristics of the CIS participant agencies, like the precomputer characteristics, held little promise for an effective reform. The lumping together of highly diverse agencies having a long history of independence from the state and hostility toward one another created at best an unstable base for reform. However, these initial impediments could have been mitigated through effective internalization of the reform.

As already mentioned, CIS was initiated by members of the governor's staff and others associated with the executive Division of the Budget in 1962–1963. It was closely associated from the very beginning with previous attempts by the governor to expand the power of state government over local criminal justice agencies—the Police Training Act (1959) and the Judicial Conference Act (1962). Thus the initiating elites were not members of the criminal justice community but political party workers and former lawyers, with neither the expertise nor the legitimacy to establish a state criminal justice information system.

CIS proceeded through two stages of internalization. The first stage featured an advisory committee composed of selected, "friendly," and well-known members of criminal justice agencies. This condition corresponds to our Notables model of internalization. For the external initiating elite, the advisory committee functioned to sensitize them to the location and nature of the opposition and served to generate support for the project. The initiating elites remained in full control of the project at this stage, although compromises over the implementation of the project were necessary (e.g., state police will not control the project; the system will be voluntary; and the CIS agency will have no operational law enforcement responsibilities).

In the first stage expertise was imported into the reform through the offices of a prestigious systems development firm in 1963. The hiring of outside technical assistance proved to be disastrous for both the technical development CIS and its political fortunes. The firm hired to perform the initial feasibility study was one of the major federal contractors for Strategic Air Command's NORAD Defense and the SAGE systems. However, the branch office assigned to assist CIS did not have the personnel to fulfill its job. Consequently, delays and errors in implementing the feasibility study were commonplace.

Moreover, the consulting firm had no experience with state government—its smaller budgets and its political in-fighting. A contemporary member of the CIS technical staff comments on the work of the systems developers:

> The only trouble with our first contractor was that they were incompetent technically and politically. CIS proceeded in

a number of stages. First, it is the wet dream of a couple of guys close to the governor. The Budget Division—they had some expertise in the field of computers—formalized the wet dream into an idea, a set of concepts. This is the Dreams, Mythology, but no-knowledge stage.

Second stage—the big federal-contract research firm comes in with the knowledge and the dreams, but their myths are unrealistic. They thought they were still working for the Air Force. The feasibility report was good, but you just don't talk to a powerful county sheriff like he is some sergeant in the Air Force. They didn't realize we had to work around a lot of political flak—and change design when resistance became too great

The third stage is now. We've fired the contractor and hired our own inside technicians, like me, to change dreams and knowledge into something that works.

In the writing of the feasibility report, and the first attempts to implement the system in 1965, the consultant firm touched a few raw nerves among sheriffs and local police departments. Sending young, inexperienced systems analysts into traditionally autonomous police agencies requires diplomacy and tact. One of the systems analysts employed by the firm recounts his introduction to the state's political mazes:

They [the CIS management group] had to spend more time projecting themselves than they did actually doing the work. They spent most of their time either justifying expenditures to the legislature or explaining the system to some local agency. We were just naïve about what was really going on—we're work-oriented people, not politicians.

Metropolis City didn't want to go along with CIS—they had received lousy service from the Bureau of Criminal Identification in Corrections and wanted nothing to do with another [sic] state system. We had to spend a lot of time in [one] county Sheriff's Department simply because he was the head of the state Sheriffs' Association. We couldn't go to some cities and really study local information needs—to see if they met CIS plan. Metropolis City was out, they didn't want anything to do with us. We couldn't go to Butte City, because of an impending state investigation of corruption there. You always have to learn something of the politics of an organization before you go in, but it's just too much when the politics starts running the project—How can you expect to build an

information system if you aren't allowed to talk with the
people who will be using it?

The hostility and misunderstanding between the consultant firm and the
CIS initiating elites resulted in the firing of the firm, and the hiring of
computer experts by the CIS agency as full-time employees in 1966. By
employing former government employees familiar with criminal justice
agencies and state politics, the CIS initiating elites hoped to be able to
convince resisting agencies, principally big city police departments and
sheriffs, that CIS had both the expertise and the experience to effectively
operate the proposed system.

TRANSITION TO A REPUTATIONAL ELITE MODEL

Internalization accomplished through coopted notables is sometimes sufficient for short-term or ad hoc reforms or as a first step toward a more
permanent structure. However, over time it becomes unstable as a reform
vehicle for two reasons. First, the reform is closely identified with external
initiating elites and in fact generally remains in their complete control.
Opposition to the reform erodes not only the substance of the reform,
(i.e., the desirability of its goals) but also its political structure. CIS was
thus attacked by local police agencies in 1963–1964, and later it was
criticized as just an attempt by the governor to interfere in local police
matters.

Second, a long-term reform effort is under pressure to stabilize its procedures and its leadership. A permanent organization is required, as well
as full-time bureaucrats to run it. These requirements of stabilization cannot be fufilled by part-time, coopted notable members of an advisory committee who retain membership in their constituencies.

A transition to a different model of internalization was necessitated by
the failure of CIS to successfully import expertise and by the requirement
for a permanent reform organization less closely identified with the governor. The mutual hostility among criminal justice agencies, and the lack of
consensus among them regarding the need or desirability of a state information system, ruled out the selection of either a Pluralist or a Collegial
model of internalization. If local agencies could have their way, it was believed by the external elites that there would be no reform at all.[26] A
Reputational Elite model was selected in the belief that it might help neutralize some of the opposition; this choice also reflected the desire of the
external elites to retain the essential goals and control of the reform.

The top management of CIS read like a police muster list: the Director and the Assistant Director, former planning officials of Metropolis City's police department; the Deputy Director for Planning, an alumnus of the city's police department; the Assistant Director for Systems Development, imported from the Chicago Police Department.

The Advisory Committee is weighted heavily in both numbers and political influence by police representatives. The court, corrections, probation, and parole associations are represented, but they have had little influence— either political or technical—over the direction of CIS.

ELITISM: POLICE DOMINANCE

The dominance of police personnel from all levels of government in the Advisory Committee and in CIS management is easily understood: an information system based on offender names, fingerprints, and criminal rap sheets requires participation of the police agencies who do the arresting. Such a system could operate without the other agencies participating, but not without police.

The first priority of CIS is and has been to bring the police into the system as active participants. However, this has meant that the information needs of the other agencies are not served. The state Judicial Conference, although represented on the CIS Advisory Committee, is largely ignored. An official of the Judicial Conference explained:

> The Judicial Conference gets little out of CIS, and they have not taken our interests to heart. We do have a limited batch-interface with CIS which operates just in Metropolis City. It is called the Criminal Statistics System and involves the exchange of information between city courts and the police files at CIS—largely just exchanges of criminal rap sheets.

> But the principal interests of the J.C. is not individual rap sheets, individual cases, et cetera, but statistical information on the flow of cases through the courts, dockets, calendaring of cases, and management information. There is a fundamental difference between apprehension or police functions and court functions. CIS doesn't understand that; they think everyone uses the same information. But that is a conceptual error— they don't have anyone who understands the courts, who knows what our problems are.

> What little we do request from CIS is [received] either late or

incorrect. Our CSS system takes delivery every two weeks from CIS. We have waited three weeks for the last batch, and the previous exchange was four weeks late. Obviously, we aren't very high on their delivery schedule.

The city corrections department also resents the dominance of police at CIS and is similarly critical of the concept that all agencies require the same kind of information. An official of the city's Department Corrections remarked:

> What do we need instant information on prisoners for? We have them here for at least a couple of months. What we could use is studies of the population, the effectiveness of programs, rates of recidivism, and so forth. Just try to get CIS to agree on doing the work! They can't even deliver to the police agencies what they've promised.

Similar views were expressed by other participating agencies. For instance, an official of the state's Crime Control Council—established under the federal Omnibus Crime Act to distribute funds to local criminal justice agencies—was critical of the traditional "cops and robbers" approach of CIS, which he attributed to the total acceptance of the "police view of information":

> There is nothing wrong with computerizing criminal rap sheets—and I don't know the political story behind that—as long as you realize what approach to crime you are going to take. Summary criminal histories give facts on individuals: actions, arrests, paroles, convictions, et cetera. It's the basis of police arrests and DA charge bringing.
>
> But what you really need to understand crime as a social phenomenon is much more. The summary criminal history contributes little understanding of the particular crime: place of crime, time of day, victim description, type of building, weapons used, and so forth. If you take a preventive approach to crime instead of an apprehension approach, then you would want information on the crime, not the criminal so much. We can prevent crime by lighting streets, building security into new architectural structures, deploying police better, et cetera.
>
> Sure, CIS might make the traditional apprehension-detention-judgment-correction process work a little faster, but it won't

transform the decision-making process. A preventive approach can prevent more crimes from happening than the CIS approach can by arresting more people. We already have too many in jail anyway.

So even if CIS was working up to its promises, it still is a traditional apprehension view of how to solve the problems facing criminal justice.

INAUTHENTIC CONSENSUS MECHANISMS: THE HOLLYWOOD STYLE

The princpial mechanisms of achieving support for CIS from local agencies have been the Advisory Committee and an extremely active public relations campaign at both state and federal levels.

After CIS was funded by the legislature, the Advisory Committee ceased holding weekly planning sessions and became a biannual meeting of officials from local agencies. The topics for discussion have changed from "How can we implement the CIS idea?" to "Now that we have built CIS, what else can we do?" In the words of the director of CIS: "The Advisory Committee was essential in the beginning for getting support from participating agencies"; however, now it is "primarily a place where we discuss new ideas such as the Automatic License Plate Scaning System." Thus the Advisory Committee meetings have become like corporate stockholder meetings at which management presents last year's accomplishments and the meeting is closed with a prayer. The Advisory Committee, subsequent to the legislative battles of 1965, was relegated to the role of a discussion circle.

There is a saying among government administrators: "Those who talk aren't doing, those who are doing aren't talking." CIS is known as far away as California as the agency with the "sexiest ads and hard sell" approach. An official of California's Department of Justice remarked:

> We are not interested in the kind of jazzy spinoffs that you see at CIS. CIS is a real Space Odyssey outfit—anybody would have to be to put all that money into things like license plate scanning and personal appearance computer files.
>
> All that stuff is a decade away. Of course we can make movies too. Hollywood is in California, you know; we're putting our money into programs, not commercials.

In Eastern State, CIS has gained a reputation among government officials as a "jet-set" agency. An administrator of Omnibus Crime Act monies commented:

> They [CIS] have a continual desire to place themselves in the technological forefront of criminal justice, even if it has little real importance for the problems at hand. They have visitors from Scotland Yard, newspapers are writing all these favorable stories about them, a monthly newsletter, two biannual publications, and two or three movies. But they aren't playing it straight.
>
> Ask people in the Office of Planning Control, or the technical staff at CIS—any of these men will document for you the fact that CIS has fallen behind in schedule on their supposed principal mission—the summary criminal histories. It is so far behind that local agencies typically find their output is not trustworthy or it is late. Figure it out: they have 600,000 criminal histories, but only 135,000 have been "cleaned" of errors. This is five years after work began.

The gap between the public relations promises and actual performance becomes increasingly visible to the participant agencies as CIS completes its first decade of life. In the words of a prominent Metropolis City police lieutenant in charge of new technological innovations for the department:

> At first we just wanted to wait and see what they could do for us—we never tried really to kill CIS, even though we could have. Now it's clear that they really can offer us little we can't provide for ourselves at lower cost and with less hassle. They are redundant: with large city systems developing, and the FBI's NCIC, who needs CIS? Maybe we wouldn't think this if their predictions in '65 were right—by now they should have had all facilities for simple criminal history transmission, but they've clearly muffed it. All this other stuff—ALPS and APADS and latent prints—is pie in the sky.

No one has tried to "kill" CIS yet—once agencies achieve a certain level of funding they rarely are eliminated—but independently the participant agencies have begun constructing their own agencies, or regional information systems, and these systems are more directly related to the problems of individual agencies.

POSTCOMPUTER PERIOD: CHANGE IN A LOW-CONTROL, LOW-RESPONSIVE SYSTEM

CIS began as part of a state-initiated reform effort to transform Eastern State's sprawling criminal justice apparatus into a more centralized system amenable to guidance by state authorities. In other states, notably California, this goal has been partly attained through the creation of a state Department of Justice—based on the federal model—with broad authority to monitor and regulate local agencies. The idea of a state Department of Justice in Eastern has been popular among academics and with study commissions of Eastern State and others generally out of elective office. For the political realist and elected official in the 1960s, a Department of Justice was out of the question—too many battles would have to be fought and too many interests would be hurt. A gradualist path toward eventual centralization was selected, and CIS was designed as one of the key "bases" for future expansion. Through gathering of information about local agencies, budget sizes, allocation of personnel, and levels of performance, it was hoped that in the future a good case could be made for major state intervention into local affairs. A former member of the governor's staff during the early 1960s explains the gradualist approach:

> The state is the crucial element of government for criminal justice administration in the U.S. because of our federal structure and the state's powers. The federal government can't do it [bring reform to criminal justice], does not do it, and doesn't have across-the-board power to do it. It has criminal jurisdiction only in aid of its enumerated powers. Local governments have only those powers given to them by the state— the state is the only layer of government that has full criminal justice powers. And the state is the only possible long-term direction, constitutionally. You can't hope to do it on the local level any more in this country, due to population size, mobility, complexity of crime problems, and the sheer mish-mash of administrative structure, the numbers of agencies, training problems, recruiting, et cetera.
>
> But it's been impossible in this state to set up the Department of Justice—and probably will be for a long time. So we work around the direct confrontation, get the money hooks into the local agencies, and pull strings later. The courts will be the most difficult to bring into state control—but we will get them. CIS is working around them—we have the police and will get Corrections and Parole. We'll keep pushing the courts for

information through the Judicial Conference. CIS will get the facts on the courts together and send them to the Budget Office. And in due course, if it works correctly, it will be possible about five years from now for the Budgeting Office to make a study that will say, "For budgetary reasons the courts must get most of their money from the state, and in order to get this money, they must do such and such." And that's when it will happen. The state Budget Office will be your control element here, backed up by the kind of management and statistical information which CIS will proivde.

The time schedule for the predicted changes, if not the entire strategy, seems to have gone awry. With major cities and counties—namely, Metropolis City and the surrounding counties—not participating actively, many criminal offenders, arrest records, and fingerprints are not represented in the CIS computer files. Moreover, the diversion of CIS agency funds to ancillary research and development projects has prevented the "cleaning up" of the data base. We have previously noted that of the 600,000 criminal histories on computer files, only 135,000 were free of errors in 1970. Finally, the CIS staff has suggested that communications between local agencies and CIS are subject to overload and breakdown, given the obsolete teletype transmission facilities that are used.

Thus it was impossible as late as 1971 for CIS to provide even the simplest kinds of information about criminal justice agencies to the governor or to other state agencies. However, if the time schedule has slowed down, the strategies of gradual penetration of local agencies and gradual increases in state control have not been forsaken.

THE USE OF POWER TO MAINTAIN CIS

In 1970 the Eastern State legislature passed a new criminal procedures law that became effective in September 1971. The new law, in effect, changed CIS from a voluntary participation agency to a mandatory one, giving CIS a great deal more control over local collection procedures.

For example, the new law requires that police departments fingerprint and photograph all persons arrested or arraigned for misdemeanors. Previously, only felons were fingerprinted. Fingerprints and photographs taken by the police must be completed according to the specifications of CIS, and the fingerprints must be forwarded to CIS.

The new criminal procedures law also affects the courts, which will not be allowed to sentence convicted offenders until the appropriate fingerprint and criminal history reports have been received from CIS. Furthermore, local criminal courts may not order recognizance or bail in felony cases unless and until the court has been furnished with a report from CIS concerning the defendant's criminal record, if any.

The new law removed many of the political roadblocks that in the past prevented CIS from realizing its goals. The completeness and quality of the data base improved dramatically, and the rates of utilization also improved. Both these factors, along with increases in the legal authority of CIS, will eventually provide state elites—the governor and the Budget Office—with the capacity and information to heighten their control over local criminal justice agencies. However, the depth and speed with which these changes occur will depend in large part on how responsive CIS becomes to local agency operational needs.

LOW RESPONSIVENESS AND INCREASING ALIENATION

As we have noted, the participant agencies in CIS do not evince a high degree of commitment to the system. Opposition, which is centered in the large urban regions of the state, has two foci: the mayors' offices and the criminal justice agencies.

CIS, unlike the regional PRIS system of Western County, does not bring status, money, or votes to city administrations. Comments by a former Metropolis City Mayoral aide for criminal justice reflect the political character of opposition to CIS in the large urban areas:

> It's the governor's fiasco in law enforcement—a program he can point to and say, "See, I've been fighting crime too." The police here hardly use it—we don't have a real time hook-up with CIS. Anyway, from what I understand it's the wrong answer to the wrong problem. The police here have their own Bureau of Identification. Anyone who read the Crime Commission Report should know the problem is catching the criminal first, or preventing him from committing a crime, not identifying him. City police have a couple of programs going right now which are really consequential for crime and law enforcement.
>
> If the governor had given us some money to pay police more, train them better, give us more equipment, it would have been more effective. The way CIS is set up, it all goes to the state. The governor gets the credit for increasing law enforcement,

CIS stock goes up, the city gets another slap in the face. Meanwhile, our housing disappears, welfare goes up, jobs are going down, and the governor won't give us the money to bail ourselves out.

The idea of automated criminal offender files being a "great leap forward" in law enforcement is not shared by local agencies. Instead, the police, DAs, courts, and corrections agencies believe that each has its own, unique information needs.

Another factor that tends to increase alienation from CIS is the system's failure to respond to the expressed needs of local agencies when it could have been of some help—for example, the failure of CIS to deliver accurate and timely information to the Judicial Conference's Criminal Statistics System in Metropolis City. Far behind schedule in the conversion from manual to computer criminal files and sidetracked in irrelevant research and development programs, CIS informed the Judicial Conference, informally, that they will not be able to comply with the criminal procedure laws of 1970 for at least a few years. Lack of computer time was the reason cited, according to a Judicial Conference official.

Prominent police agencies in the metropolitan areas report lack of service from CIS, failures of equipment, and frequent jamming of the communications lines. In addition, the information received from CIS is of low reliability due to the number of errors that were present on the old manual files and were not expunged from the computer files.[27]

A third factor that has tended over time to increase the alienation of local agencies from CIS is the sense of "rising expectations" with regard to use of computers and electronic data processing in criminal justice. Illustratively, police departments in the large urban areas are urged by major computer and systems development firms to apply the "latest techniques" to their work, to "modernize" their operations, through the use of computers. The "bandwagon" effect, which has led to "over computerization" in some areas of government, is supported by the growth of regional and municipal criminal justice applications of computers elsewhere in the country. Among the most famous police computer applications are: Los Angeles's Oracle Project, Santa Clara County's LOGIC, Kansas City's Police Command–Control System, San Francisco's Command Control, and the Criminal Process System of Dade County, Florida.

One impact of CIS has been precisely to prevent the development of municipal and regional criminal justice information systems by shunting state support and funds to CIS. Among the CIS management group this is considered to be a latent benefit of CIS. The director commented:

> It's true to say that the resistance to CIS is in the urban areas.
> Why? I don't really know. I suppose jealousy. But we have
> been able to prevent the growth of a lot of patchwork systems.
> [One] county wanted to build its own system; other counties
> wanted their own operation.

What is considered to be a benefit at CIS is resented by the localities, for it drains away from their agencies' state and federal funds for the development of local projects, and robs them of the prestige that comes from "having our own system."

The low responsiveness of CIS to local needs for information services, its failure to deliver on promises, and the fact that it does not deliver "political payoffs" to local political interests—all these factors have led to increasing alienation from the system. One way to measure this alienation is to note the number and the location of computer projects being developed outside CIS by local agencies and jurisdictions.

LOCAL ANSWERS TO THE FAILURES OF CIS

Responses to alienation are many and different. Resignation and apathy are frequent responses to alienation by social units, as are self-initiated social projects that reduce alienation by fulfilling the needs of those units. In the large metropolitan areas, principally Metropolis City, a number of computerized information systems are being developed and funded, with the help of foundations and some federal money.

The mayor of Metropolis City initiated in 1968 the Criminal Justice Automation Task Force, funded by the Safe Streets Act of 1969. The Task Force is presently writing a feasibility study for a criminal justice information system that would coordinate the flow of criminal offenders from police, DAs, courts, and Corrections in the city. Using a data base similar to CIS (offender name, criminal history, and fingerprints), the proposed system would decrease the time required to process offenders and would develop statistical information to aid in budgeting and planning within the mayor's office.

A second large project begun in the city is the Judicial Conference's Judicial Data Center, which is paid for by the city and a private fund. The Center began operation in 1970 by automating the city's court dockets and calendars. According to Judicial Conference officials, the Data Center has been successful in leveling out the flow of criminal offenders and decreasing the average time a defendant must wait for trial. In 1972 the Data Center began collecting information on the productivity of city judges (i.e., numbers of cases handled per unit time and disposition of cases and hours spent on the bench).

The pride and joy of the city's police department is the Radio Inquiry Network (RINT). RINT is a computerized command-control system that allows a centralized dispatcher to direct specific patrol cars to reported crime scenes; it also gives police managers a tool for measuring the effectiveness of patrol cars, precincts, and divisions in terms of response time and apprehension rate.

All the police department's computer applications are operated through a central computer in the Electronic Data Processing Division of the city police. The EDP Division's director, a fiercely proud Irish career officer, expresses a prevalent city police attitude toward CIS when he says, "CIS? Anything they do, we do better and cheaper, so who needs 'em?"

CIS IN PERSPECTIVE

The CIS case is illustrative of a centralized information system that has the political consequence of centralizing administrative authority. But as we have attempted to show, this is not an unintended consequence of the use of a new technology; rather, it follows from the conscious political goals of administrative officials' in a state government. Specifically, the CIS information system is designed to be the first step in the creation of a state department of Justice with broad regulatory and supervisory control over local criminal justice agencies throughout the state. Five years after the initiation of CIS, the governor engineered the passage of a state law requiring all criminal justice agencies to consult the centralized data bank before taking formal action with agency clients. Without a system like CIS, such a law would not have been possible, thus state regulations of local agencies would not have been possible. The centralized data bank in this case serves as a useful fill-in prior to political reform.

As in Western County, where computers found similar centralizing uses, resistance to CIS was extensive and very strong. Indeed, overt and public resistance to CIS was stronger than that to SSIS. This may be partly because in CIS we are examining relatively independent state and local agencies, supported by local politicians and legislators, whereas the user agencies in Western County were less independent and lacked a strong base of public and political support. Resistance to the SSIS system was more covert and was not expressed in public remarks.

Although the aforementioned differences in political systems explain perhaps the very high level of resistance to CIS, the sources of that resistance
to a centralized information system appear to be similar in both case
studies. Thus it appeared to me that the initial characteristics of the agencies that the system was attempting to link were partly responsible for the
high resistance to CIS. The user agencies involved, although all members
of something loosely called the "criminal justice system," were very different in terms of the kinds of activities they performed, the ideologies and
values informing those activities, and the kinds of personnel employed.

That the user agencies were highly differentiated suggests that it would
be extremely difficult for those agencies to voluntarily agree to participate
in a common data bank, on the kinds of information to be stored there,
and on the purposes the data bank would serve. Whereas in the PRIS case
study voluntary agreement about the information system was produced
quite easily among very similar police agencies, in CIS there was from the
beginning a very low probability that police officials, judges, district attorneys, and corrections officers would agree about the kind of information
system to have.

Other social factors not conducive to acceptance of the CIS system by
user agencies were the long-standing pattern of hostility among the participants and their social isolation from one another. As noted, Eastern
State is traditionally "balkanized," especially in criminal justice. There are
no powerful statewide police associations, and the state-level coordinating
council of the judicial branch was relatively recently. Within functional
areas, cooperation among criminal justice agencies in various regions of
the state is virtually absent.

These factors, we suggest, helped prevent an initial consensus on the
need for an information system such as CIS. Moreover, other factors related to the manner in which CIS was constructed strengthened resistance
and contributed to its centralizing effect.

From its very inception by the governor's staff, CIS has limited participation by user agencies in its design, implementation, and operation. The
governor's staff selected notable personages who presumably guided the
design of the system and recruited a reputational elite to operate it, including only persons friendly to CIS and excluding factions and persons that
disagreed with the staff. In large part, as we suggested, participation was
limited precisely because the initiating groups recognized that the user
agencies were hostile to one another.

The limited participation of user agencies has two important effects.
First, resistance by user agencies was higher than it might have been if
broader participation had been allowed. Resistance focuses not just on the

information system, but on the political process of its construction. Second, the CIS information system failed to provide useful information services to many of the user agencies. Thus the courts and large city police agencies claimed the product of CIS to be a lot of information they could not use. CIS incorporated the kinds of information service that will be useful in building a state Department of Justice.

Initiated and controlled by members of the governor's staff (or persons selected by them), the CIS system is suggestive of the kind of reform we have called a Reputational Elite. One feature of that model is the restricted participation of constituents, which results in the reform serving the interests of those who began it. In the case of CIS, this kind of reform has probably increased resistance to the information system and has likely assured that the governor's interest in expanding the authority of the executive branch over local agencies will be served. In this sense the process of reform has been supportive of an increase in administrative centralization.

1972—A Sequel

A re-examination of CIS in the middle of 1972 seems to indicate that the system has begun to solve many of its more vexing problems. This judgment follows from two events. First, in the period 1970–1971, and continuing into 1972, a budget crisis in Eastern State resulted in the CIS budget being cut just when the system was expected to become fully operational and capable of handling the increased demand for its services brought about by the new criminal procedure law. Second, in a tight budget year, CIS was under great political pressure to respond to complaints from city courts and police.

Insufficient budgeting and increasing complaints of ctiy officials and criminal justice personnel, especially in the courts, has forced CIS to re-allocate its resources to serve the more pressing needs of city agencies. Specifically, CIS management has removed equipment and machinery from low-demand areas to high-demand city areas. This seems to represent, a shift in phase for CIS: the political allocation of resources called for during the building or initiating of a reform giving way to the functional allocation needed for system maintenance.

In reallocating its hardware, CIS has also made a very acceptable response to complaints of city jurists that they are not included in decision making at CIS. This has involved holding long sessions with some of the city's more powerful judicial figures and changing CIS procedures to accommodate them. Among other improvements, an on-line printer was installed in Metropolis City to print out requests there as soon as they are printed out in the state capital, and additional receiving stations have been installed to answer the city's high demand for service.

As of 1972 CIS was becoming much more responsive to its customers' requests than it had been initially. This was partly because of the increasing visibility of customer complaints and the tightening of the state budget, which endangered any program that appeared to be faltering. Also, many of the complaints against CIS originated with city police officials, whose empires declined as CIS assumed many of their functions (in particular, the city's Bureau of Criminal Identification was reduced to an applicant-licensee data bank). As these complaints subsided, however, greater attention was paid to more serious complaints of the courts. And last, improvements in programming and computer capacity allowed CIS to begin living up to its promises of fast and accurate information delivered from the state to local agencies.

The Division of Criminal Justice Services—1972

The role of CIS in creating a state department of justice was clarified in 1972. A bill passed by the state assembly and approved by the governor created in the executive branch a new department, responsible for coordinating state criminal justice programs. The following statement was released by the governor's office on May 22.

> The bill, adopted on my recommendation, creates a new Division of Criminal Justice Services in the Executive Department and combines in it the functions now performed by the Division for Local Police in the Office for Local Government, the Criminal Identification System, and the Division of Criminal Justice in the office of Planning Services.
>
> While enforcement of the general criminal laws of the state has traditionally been viewed as principally a local responsibility, the state has serious obligations to provide all appropriate technical assistance to improve the capability of localities to meet this responsibility and to assure the safety of all our citizens.
>
> The combination of the three merged agencies will better enable the state to concentrate its efforts to strengthen criminal justice programs in a single, well-coordinated thrust. This

legislation will unite planning, analysis, local police training and standard setting, information gathering, and dissemination functions in an agency that has a grant-in-aid authority, which in turn can enhance the opportunity for realization of the goals of those functions at the local level.

John Williams, a former aide to the governor and the person responsible for much of the early work on CIS predicted to me in 1970 that "one day the governor will simply announce the creation of a state Department of Justice needed to coordinate the CIS and the other state programs. And that will be that." This prophecy was fulfilled perhaps sooner that even Williams had imagined.

NOTES

1. On the problems accompanying the creation of a new agency, see Anthony Downs, *Inside Bureaucracy,* Boston: Little, Brown, 1967, Chapter 3.

2. A Republican party worker who was chiefly responsible for the initiation of CIS remarked that a large computer firm had offered to develop a workable latent-finger-print-analysis program for $10 million (twice the CIS annual budget). Development was expected to take five years for a prototype and ten for an operational model.

3. Eastern State Criminal Identification System, *1969 Annual Report.*

4. Federal Bureau of Investigation, *National Crime Information Center,* Washington, D.C.: Government Printing Office, 1968. As of April 1971, the FBI had successfully obtained from Congress the authority to subsume SEARCH into its NCIC national network, thus asserting its authority over all interstate exchanges of criminal information. See *World News,* February 20, 1971.

5. On the difficulties of defining organized crime and gathering systematic intelligence on its operations, see President's Commission on Law Enforcement and Administration of Justice, *The Challenge of Crime in a Free Society,* Washington D.C.: Government Printing Office, 1968, pp. 448–465.

6. See Donald Cressey, *Theft of a Nation,* New York: Harper & Row, 1969.

7. These opinions, paraphrased from interviews with former members of the governor's staff and the Budget Division, are supported by Bruce Smith, *Police Systems in the United States* 2nd ed., New York: Harper & Row, 1960, pp. 65–80. Smith discusses various attempts by local and state politicians to exert external control over police agencies to ensure their integrity. By and large, Smith concludes, attempts at external control do not work and only open the door for more "political interference." Smith, with other police professionals, argues for greater professionalism and education among police and reliance on normative commitments of police officers to preserve police integrity.

8. Philip Zelznick, *TVA and the Grass Roots,* Berkeley: University of California Press, 1953. For a discussion of the consequences of failing to coopt important local interests into antipoverty projects, see Peter Marris and Martin Rein, *The Dilemmas of Social Reform,* New York: Atherton, 1967, pp. 139–163, 224–238.

9. For a discussion of the relation between professional police managers and political reformers, see James Q. Wilson, *Varieties of Police Behavior*, Cambridge, Mass.: Harvard University Press, 1968, p. 259; for a discussion of professionalism among city employees and political reform, see Wallace Sayre and Herbert Kaufman, *Governing New York City*, New York: Russell Sage, 1960, pp. 400–410.

10. For a discussion of the period, see Richard Hofstadter, *The Age of Reform*, New York: Random House, 1955, pp. 4–12.

11. The concept of a criminal justice system first received wide public exposure through the work of the President's Commission on Law Enforcement and Administration of Justice, especially the *Task Force Report: Science and Technology*, Washington, DC.: Government Printing Office, 1968, Chapter 5.

12. Roscoe Pound, *The Development of Constitutional Guarantees of Liberty*, New Haven, Conn.: Yale University Press, 1967, Chapters 3 and 4.

13. See Arthur Niederhoffer, *Behind the Shield*, Garden City, N.Y.: Anchor, 1969, Chapter 1.

14. Fred J. Cook, *The F.B.I. Nobody Knows*, New York: Macmillan, 1964.

15. On police promotion and lateral entry problems related to Civil Service pension regulations, see President's Commission, *The Challenge of Crime in a Free Society*, *op. cit.*, pp. 283–284; and *Task Force Report: The Police, op. cit.*, Chapter 5.

16. For a discussion of the role-related attitudes of various criminal justice personnel, the police, district attorneys, and judges, toward one another, see Jerome Skolnick, *Justice Without Trial*, New York: Wiley, 1967, and Niederhoffer, *op. cit.*, Chapter 6.

17. President's Commission, *The Challenge of Crime in a Free Society, op. cit.*, pp. 70–83.

18. See "The Administration of Complaints by Civilians Against the Police," *Harvard Law Review*, **77** (January 1964), pp. 499–519.

19. Niederhoffer, *op. cit.*, Chapter 2, and Skolnick, *op. cit.*, Chapter 3. See also Nicholas Alex, *Black in Blue—A Study of Negro Policemen*, New York: Appleton-Century-Crofts, 1969, Chapter 4, and William A. Westley, "Secrecy and the Police," *Social Forces*, **34** (1956), pp. 254–257.

20. William A. Westley, *Violence and the Police*, Cambridge, Mass.: M.I.T. Press, 1971.

21. Emile Durkheim, *The Division of Labor in Society*, New York: Free Press, 1966, pp. 356–357.

22. James D. Thompson, *Organizations in Action*, New York: McGraw-Hill, 1966, pp. 256–257.

23. David T. Stanley, *The Higher Civil Service*, Washington, D.C.: Brookings Institution, 1964, pp. 31–37.

24. Robert W. Hodge, Paul M. Siegel, and Peter H. Rossi, "Occupational Prestige in the United States: 1925–1963," in Reinhard Bendix and Seymour Martin Lipset (eds.), *Class, Status, and Party*, 2nd ed., New York: Free Press, 1966, pp. 324–325. See also Alfred Kadushin, "Prestige of Social Work," *Social Work*, **3** (April 1958), p. 40.

25. The compromise between central funding and voluntary local participation arrived at in the CIS case parallels in consequence that achieved in federal community Action Projects. In a desire to encourage local participation in their programs, the federal agencies abdicated political and administrative control. A good deal of "local activity" and conflict among competitors for the spoils resulted, but very little authentic change was accomplished. See Peter Marris and Martin Rein, *Dilemmas of Social Reform,* New York: Atherton Press, 1968, especially Chapter 5.

26. As described by one of the principal organizers of CIS, the political strategy with regard to the courts, the district attorneys, and the parole and probation departments—which were all ambivalent at best to the CIS idea—was to "go around them" (i.e., to begin with the police and corrections agencies, where support was more solid, only later pressuring the courts and district attorneys to utilize the system).

27. Thus a principal complaint of Metropolis City and adjacent county bureaus of identification is that most of of the CIS information is inaccurate and unreliable. The NCIC, to which the large cities have access through remote terminals, is found to be more reliable and receives more use.

APPENDIX

Design Specifications

The design specifications of the CIS system were written by an internal staff of programmers (see Figure 6 for a general flow chart of the CIS system). The computer equipment is capable of operation with several billion characters of on-line storage in random access files; terminal equipment includes visual display input/output, key-driven input devices capable of receiving and preparing hard copy output, and internal processing ability to handle complex calculations.

Software requirements includes a sophisticated operating system for the processing of inquiries from remote terminals in real-time mode, high-order procedural language compilers, and an executive control system that simultaneously serviced and processed remote terminal inquiries, performing batch-type processing and executing lengthy program compilations. The CIS design, briefly, is a large-scale real-time computer capable of operating in a multiprogramming environment. Specifications were drawn in 1965–66, and the system was up in 1969.

CIS Data Base

The CIS system in 1973 contains several separate files that previously had been maintained in manual form by diverse agencies at the state level. In addition, at the direction of the legislature CIS has created new files primarily concerned with civilian license applications and data on employees of private organizations dealing in financial securities. The following items compose the data base of CIS:

Summary criminal history of convicted felons
Fingerprints (convicted felons)
Fraudulent checks
Name file (convicted felons)

Warrant/wanted notifications
Missing persons (name and descriptors file)
Securities personnel (name file and fingerprints)
Civilian license personnel (name file and fingerprints)

Hardware of Central Installation

The CIS system contained the following hardware and capabilities as of 1970:

Description	Quantity
Basic processor—Burroughs 6500	1
Core memory (32 K)	1
Floating input-output channels	2
Card reader and control (800 cpm)	1
Card punch and control (100 cpm)	
Printer and control (700 lpm, 120 pp)	1
Printer and control (1040 lpm, 120 pp)	1
Console and control	1
Tape control	1
Tape drive (72 KB 9 Ch 800 BPI)	2
Disk file control	2
Electronics unit	1
System disks Mo. (12 M Chars. 20 MS)	1
Disk file exchange	1
Terminal control unit	1
DT Term unit	1
Expansion unit	1
DT control unit	2
TT 35 terminal	16
TT adapters	16
Multiplier and extender	1
BDU line adapter	1
Display unit II plus tab feature	9
Data memory bank (108 M Chars 60 M)	1
Disk increment (36 M Chars)	37

Software

The Burroughs B6500 employed by CIS utilizes a COBOL program to accomplish its diverse tasks. Modifications to the program are written by an internal staff. Figure 7 shows a flow chart of a simulated name and summary criminal history retrieval.

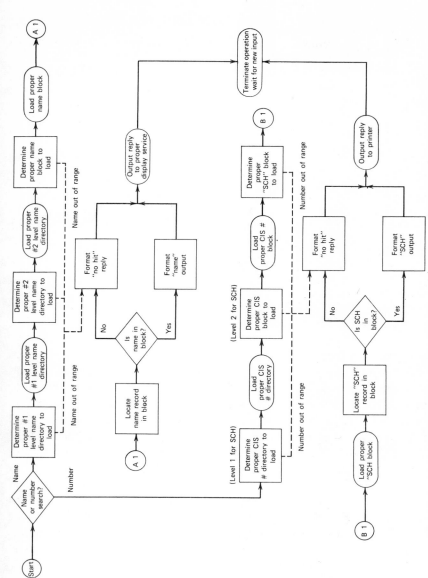

Figure 7. Flow of simulated name search and summary criminal history (SCH) retrieval.

275

TEN

Criminal Information Network of Western State

The Criminal Information Network (CIN) is a statewide system designed to transfer information on criminals among local, regional, and state criminal justice agencies in Western State. Begun in 1964 in an effort to broaden telecommunications among agencies in the state, CIN has expanded its functions to those of a real-time storage bank and clearinghouse for criminal information. In most technical respects, it is a mirror image of CIS in Eastern State; and indeed, the director of the Division of Law Enforcement, State Department of Justice, indicated to me that CIS served as a prototype for the design of CIN. Unlike CIS, however, CIN has not incurred the opposition of local politicians and agencies. Rather, the first three years of operation suggest that CIN is far more successful in gaining the active support of local agencies and political jurisdictions. The reasons for its relatively greater success are different initial conditions and more effective adaptation and maintenance mechanisms.

Planning for CIN began in 1964 within the Law Enforcement Division of the state Department of Justice. The system has two major components: a set of automated files and a new computerized telecommunications network. The first file to be automated was a "warrant/wanted" file, which lists issued warrants for serious felonies and suspected felons. In 1969 there were 50,000 individual warrants listed in this file. The second file to be automated was a criminal offender file composed of fingerprints, names and aliases, and summary criminal histories. This file is exactly the same as the comparable CIS file, and in 1970 it contained approximately 40,000 individual criminal histories.

One fault of the CIS system that was apparent to Western State officials was the absence of a high-speed communications network connecting local agencies with one another and with the state data bank. To eliminate this bottleneck that might prevent full utilization of the CIN data bank, an obsolete teletype network was replaced with a computer-based telecommunications network called SLETS (State Law Enforcement Telecommunications System). Each local agency in the CIN system is connected through dedicated telephone lines to one of two message switching computers in either Hilltown or in the state capital (in the northern and southern regions of the state, respectively). Messages sent by local agencies to other local agencies or to the state Department of Justice, are routed through these message switching computers and then sent to the appropriate destination. The SLETS system is 100 times as fast as the older teletype and has nearly 1000 times more information capacity. In addition, SLETS provides a previously unattainable capability—namely, the transmission of information between local agencies. Previously, teletype messages were "all points bulletins" with no selectivity of destination.

Besides connecting local agencies, SLETS links local agencies to other state and national computer files such as the Department of Motor Vehicles Stolen Auto file and the FBI's National Crime Information Center in Washington.

DIFFERING INITIAL CONDITION: POLITICAL SYSTEM EFFECTS

There are great differences in political history, Civil Service traditions, and political organization among the states in the federal system. Dissimilarities in the political and administrative traditions of states have been said by political scientists and historians to reflect differing social class, ethnc, religious, and economic factors that differentiate the several regions of the country.[1] Regardless of their origins, these historical differences in political and administrative structure affect the manner in which individual states adapt to changing social conditions within their boundaries. In Western State, the state government has always played a much larger role in the affairs of local criminal justice agencies than is true of Eastern State, and this dominance affects the agencies' operating authority and funds, (as well as the establishment of state standards). Partly because of this, local agencies resisted the state-initiated CIN project hardly at all (compared with the opposition of their colleagues in CIS). Indeed most of the Western agencies believed CIN to be a legitimate extension of the state's traditional authoritative role as a coordinator of local agencies.

To understand the different state–local agency relations that characterize Western State and to distinguish it from Eastern State, we must briefly digress into political history.

HISTORICAL BACKGROUND

The Western Machine

During the Reconstruction era, New York City Democratic party boss William Marcy Tweed, having selected the state's governor in 1868, was attempting to control his party's presidential nomination. At the same time Western State was experiencing the growth of a new kind of political machine, unmatched anywhere else in the nation. Immortalized in *The Octopus* by Frank Norris, the Western machine originated from the Political Bureau of the Southern Pacific Railway, which represented the interests of the "Big Four" railway magnates—Huntington, Crocker, Hopkins, and Stanford.[2]

The most heavily capitalized corporation of its day, the Southern Pacific depended for its existence on a nearly complete monopoly of railway traffic west of Salt Lake and in California, Oregon, and Washington. For the cash flow required to serve the company's huge debts, management relied on discriminatory rate structures, enforced by an annual audit of customers' accounts, whereupon rates were pegged according to the customers' profits. The power of the Southern Pacific to determine the economic future of an entire town is illustrated by the result of the company's threat to build around Los Angeles: the city handed over $600,000 plus sixty acres to the railway.[3]

By 1900 the Southern Pacific owned 85% of California's tracks and more than one-half the river and ocean shipping lines, ferry services, and urban mass transportation lines.[4] In the eastern United States during this period the railroads were circumscribed somewhat by the presence of other large organized industrial interests, creating a limited pluralism; in the western states, however, small unit agriculture was the only industry of any size, and the small farmers of wheat and citrus fruits were hardly a match for the Big Four.

It would have been strange indeed if this great economic power did not translate itself into political influence, and one contemporary commentator on western politics wrote that the Republican party was but a pseudonym for the Southern Pacific Railway.[5] Through the Political Bureau of the Southern Pacific were channeled the funds and favors necessary to control the state senate and the Republican party. Up to 1910, the Southern Pacific was the only organization allowed to have paid lobbyists on the senate floor during debate, and in some instances there were more SP lobbyists than senators involved in the discussions. Although control of the governorship automatically signaled control of the state judiciary, in the 1880s the Southern Pacific was even successful in appointing a former state justice to the U.S. Supreme Court.

The Heavenly City and the City of Sin

That Western State is popularly thought of as a land of political extremes is in part explained by the early and complete domination of the railways and by the reaction to that domination which arose after the turn of the century.

By 1900 the population of Western State was growing at a rate of 60% per decade. Whereas the early immigrants had come from the urban areas of the East, settling in the northern part of the state, the population spurt begun in the 1890s originated in the Middle West. By 1910 60% of the state's population was from the Middle West, and these people tended to settle in the agricultural regions of the southern half of the state, especially the Hilltown area.[6]

Besides making Hilltown the largest city in the state, the middle westerners brought with them Protestant fundamentalism, and its political expressions of populism and progressivism.[7] Mill City in the north, by contrast, retained its European and Catholic character. Boss-run Democratic politics control made of Mill City almost a mirror image of Eastern City politics. Despite its nickname—the "Paris of the West"—Mill City in the early 1900s was notorious for its toleration of organized crime, prostitution, gambling, and unions, and for selling of franchises to utilities and the railroad. After a mass strike of 1901, Mill City became forever after a closed shop union town.

The Lincoln League and Progressive Reform

In 1906 a new group of politicians emerged in Hilltown to challenge the Southern Pacific, the northern labor unions, and the Republican party, which had dominated state government with Southern Pacific backing. Successful in the mayoralty campaign of Hilltown in 1906, the group of fifteen journalists, lawyers, and independent businessmen formed the Lincoln Republican League in 1907 for "the emancipation of the Republican Party in Western State from domination by the Political Bureau of the Southern Pacific" and to organize the votes needed to nominate Theodore Roosevelt for President in 1908.[8] The insurgent Republicans failed in 1908 to capture the state party organization or to pledge Western State to Roosevelt. In 1910, however, they were successful in electing the governor, on the Progressive party ticket, and there followed a series of political and administrative reforms that radically changed the government of the state.

"Give Us A Square Deal, for Christs Sake"

Chaplain's invocation at the Western State Congress

It has been said that Western progressivism was heavily influenced by the religious tradition of New England. The Western Progressive was typically Protestant, often a Congregationalist from the southern region of the state. He was born in the Middle West, had a northern European name, and with few exceptions, was from a native American family. Three of every four had a college education; one-half were lawyers, one-quarter journalists, one-tenth business men and real estate operators, and the rest doctors and bankers.[9]

Steadfast in the belief that there was a moral and political middle ground between the positions of organized big business and of organized labor, the Lincoln Republicans enacted much substantive legislation designed to minimize the influence of both capital and labor over state politics. Robert La Follette of Wisconsin was one of their heroes, and the initiative, referendum, recall, direct primary, short ballot, and home rule constitutional amendments were enacted because of their efforts.

The Progressives next began a movement of administrative reform which continues to the present, allowing the state to exercise more and more control over local governments and administration. A bill reforming the criminal procedure law introduced state judicial review of local judges and popular recall of judges. A state Board of Control centralized budgeting in the state government, removing ultimate budgetary authority from individual agencies and giving it to the governor. A state Civil Service Commission was established to replace political appointees to investigatory and regulatory commissions with persons of demonstrated competence in such fields as tax law, the economics of monopolies, and labor negotiation. For the first time in the history of the state, a Railroad Commission reduced the rates and profits of a railroad.

With the decline of the Progressive machine in 1916, many of the administrative reforms lost their steam. Ultimately the reforms depended as much on honest men as on statutory authority. Nevertheless, the Progressive reforms of the period were successful in changing the image of state administration from that of a gang of "boodlers and grafters" to that of an efficient and honest civil service. Insofar as this was true, the Western State reforms preceded by a decade similar reforms enacted in Eastern State in the late 1920s. Significantly, this lead time still exists, especially in the administration of criminal justice.

Progressive Reforms: Centralization of Criminal Justice Administration

The reform movement declined with the Progressive party after 1920, and in the years between 1920 and 1942 few important administrative changes occurred in Western State government. This period saw the diversification of the state's economy from largely agro-business to include aviation, electronics, and shipping; in addition, the railroads' political influence began to decline. A Democrat was elected governor in 1938 for the first time in the state's history. In the same election, however, an insurgent Republican won the post of attorney general. The successful candidate possessed a phenomenal reputation with both Republicans and Democrats as a man who blew the whistle on dishonest politicians and organized crime syndicates. He was the only attorney general to win a majority of the Republican, Progressive, and Democratic party ballots in the same election. He had begun his public career as a county district attorney in 1924, his last official act in that capacity being the indictment of an entire city board of supervisors for taking kickbacks on city contracts. As attorney general and later as governor (1942–1950), he reshaped the administration of criminal justice in the state.

The most far-reaching of the Republican governor's criminal justice reforms involved the creation in 1944 of the state Department of Justice out of a number of independent state agencies. Directed by an elected attorney general, the Department of Justice is organized into four divisions: law enforcement, criminal law, civil law, and administration. The criminal and civil law divisions are both involved in the prosecution of individuals for violation of state laws—typical functions of an attorney general. The Division of Law Enforcement represented, however, a significant aggrandizement of state authority over local criminal justice agencies. This division established a state repository for all information on convicted felons in the state and imposed standards on the collection of criminal information at the local level. The division was also empowered to investigate local crimes, and more importantly, local police, courts, and district attorneys.

Accompanying the "stick" of greater state control over local agencies were "carrots" in the form of state grants to induce local agencies to increase the training and competence of their officers, to adopt new procedures of police work, and to cooperate with other local agencies. These practices were enforced in 1943 by the Mutual Assistance Act, which required local police and fire agencies to come to one another's aid regardless of jurisdictional boundaries, with agency expenses paid by the state. The creation of the state Youth Authority to separate juvenile offenders from imprisoned adult criminals and the strengthening of the state Department of Corrections' authority over county and city prisons completed the Republican governor's reform package in criminal justice.

The changes in the administration of criminal justice in Western State in the late 1940s preceded similar attempts in other states, including Eastern State, by at least a decade. Whereas in Eastern State the development of a state criminal identification system, CIS, was intimately connected with a bitter debate over the proper role of the state in the administration of local agencies, in Western State the two issues were separated by twenty years. The result is that in Western State local criminal justice agencies—police, district attorneys, courts, and correctional institutions, in particular—had come to expect the state government to play a large role in coordinating and standardizing local agency behavior and in providing funds and technical assistance to achieve these ends.

CIN: CONDITIONS OF INITIATION

With one significant exception, CIN agencies evince the same characteristics as Eastern State's criminal justice agencies. They can be characterized first as being of low homogeneity. In terms of the tasks they perform, their rank in a hierarchy of prestige and power, and status-role requirements of members, the state's police, courts, and corrections agencies are as different from one another as are their counterparts in Eastern State. Likewise, the level of internal integration of criminal justice agencies in Western is high when compared with other agencies of government. Police and corrections officers exhibit high levels of agency loyalty; judges and district attorneys, very high levels of occupational loyalty.

Other things being equal, then, we might expect the initial levels of homogeneity and internal integration among the CIN agencies to generate much resistance to the efforts of a state executive agency, the Department of Justice, to more closely integrate these agencies in a criminal information network.

However, initial resistance to CIN was quite low, and it remains very low when compared with CIS in Eastern State. Aside from differences in manner in which it was organized (discussed below), one difference stands out. That is, the CIN agencies were characterized initially as much more interdependent than the CIS agencies.

The higher initial interdependence of the CIN agencies has two explanations. First, local criminal justice agencies were historically much more closely integrated by virtue of the existence of a state Department of Justice—an element missing in Eastern State. Besides enforcing and funding cooperation among local criminal justice agencies through the Mutual Assistance Act of 1943, the state Department of Justice established standards of performance and training for local agencies.

As the second factor in the high initial interdependence of local criminal justice agencies in Western State, we note that the local agencies are less highly integrated into their local political jurisdictions than in Eastern State. For instance, whereas cities in Eastern State have authority over local criminal justice agencies (with the sole exception of police), Western cities do not, and courts, DA's offices, and parole, probation, and corrections agencies are organized on a county basis. City agencies have been therefore the creation of county authorities, which coordinate the city agencies on a regional basis. Consequently, local agencies have been more interdependent with other regional agencies.[10] An important base of opposition to CIS in Eastern State arose from historically autonomous "big city" agencies, which in Western State simply do not exist.

The CIN program, which envisaged the automation of existing Department of Justice files, with the addition of some new elements such as a state wanted/warrant file, did not arouse the suspicions and hostilities of local agencies—mostly because it did not involve any significant changes in the political or administrative arrangements between the state and local agencies. In the words of the Director of Law Enforcement at the Department of Justice (DOJ):

> The kinds of paranoid and suspicious internecine warfare which I know goes on in Eastern State simply doesn't exist here, although I don't really know why. Part of it is explained by the cooperation which has gone on between state and local agencies for a long time encouraged by us at the DOJ. We've

preached cooperation among local agencies, consolidation
of city and county, county with regional service for decades.
We don't have any prima donna city-states. The large cities
have always supported state coordination of criminal information—I mean, they benefit from it, so why not? It doesn't
cost them anything and generally results in local agencies
doing a better job.

Computerization of the state files meant to local agencies nothing more
threatening than only an increase in the speed with which they could use
state criminal offender files.

THE DEVELOPMENT OF REGIONAL CRIMINAL SYSTEMS IN WESTERN STATE

One example of the extent of regional interdependence and cooperation
among local criminal justice agencies is provided by the growth of regional
information systems. The development of criminal justice information systems in Western State follows a pattern quite different from that in
Eastern State. In Eastern State criminal justice information systems are
conceived, initiated, developed, and controlled by state elites. In Western
State, regional coalitions of law enforcement agencies (police, DAs, and
county sheriffs) are the first to develop information systems. The Western
County PRIS system, begun in 1965, was the first. Serving Western County
initially, it gradually expanded to include police, courts, and DAs in nine
counties surrounding and including Hilltown. The PRIS system, described
in Chapter 8, provides the region with wanted/warrant information and
communications with state and federal systems. A neighboring county began building its LOGIC system (Local Government Information Center),
based largely on PRIS and another county inaugurated its own Regional
Police Information System in 1968.

The regional systems just mentioned were initiated, controlled, and paid
for by local governments—cities and counties. Internal elites—county
sheriffs and city police—were the principal movers behind these criminal
justice information systems.

The regional systems tend to be more responsive to the needs of local
agencies, which pay for them, and they are more flexible in meeting these
needs. That is, the regional systems provide more than computer files to
local agencies. Local police, for instance, can call on the regional systems

to perform special tasks such as manpower studies, court docketing pilot programs, and crime frequency studies.

Elitism initially characterized the regional systems, which were developed largely by police agencies. However, the computers are owned and operated by civilians in county data processing centers. Courts and county DAs have just recently begun to obtain directorship on police information system boards and to receive computer services from these systems. Elitism is declining within these systems.

THE REFORM PROCESS: A PLURALIST COALITION

The existence and popular success of the regional criminal justice information systems was a *fait accompli* that Western State had to accept when it began to develop the statewide CIN system in 1966. The Department of Justice had broad authority and could have banned these systems, but this path would have been politically costly and economically unwise; the local system existed, had the support of local political elites, and represented a sunk historical cost.

On the other hand, the regional systems were not compatible with one another because of the use of different equipment and different formats for storing information. The regional systems could not talk with one another, as the programmers say. To the state, interested in coordinating local agencies, the prospect of further unregulated development of regional systems was anathema:

> Achievement of the benefits of CIN will be delayed or thwarted by failure to act on CIN implementation at the earliest opportunity. . . . Local or regional agencies will continue to develop and build costly automated information systems which because they offer only partial solutions, must subsequently be modified or abandoned as total state or national systems are developed. . . . Fragmentation of files and duplication effort between levels of government will grow as crime rates and population increase. The opportunity to influence properly the development of effective nationwide criminal history transcript exchange programs may be lost.[11]

In the early stages of CIN development, the Department of Justice was aiming for the ultimate replacement of the regional systems with a statewide system.

THE 1964 SLETS CONFERENCE

The first element of the CIN system to be designed and implemented was a computer-based telecommunications system that would connect local agencies with the state government. Implementation of SLETS required the adoption of a uniform information storage format by local agencies and regional information systems. Since legislative approval was required to obtain funding for SLETS system, interest groups affected by SLETS had the opportunity to prevent appropriations being made to SLETS programs.

To organize support for the SLETS project among key interest group, and to write the technical specifications of the project, an Advisory Committee was formed in 1964, composed of members of the Peace Officers' Association, the state Sheriffs' Association, the League of Cities, the County Supervisors' Association, the State Highway Patrol, the state departments of Motor Vehicles, Justice, and General Services, and the chairman of the governor's Communications Advisory Commission. The Department of Justice told the committee that it desired to establish SLETS as the first stage in a statewide criminal information system, which would eventually replace the local and regional systems being developed at the time. In the initial proposal each local agency would have a SLETS communication console in its office, providing direct access to the state files in the state capital and national files in Washington.

The state's proposal encountered the stiff resistance of several powerful interest groups who by 1964 had already decided to support regional systems. The Peace Officers' Association and its Electronic Data Processing Subcommittee favored the development of PRIS in Western County and similar systems in other counties. In turn, the regional systems were supported by the county supervisors and the county sheriffs. The supervisors and sheriffs are elected officials in Western State, typically heading their county's political party. Thus both groups have powerful lobbies in the state legislature. An official of PRIS system in Western County, who was a participant on the Advisory Committee, commented:

> The state's proposal was supported by the governor's representative of DOJ, and the Department of Motor Vehicles. These are all state people and they don't see the local agencies' view. But the regional systems—the supervisors and sheriffs and peace officers—weren't about to participate in the dismantling of what they just built up. We were all for coordination—we knew at the regional level that a real problem was developing as all of us were going our own merry way with equipment and formats, and so forth. But misdemeanors and

scofflaws were regional and local concerns which the state couldn't serve, besides which, we provide for a lot of local computer services to the agencies. The state's system couldn't replace us. And they couldn't have received appropriations without our support.

A compromise proposal was agreed on whereby the SLETS system would work through existing regional information systems with terminals placed at the regional headquarters and with local agencies inquiring through the regional system to state files. The local regional systems would build and control the local networks used by local agencies, although accepting state standards for the type of equipment used and the format for handling data.

The compromise arrived at in establishing the SLETS system created a *de facto* division of labor between the state and the developing regional systems, a division of labor that was later reinforced by decisions involving the CIN system. Accordingly, the state was given the responsibility and authority for controlling all interregion and region–state criminal information processes, and the regions and localities were placed in control (within guidelines established by the state) of intraregional criminal information processes.

THE CIN SYSTEM: 1966–1970

In 1966 the Department of Justice, under pressure from the governor, hired the nearly bankrupt aerospace firm, Lockheed, Inc., to design a statewide criminal justice information system that would utilize the SLETS system to connect local and regional agencies to fully automated criminal files. According to a Department of Justice official, the study was a disaster:

Lockheed was new to the contract study business, and they received the contract largely to bolster their failing aerospace business. Their solution to our problem was to computerize everything. They just sent out teams of researchers to local agencies and wrote down what each agency wanted computerized. They ended up suggesting a huge state criminal justice system, way beyond present capabilities and needs and with no discriminating look at just what was really important and what wasn't.

The consultant's proposal was for a statewide system similar to CIS in Eastern State, with the state replacing all local systems and providing for a totally centralized information utility. A Department of Justice official remarked, "We patted them on the back and sent them on their way in 1969."

During 1968–1969 the regional systems in Western, Southern, and Vista counties became operational with strong local support. Any state effort to replace them would again be resisted by local users and supporters of these systems. The regional systems typically supplied local agencies with a wanted/warrant file for local offenders, crime frequency reports, and a intraregional communication network connecting local agencies.

Meanwhile, Department of Justice personnel conferred with representatives from the regional systems to determine what the state logically could and should perform and what functions should remain regional or local. From these conferences it was decided that the state should computerize its summary criminal history file, which was currently a manual file. This, it was argued, was something the regional systems could not do and was traditionally a function performed by the state. The agreements reached by 1969 formally established the principle that the state was only a partner to local efforts and was restricted to fulfilling its given statutory responsibilities:

> The program is envisioned as an expanded responsibility of the state Department of Justice in serving as the central record repository and information center for criminal justice agencies throughout the state as provided by existing statutes. . . . Neither the expanded responsibility of the Department of Justice nor the use of SLETS should be interpreted as precluding the development or use, as part of the total CIN program, of local or regional communications and information processing capabilities. However, it will be necessary for these systems to adhere to certain minimum standards in order for data to be meaningfully exchanged.[12]

The implementation of the CIN project proceeded in two stages. The Department of Justice hired full-time systems design experts from other areas of state government, persons familiar with state bureaucracies and qualified to build a complex computer information bank. This group of design personnel worked only on the state's manual files in the capital. Implementation of standards and local and regional communication linkages with the state files were left to the regional systems. Figure 8 illustrates the extent to which the CIN system is really a partnership between the Department of Justice and regional criminal information system.

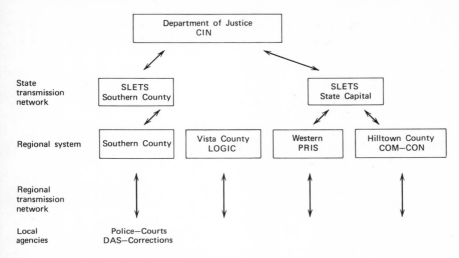

Figure 8. A model of the CIN system.

The Pluralist Model

The SLETS negotiations in 1964 and the CIN initiation period of 1968–1969 led to the creation of a coalition between state, regional, and local authorities to provide the entire state with a workable criminal justice information system, compatible with both state and regional interests.

A consensus on the goals of the CIN–SLETS system was reached in both cases through the inclusion of key interest groups in the early policy-making process, fulfilling the conditions for the Pluralist model we discussed in Chpater 3. In the SLETS program, consensus was arrived at formally by an advisory committee composed of representatives from affected interest groups. In the CIN example, negotiations between the state and regional systems were largely informal, following closely Selznik's paradigm of informal cooptation. It was the cooptation of such key interest groups, whether formally or informally constituted, that resulted in agreements in which both regional and state parties gained. The state achieved its goals of setting state standards for the storage and interchange of criminal information among local agencies and with the state; it also established requirements for compatibility of equipment and indirectly managed to assert some control over the regional systems. The regional systems in turn obtained formal state recognition of their authority over selected local information processes, such as command and control systems for their

regions, regional wanted/warrant files, as well as operational control over
regional communication networks—those which connect local agencies to
the regional system.

A similar consensus on the division of labor and authority between state
and region was developed to implement the CIN system. After an initial
flirtation with imported expertise—the Lockheed study—the Department
of Justice hired its own full-time consultants to automate the files in
the capital and in the SLETS centers in Southern County and the capital.
The regions in turn were given authority to implement the regional CIN
projects, which involved informing local agencies of the new information
formats for inputting into the system, enforcing the state standards, and
operating the regional equipment of CIN. Implementation relied at the
regional level on local experts.

CIN Maintenance: Control and Commitment Mechanisms

The maintenance of a reform project, besides requiring the use of resources for continual adaptation to a changing environment, calls for the
use of resources both to exert control over participating units and to maintain their commitment to the reform. As we noted in connection with the
CIS case (Chapter 9), control over resisting participant units eventually
takes the form of compulsion. This in turn resulted in very low commitment to the project. In the CIN case compliance with state standards and
procedures was voluntarily arrived at and never presented a problem to
the reform. This is largely because the inducements offered by the reform
to participants have functioned to maintain and increase commitment to
CIN. Besides the direct benefits of participating, such as faster communications with other local agencies and more complete information on criminals from a state agency at no cost to the regional systems (CIS participants had to pay for services rendered), the Department of Justice has
encouraged the further development of regional information systems
through providing technical assistance and funds for new projects. The
Southern City Police Department, for example, has received technical
assistance from the state in building its regional wanted/warrant file and
funds to develop a command-control network for the county. The prevailing attitude of high commitment to the CIN system was illustrated by a
Southern City police captain, director of the Department's Planning and
Development Division:

> State–local relations are not a problem so much in this state,
> especially in the criminal justice area. They [the state] do what

they can do best, like CIN or SLETS, and we do what we
can do best. As long as they stay out of our way, let us do
our job, we have no complaints. In the past—I mean to date—
they have encouraged us to develop as many innovations as
we can. We're working on a command-control system, a
regional wanted/warrant file, a *modus operandi* automated
file, and so forth. The state is going to provide us funds to
develop these systems through Omnibus Crime Act money.
We get a lot out of CIN—it doesn't cost us anything and
really extends the usefullness of our own systems.

The Hilltown regional system, also receiving development money and
assistance from the state Department of Justice, evinces a relatively high
degree of commitment to the CIN project. A planning officer said:

Unlike the CIS system in Eastern State, CIN is based on
common sense. Our relation with them is more like a state–
federal one, really, insofar as they provide guidelines and direction but we still run things on the local level and gear our
work to fulfilling the needs of local, on-the-job agencies and
patrolmen. Some things the state has to do—like a summary
criminal history file and state-wide communications—but some
things can only be done locally by people close to the operating problems of line agencies. You need both state and
regional or local systems, really, which is why CIS got into
trouble, trying to prevent regional systems from developing.

It would appear that the traditional roles of the state—as coordinator
of local agencies in criminal justice and as a standard-setting force—is well
accepted by local agencies. Thus the state does not need to compel compliance with its standards. Moreover, the use of positive inducements, such
as technical assistance and additional funds to support regional systems,
not only gives the state another means of influencing or controlling regional
systems, it increases the commitment of the regional systems to state-
initiated reforms, such as CIN.

CIN IN PERSPECTIVE

Two findings are illustrated by the CIN case study. First, as with the PRIS
study, a centralized information and communications system does not ineluctably lead to a higher level of administrative centralization. Second,
under appropriate conditions the technology can be made to conform to an

already-present set of administrative and political relationships. Information technology is malleable.

In the CIN case the existence of regional information systems serving local agencies and supported by local law enforcement and elected officials was a crucial factor in shaping the state system. These regional groups were mainly responsible for inhibiting the state in 1964 from designing a fully centralized communications network (SLETS), which would have removed from local and regional control existing communication and data processing capabilities.

Regional and local law enforcement groups were quite strongly opposed to the state's original intentions and to the later Lockheed study in 1968. Over time, as Department of Justice planners accommodated to local groups, resistance declined. Our narrative ends with CIN performing many of the same functions as CIS and involving many of the same types of agencies, but with far less resistance. We have suggested that two factors account for this lower level of resistance. Differing state political histories and state-local relationships created dissimilar initial conditions in the CIN and CIS cases. Second, the political process of building the CIN system was also conducive to lower resistance.

Although homogeneity among criminal justice agencies is low in Western State as in Eastern State, two initial conditions distinguish the user agencies. The first is a higher level of interdependence in Western State among criminal justice agencies. Since 1950 the state, through its Department of Justice, has played a large role in coordinating and standardizing local criminal justice agencies. The existence of a state Department of Justice was in turn related to the growth of statewide professional associations of police administrators, judges, and district attorneys. This social network of law enforcement personnel, which predated the computer, suggests that the user agencies in Western State were much more closely related and interdependent than their counterparts in Eastern State. Second, it suggests a lower level of internal integration than in Eastern State. Local agencies in Western State are subject to county and state authorities, which have mandated cooperation among the local units.

These initial factors, we suggest, were more conducive to an early consensus on the need for a system like CIN and to the relatively low level of resistance to its construction. Other factors related to the social process of its construction were important to the low level of resistance, as well as to the decentralized character of the system.

Following flirtations with a highly centralizing system in 1964 and with an inappropriate consultant's study in 1968, the Department of Justice tended to accommodate its designs and goals to the interests of regional and local groups. We have called the process by which this occurred a Pluralist model of reform, in which important and powerful local groups are coopted into the early stages of a reform to shape its design and implementation. In this respect the CIN project stands in marked contrast to the CIS experience. There are no regional systems Eastern State, largely because of the refusal of state leaders to recognize local and regional interests coupled with their refusal to allocate funds from the Omnibus Crime Act of 1968 for such purposes: CIS was expressly designed to inhibit regional systems from developing. The units of CIS are strictly local agencies. Although CIS imposed state standards on local information storage process after voluntary efforts failed, it does not encourage local and regional collaboration among criminal justice agencies. Each local agency tends to bargain with the state as a self-sufficient unit.

Perhaps it could be argued that CIN has expanded the traditionally large administrative authority of Western State's Department of Justice over local agencies. CIN represents one more area—namely, criminal information storage and retrieval—in which the state adopts a coordinating and standard-setting role in the life of local agencies.

Simultaneously, however, CIN has functioned to increase state support for local and regional innovations such as regional wanted/warrant files and the automated *modus operandi* files in Southern City. The state has guided the strategy of developing a statewide criminal information system, but it has encouraged the regions and localities to develop independent tactical information tools suited to local needs. Rather than centralizing administrative authority, the substantive political impact of CIN seems to have been as follows: the state has created the ground rules for closer cooperation among regional and local agencies without taking away their ability to adjust to local needs.

NOTES

1. On religious and cultural factors in the political life of different states, see Richard Hofstadter, *The Age of Reform,* New York: Random House, 1955, Chapter 1, and Seymour M. Lipset, *The First New Nation,* Garden City, N.Y.: Anchor, 1967, Chapter 4. See also Daniel J. Elazar, *The American Partnership,* Chicago: University of Chicago Press, 1962.

2. Frank Norris, *The Octopus.* New York: Doubleday, 1901. See also Oscar Lewis, *The Big Four.* New York: A. A. Knopf, 1946.

3. George E. Mowry, *The California Progressives,* New York: Quadrangle Books, 1963, p. 9.

4. *Ibid.,* p. 10.

5. Edward A. Dickson, in *The Los Angeles Express,* 1906, cited in Mowry, *op. cit.* p. 60.

6. Mowry, *op. cit.,* p. 7.

7. Hofstadter, *op. cit.,* Chapter 1.

8. Mowry, *op. cit.,* p. 70.

9. From a survey of 100 Progressive party organizers at a Brighton meeting in 1907.

10. See John C. Bollens, "Administrative Integration," *Public Administration Review,* **11** (1951).

11. State Department of Justice, *CIN 5 Year-Implementation Plan,* 1970.

12. *State Criminal Justice Information, Final Report, op. cit.*

APPENDIX

Design Specifications

The CIN system is really two different systems composed of SLETS (State Law Enforcement Transmission System) and CIN (Criminal Information Network). SLETS is a high-speed data transmission and switching system that allows one agency to communicate with central files, other agencies, or all agencies in the system using free text messages. As Figure 9 indicates CIN is a family of on-line, real-time systems related to specific criminal justice needs, including a wanted persons file (WPS), an automated property system (APS), an automated firearms system (AFS), and stolen vehicle and criminal history systems (SUS and CHS).

Data Base of Criminal Information Network

Wanted Persons System (WPS)

Warrant-issuing agency	
Name of person and description	71,000 persons
Reasons for want	2 Univac Disk 70/590 units
Birth, number, social security number	
Driver's license number	

Automated Property System

Law enforcement status (stolen, lost, found)	
Serial number	650,000 records
Category code, including brand name	8 Univac Disk 70/590
Description	

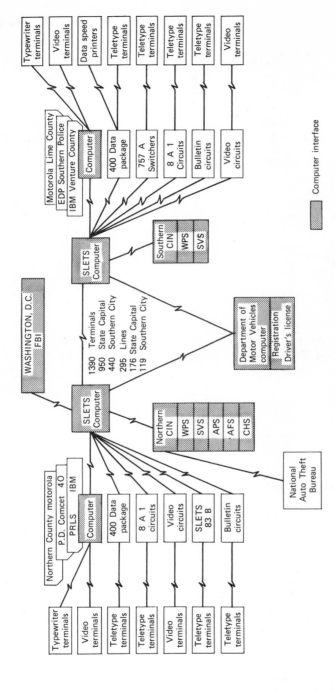

Figure 9. The CIN system plan.

Automated Firearms System

Firearm status (purchased, stolen, lost,
   found, pawned)
Serial number
Purchase information (person, address,   2.85 million records
   criminal record number)   16 Univac Disk 70/590

Stolen Vehicle System

Vehicle status, (stolen, lost, found)
Serial number
Engine number   170,000 records
Description   2 Disk Univac 70/590

Criminal History System

Personal data
Rap sheet (criminal history in Western
   State)
Supporting data (data that allow automatic
   inquiries into stored data based on   141,000 persons
   partial personal descriptors, includ-   16 Univac Disk 70/590
   ing *modus operandi*).   (ultimate size = 2.2 million)

Hardware

SLETS Telecommunications System

Description	Quantity
Univac Spectra 70/46 computers in southern part of state	2
Univac Spectra 70/46 computers in northern part of state	2
Teletypewriters in 450 locations	900
Model 33/35 teletypewriter operating as dial terminal through 400 data pack or 757A line switcher	1
Model 35 teletypewriter as controlled terminal on 8A1 circuit	1
Model 28 teletypewriter as controlled terminal on 83B3 circuit	1
Department of Motor Vehicles RCA 70-45 using three 2400-bps lines	1
Highway Patrol IBM 7740 utilizing four 150-bps lines	1
Department of Justice RCA 301 utilizing two 1800-bps lines	1
Center-to-Center as utilizing two 2400-bps line parts operating as two full duplex lines	1
Monitor terminals each center for operator control	3

Criminal Information Network, Northern Center (Southern is similar)

Description	Quantity
70/46 Univac main processor, 262 K	1
70/60 Univac main processor 655 K	1
CCM (On-line)	5
CCM (Backup)	5
564-2 Disk Storage	3
Magnetic tape drives	2
Printer	1
590-8 Disk storage	1
590-6 Disk storage	2
Magnetic tape drives	4
Card reader	1
70/60 Univac backup main processor	1

Software

Private consultants, under contract to RCA, developed the SLETS software package. Approximately twenty man-years were required. Design goal of the system was to switch approximately 17,000 messages per peak hour, with 24-hour retrieval and 24-hour operational capabilities. Average message length was established as 174 characters, with no upper limit on message size.

The message system runs under a standard RCA TDOS Executive with minor modifications made at execution time to permit automatic switchover between processors. The TDOS Executive permits multiprogramming in the background while the communications system is operational.

The interfaces to existing computer systems are all programmed using poll, call, and acknowledge logic. However, the number of responses to an inquiry is variable, as are the details of the interfaces. Intercenter message transmission employs a highly efficient, free-wheeling logic, with no acknowledgment required between messages.

Message segments are recorded as they arrive, along with their corresponding journals. Segments are forward linked, with the linkage occurring after the segments have been recorded. All incoming data are recorded twice on disk for backup and a third time on tape for off-line statistical processing.

Multiple addressing and group code addressing permit addressing up to sixty stations for each message. Queueing to stations (including other computers) is performed by priority. Traffic for circuits on intercept may be alternately rerouted or held indefinitely; when the station on-line can again accept traffic, the operator at the monitor may elect to reenter intercepted traffic or to deliver it off-line.

PART THREE

ELEVEN

Conclusion

It is generally agreed that the radical political reform and community action projects of the 1960s failed to redress the problems of social and economic inequality. It must now be concluded that the administrative reform projects of this era have also failed to achieve their announced goal of developing and implementing new public policies for dealing with the problems of urban life.

The simple truth is that computers cannot decrease the incidence of crime; they cannot educate people, raise the incomes of those living in poverty, or increase the supply of housing. If current patterns of utilization by state and local governments continue, it is doubtful that computers will even be able to contribute to the solution of these problems. The so-called information crisis—touted by computer firms, professional data processors, and hopeful politicians as the root of governmental problems in the 1960s—now appears to have been related only indirectly, if at all, to the "urban crisis."

If the activities of government are divided among operational activities of line personnel, management control activities, and strategic planning, our research shows that the principal contribution of computers in local governments has been to collect, store, and process information useful in the day-to-day operations of line personnel; in some limited cases, management control has been improved. On these grounds alone, the enormous computer-related expenditure of wealth and manpower by local governments may be justified.

At best, however, the impact of computers has been to increase the efficiency of line personnel acting within the context of traditional public policies. Policemen can now make more efficient and thorough arrests based on better information; more stolen automobiles are recovered; welfare and medical assistance programs have less fraud; budgets are more current and more thorough.

None of this progress has called forth any reformulation of our society's criminal justice, medical, or welfare programs. The computers have simply failed to engender new Principiates armed with the right information at the right time and capable of developing new strategies and policies for coping with the problems of an urban society. Neither have the computers created a ground swell of public opinion supportive of new public policies. Indeed, it is possible that the appearance of "modernism" and rationality created by the machines and their propagandists has narcotized the public into acceptance of the status quo.

With this perspective on the effect of computerized information systems on public policy, we must ask why their impact has been limited; and we should ask whether it could be changed. Three reasons are apparent.

EARLY STAGES OF DEVELOPMENT

First, our research focuses on the early stages of development and implementation in the history of third and fourth generation computers. Over time, however, applications have become more sophisticated, beginning in the mid-1950s with office automation to on-line, real-time systems that affect ongoing transactions of line personnel and provide managers in the mid-1970s with a great deal more information on the organizational process. It can be argued that with new developments in hardware and especially software capable of tailoring and selecting information needed by political executives, computers will in time become an essential part of the policy-formation process.

LACK OF A THEORY OF INFORMATION

The sanguine stage theory just outlined assumes lack of hardware and software to be a principal impediment to the realization of early predictions for the computer. Perhaps more fundamental is the absence of a theory of information capable of suggesting what kinds of information are required by the nonroutine decisions typically made by political executives. What is lacking is a theory of the policy-formation process that suggests the role played by new information and knowledge in the creation of public demand for new policies as well as in the making of executive decisions with regard to alternative public policies.

It must be remembered that the principal criteria for computerizing information files in the systems we examined were convenience and utilization. By and large, existing information files were computerized and existing information flows were expedited. If several agencies used the same basic information, it was assumed that a centralized computer file was justified. This apparently pragmatic policy often backfired: several agencies might use the same piece of information, but its relative value might be very different for each agency. The result quite frequently was computerization of existing files containing information that was of little value to specific agencies.

One interview during my research illustrates the point. A young manager of a large county probation agency, recently graduated from a prestigious business school, described how the computer came to his agency under the aegis of a powerfully connected data processing bureau:

> It was a process of getting the mostest for the leastest: once they found out we had a large manual file of probationers' names and addresses, and that we occasionally had to know if one of our clients was arrested or on welfare, they simply added our files to the Central Index file. What they didn't know is that this information is of little value to us. What we really need to know is how our clients are affected by agency decisions. Do we make any difference by sending a man to jail or continuing him on probation? We can't make rational decisions without this information. We simply got computerized!

The seemingly pragmatic policy of rendering accessible to computer uses the data in whatever large files exist has meant that much useless information is efficiently stored and potentially retrievable. Eventually this policy will run out of files that can be economically computerized. The difficult question of what new information and what new information flows are needed to inform public policy will then arise. The lack of theoretical understanding of the role of information in public policy formation will become more apparent.

The development of a theory of information, of course, is an interdisciplinary problem requiring years of work by social scientists and management scientists. In American business and management schools, information collection, storage, and display are currently viewed as costs, and the computer is viewed as an instrument for reducing information costs. Almost every large computer installation in a private or public organization is preceded by voluminous cost-benefit studies, which invariably conclude that computers are faster and cheaper than clerks. But as one manager of a large firm remarked after reading such a report, "They don't seem to realize we need new products and new markets, not just lower costs."

With the kind of theories now prevalent in business schools, the automobile would still be a carriage and airplanes would have flapping wings. Clearly, a second major impediment to full realization of the computer's potential is the absence of more sophisticated information theory.

LACK OF POLITICAL COMMITMENT TO CHANGE

The lack of hardware/software and the absence of a coherent theory of information may be overcome. Yet the impact of the computer has been limited for a yet more fundamental reason: the lack of political commitment to social policy change. Neither the bureaucratic nor the professional groups who vied for control of the computer in local governments were committed to securing far-reaching changes in public policy. Moreover, those professional groups committed to social policy change were typically overwhelmed by the political clout of administrative reformers anxious to fill the ever-larger memory cores of third generation computers. A closer examination of bureaucratic and professional groups is warranted because together they shaped the development of local governments' use of computers in the late 1960s and early 1970s.

Bureaucratization of Local Government

Of continuing fascination to Western political thought since the nineteenth century has been the prospect of removing politicians from politics and replacing them with a rational calculus of administration.[1] Bentham's reduction of the best government to the provision of the greatest good for the greatest number is echoed in Marx's vision of the utopian state as a rational administration of things.

No doubt these early versions of rational government received support from the rapid advance in factory-machine technology in the nineteenth century, the growth of large nation-state bureaucracies, and the rise to positions of political importance of a professional class of lawyers, engineers, and civil servants who increasingly built, controlled, and administered the new social units. In the United States these developments occurred somewhat later than in Europe. Nevertheless, in the first decades of the twentieth century the success of the private corporation in mobilizing and allocating labor and capital spawned a political movement, organized largely by professional and middle-class citizens, which argued that government was essentially a corporation, not an arena for competing political interests.

Coupled with the growth in government functions since the turn of the century and the increased size and complexity of its undertakings, the ideology of rational government that informed progressivism led to the aggrandizement of executive authority vis-à-vis legislatures and government agencies, as well as the insulation of that authority from partisan politics. This aggrandizement of executive authority in local government takes varying forms, including the restoration of appointive powers to elected executives, the establishment of county and city managers, and the introduction of at-large election and non partisan electoral systems. In state political structures, aside from the restoration of gubernatorial appointive power, executive authority was enhanced through the centralization of budgeting under the executive and the use of state executive departments of welfare, education, highways, and justice, among others, to control local agency budgets, procedures, and standards of performance.

Whereas in the late nineteenth century the principal integrative mechanism of local government was the power of a political machine and its boss, in the twentieth century administrative authority and bureaucratic procedures became the chief mechanism of integration.

Professionalization of Local Government Agencies

A related yet independent theme of local government since the end of the nineteenth century has been the increasing professionalization of government agencies. The trend toward professionalization is related to the growing emphasis on bureaucratic procedures of recruitment and daily operation, which stress appointment according to widely accepted norms of achievement and competence, behavior in accordance with established rules and regulations, and hierarchic subordination to legitimate authority.

Although professionalization and bureaucratization have historically proceeded hand in hand, they have come to represent differing values, political interests, and systems of action within local government. The bureaucratic orientation fostered by executive reformers has stressed subordination of public servants to legitimate political authority, public accountability, adherence to formal rules and regulations, dedication to a political unit (e.g., the agency), and efficiency. Professionalization in local government, as elsewhere, has emphasized action in accordance with a given body of specialized knowledge, independence from political and lay review, reliance on professional judgment and collegial authority, and dedication to service and professional ideals.

The success of government workers' attempts to achieve professional status has been related in part to their political influence. The growth of large and powerful professional associations that have lobbied successfully for specialized training and formal degree in nursing, social work, and police science as a condition for Civil Service appointments in many local governments provides some indication of their success. The failure of the same groups to achieve full professional status rests in part with the lack of public acceptance of certain specific functions (e.g., welfare) and public disbelief in the existence of certain specialized bodies of knowledge (e.g., police science).

The differing orientations of administrative reformers and professional employees of government agencies account for one of the principal contemporary cleavages in the structure of local government—a cleavage that became all the more obvious in periods of crisis. After the urban upheavals of the 1960s, many reform mayors supported the idea of civilian police review boards and greater executive control over police agencies in the name of accountability and efficiency. They were bitterly—and successfully—opposed by police professional organizations, which appealed- for autonomy from lay review in the interest of professionalism and to preserve impartial enforcement of the law. The decline in popularity for welfare programs in the 1960s led reform mayors and governors alike to seek greater executive control over social service budgets and procedures (such as the assignment of caseload), once again invoking efficiency and accountability. They too were bitterly opposed by welfare and health employees, who mounted strikes and demonstrations to show their concern for client needs and their desire for professionally acceptable caseload levels.

The Third Generation Options

With the development in the early 1960s of a third generation of computers and their use as a tool for centralizing and rationalizing strategic defense forces in the United States, many political scientists, systems analysts, computer firms, and politicians began to look for applications of the new technology to problems of local and national government. If the Pentagon had a management information system capable of improving its decision making, efficiency, and effectiveness, why not national and local government? The idea of a Total Unified Information System for state and local government, developed by two RAND Corporation theorists in 1962, President Johnson's call in 1965 for PPBS (Planning, Programming, Budgeting System) budgeting in federal agencies, and the proposal for a National Data Center in 1968, all emanate from the euphoria that surrounded the successful military applications of the technology in the late 1950s.

Whatever their capacity for improving the quality of local government decision making through the talents of that mythical leviathan, the management information system, the third generation computers were strongest in accounting and inventory control applications. However, what or who was to be accounted for or inventoried in local government became a matter of some contention.

The new technology presented administrative reformers in local government with a host of options. For the Board of Supervisors and the county administrative officer of Western County, information technology could be used to increase executive control and review capacity over agency budgets; specifically, it could serve to regulate more closely social service agency procedures and expenditures for welfare recipients. Greater efficiency and reduction in welfare fraud became the rationale for selection of this option.

For the governor of Eastern State, the technology afforded a new opportunity for the state executive to gain greater control over local criminal justice agencies (especially local police forces), to establish state standards enforced by dependence on state funds, and to act as a first step toward an eventual state Department of Justice. In Western State, similarly, the new technology represented an opportunity for the Department of Justice to standardize and more closely coordinate local and regional police information procedures.

To local government agency managers and professional employees, the technology presented a different set of options. It gave the welfare professionals of Western County opportunities to assess the welfare needs of the county population, to inventory the unmet needs of that population, and hopefully to increase the speed and effectiveness of welfare services to clients. For Health Department professionals and managers, information technology offered the potential abilities to identify more rapidly the health needs of specific groups in the county and to deliver health services to needy groups more efficiently. Similarly, county Probation Department managers and caseworkers were desirous of using the technology to help clients find jobs, to analyze internal decision making vis-à-vis clients, and to conduct follow-up studies of clients. Local police agencies in turn wanted to utilize the technology to increase local arrest rates and thereby the efficiency of their forces, and in some cases to improve the deployment of their forces.

Whereas the administrative reformers perceived information technology as a tool of centralization of authority, closer supervision, cost reduction, and standardization, agency managers and professionals were more likely to interpret information technology as an opportunity to improve the quality of their services to clients.

The introduction of information technology to local government created another stage on which the cleavage between the professional and bureaucratic orientations could develop into open conflict. The results of this conflict, the selection of which options the new technology would serve, depended little on the technology per se.

The Political Process of Goal Selection

With the exception of cases involving local police agencies, administrative reformers generally won out over professional groups and interests. The single most important factor in determining the uses of information technology in local government has been the relative political strength of administrative reformers as against agency managers and their professional employees. Where administrative reformers possessed sufficient legislative strength, public support, and legal authority, the technology came to be used as a tool for obtaining greater executive control over line agencies. This is illustrated in two of our studies—the SSIS, the CIS systems. In Western County the public unpopularity of the social service agencies, the broad legal authority of the county administrative officer, and the relative weakness of social worker unions and professional association of nurses, combined to ensure agency managers and professional employees little if any voice in the uses of the SSIS system. In Eastern State, the only significant opposition to legislative authorization of the governor's proposal for a statewide criminal justice information system came from the sheriffs' association. Once the sheriffs were placated, local police associations were unable (despite sincere efforts) to prevent adoption of the CIS plan by the legislature.

Where government agencies had sufficient public support and legislative strength, however, they gained important concessions from administrative reformers and in one case complete control over the uses of the technology. The CIN and PRIS systems illustrate this finding. In Western State, local police agencies were the first to establish regional information systems;

these in turn were politically popular in local constituencies and were supported by powerful police political lobbies, principally the Peace Officers' Association and the county sheriffs. State administrative reformers attempting to extend state control over police information procedures through the CIN system were forced to accept these regional system as *faits accompli*. They also had to allow regional and local systems to continue development of tactical information tools, and they were obliged to permit significant regional and local control over the CIN system itself. Information technology in this situation was used to foster agency and professional goals best described as "effective law enforcement"—that is, higher arrest rates for relatively minor infractions of the law, better protection of police personnel (e.g., by giving greater warning to policemen of approaching cars suspected of being occupied by armed criminals), and reduction in response time to calls for assistance. The state executive branch gained also through agreements on the compatibility of regional systems and adoption of uniform information procedures.

From the example provided by PRIS, we see local agencies and their professional staffs given complete control over the development of the technology. This occurred largely because local police agencies in conservative, affluent, and "reform politics" constituencies are something of a sacred cow. Local politicians take very seriously the possibility that interference with police operations for any reason may bring on charges of "playing politics with the police." Supported by the police officers' association and the elected county sheriffs of three surrounding counties, the PRIS system developed with no supervision of county political executives. Increased warrant service for minor traffic violations and dangerous persons computer files are the principal products of the system. Compatibility with other regional, state, and national information systems in criminal justice was of secondary importance to local agencies.

Briefly, where local agencies and their professional staffs possessed sufficient political strength, information technology was utilized to improve the self-perceived quality of service and working conditions of employees. Notions of efficiency, standardization, and subordination to central executive review received less urgent consideration.

TECHNOLOGY AND SOCIETY

Technique, as I believe I have shown, is totally irrelevant to this notion, and pursues no end, professed or unprofessed. It evolves in a purely causal way: the combination of preceding elements furnishes the new technical elements. There is

> no purpose or plan that is being progressively realized. There
> is not even a tendency towards human ends. We are dealing
> with a phenomenon blind to the future, in a domain of integral
> causality. Hence, to pose arbitrarily some goal or other, to
> propose a direction for a technique, is to deny tenchnique
> and divest it of its character and strength.[2]—Ellul

> For our society is leaving the phase of spontaneity and is
> entering a more self-conscious stage; ceasing to be an industrial
> society, it is being shaped to an ever-increasing extent by
> technology and electronics, and thus becoming the first tech-
> netronic society.[3]—Brzezinski

Contemporary writing on the relation between society and technology is
reminiscent of the early descriptions of the role of bureaucracy in reshap-
ing nineteenth-century society. Pessimistic observers of modern technology,
especially electronic computers, conclude that technology is developing independently of human designs and purposes; ultimately, according to
thinkers such as Ellul, technology will rob men of their freedom and dig-
nity, replacing those qualities with logic and regimentation. Optimistic observers of our technology, such as Brzezinski, conclude that although new
problems will surely be created by the use of some technologies, such traditional problems as the production and distribution of material goods will
be solved. Some even believe that politics as a contest of differing interests
and values will be replaced by a more rational means of arriving at collective decisions, relying more on analytic models and techniques than on
ideology.[4]

Both contemporary schools, if they can be called schools, rely on the
premise that through some inevitable principle of "reason," technology
works on society to determine its fundamental structure, course, and content. Echoed in both views are the words of Robert Michels describing the
implicit, or rather the inevitable, consequences of bureaucracy for democratic institutions:

> Organization implies the tendency to oligarchy. . . . As a
> result of organization, every party or professional union
> becomes divided into a minority of directors and majority of
> directed. . . . It is indisputable that the oligarchical and bureau-
> cratic tendency of party organization is a matter of technical
> and practical necessity. It is the inevitable product of the very
> principle of organization.[5]

Current research suggests that under certain political and social conditions, bureaucracy can be used as a tool by the directed to control the

directors, and in some cases to protect the directed.[6] In this book we have suggested similarly that information technology is a malleable tool whose ultimate social meaning, content, and consequences are highly subject to the influence of the specific political values and interests that inform its use.

We have focused on the cleavage between bureaucratic and professional interests insofar as they influenced the uses of information technology in local government; implicit in this finding, however, is the notion that other values and interests could be served by the technology as well.

Bureaucracy, insofar as it emphasizes efficiency as against social equality, and professionalism, insofar as it stresses the received wisdom of the profession as against the aspirations of disenfranchised groups in the society striving to attain social equality may both be irrelevant to those groups in society striving to attain social equality. The criminal offender information systems in Eastern and Western states, the social service information system of Western County, and the wanted/warrant system of the Western County police bear at best a distant relation to the need for an adequate welfare system in the United States and to the need for an equitable system of criminal justice.

Far from representing a dynamic force in local government, the information systems we describe—and we suggest that these are not atypical applications—illustrate the use of a new technology to further the political aims and interests of established and limited groups in the society. Whether the technology is used to produce higher arrest rates for minor infractions of the law or to prevent welfare fraud, the result is a kind of technical rationality in which the relation between means and ends becomes obscured. Thus our perception of the relation between the prevention of welfare fraud and the presumed goal of welfare agencies—namely, the provision of welfare services to needy persons—becomes dimmed by the very success of a technology in achieving a welfare system free of fraud.

Clearly computer technology has evolved to the stage at which it could be effectively utilized to further the values and interests of less established groups in the society. A regional job bank for unemployed persons, quarterly surveys of the welfare and health needs of county and state populations, closer surveillance of the billing practices of outside professionals paid by government for social services, close surveillance of the hiring practices of firms supported by federal contracts, and annual surveys (publicly available) of the distribution of police services within local communities, are a few potential uses of information technology that are directly related to societal needs.

The extent to which information technology will be used to help meet these broader social needs is a political, not a technological question. By raising to the level of societal consciousness the specific values and in-

terests that have shaped the uses of information technology in local government to date, we hope to have contributed to the society's ability to select
future uses of the technology, thus to shape its own future.

NOTES

1. Sheldon Wolin, *Politics and Vision*, Boston: Little Brown, 1960, pp. 357–361.

2. Jacques Ellul, *The Technological Society*, New York: Random House, 1967, p. 97.

3. Zbigniew Brzezinski, "The American Transition," *New Republic*, **157** (December 23, 1967), p. 18.

4. This I take to be the gist of articles by Daniel Bell on the changes taking place in contemporary American society. See, for example, Daniel Bell, *The End of Ideology*, New York: Free Press, 1966, pp. 393–408, and "Notes on the Post-Industrial Society II," *Public Interest*, 1967.

5. Robert Michels, *Political Parties*, New York: Free Press, 1962, pp. 70–72.

6. See Seymour M. Lipset et al., *Union Democracy*, Garden City, N. Y., Anchor, 1962; and also Alvin Gouldner, *Patterns of Industrial Bureaucracy*, New York: Free Press, 1954.

SELECTED BIBLIOGRAPHY

The bibliography contains references to selected chapters where the author believed
that readers may desire additional background information. More detailed references
can be found in the Notes following each chapter.

Selected Bibliography

Chapter 1

Batchelder, Allan, "Decline in the Economic Relations of Negro Men," *Quarterly Journal of Economics,* **68,** (August 1964).

Bell, Daniel, "Notes on the Post-Industrial Society II," *Public Interest,* 1967. Number 8 (Summer 67)

Bell, Daniel, *The End of Ideology,* New York: Free Press, 1960.

Black, Harold, and Edward Shaw, "Detroit's Data Banks," *Datamation,* **13** (March 1967), pp. 25–27.

Blauner, Robert, *Alienation and Freedom,* Chicago: University of Chicago Press, 1967.

Blatt, H., "Organizing for Information in Nassau County," *Public Management,* October 1967, pp. 292–299.

Blumberg, Paul M., *Industrial Democracy: The Sociology of Participation,* London: Constable, 1968.

Bright, James R., "Does Automation Raise Skill Requirements?" *Harvard Business Review,* **36,** (July–August 1958), pp. 85–89.

Califano, Joseph, Testimony before a Senate Labor Sub-Committee, cited in *The New York Times,* editorial, December 25, 1969.

"Census," *International Encyclopedia of the Social Sciences,* Vol. 2, New York: Macmillan and Free Press, 1968.

Chartrand, Robert L., "Congress Seeks a System Approach," *Datamation,* **14** (May 1968), pp. 46–49.

Chiera, Edward, *They Wrote on Clay,* Chicago: University of Chicago Press, 1968.

Chrimes, Kathleen M. T., *Ancient Sparta,* Manchester: University of Manchester Press, 1949.

Cloward, Richard, and Lloyd Ohlin, *Delinquency and Opportunity.* New York: Free Press, 1960.

"Computers," *Encyclopedia Britannica,* Vol. 7, 1971.

de Sola Pool, Ithiel, Stuart McIntosh, and David Griffel, *On the Design of Computer-Based Information Systems,* Cambridge, Mass.: M.I.T. Press, 1968.

District of Columbia, Executive Office, *Manual for the Users of the District of Columbia Real Property Data Bank,* Washington, D.C.: Government Printing Office, November 1967.

Drew, Elizabeth, "HEW Grapples with PPBS," *Public Interest,* 1967, pp. 10–21.

Dunn, Edgar, "The Idea of a National Data Center," *The American Statistician,* **21** February 1967), pp. 21–27.

Etzioni, Amita, *The Active Society,* New York: Free Press, 1966.

Federal Bureau of Investigation, "A National Crime Information Center," *FBI Law Enforcement Bulletin,* Washington, D.C.: Government Printing Office, May 1966.

Ferry, W. H., "Must We Re-Write the Constitution to Control Technology?" *Saturday Review,* **51** (March 2, 1968), pp. 50–54.

Gordon, Mitchell, *Sick Cities,* Baltimore: Penguin, 1965.

Gyarfas, Mary, "Social Science, Technology, and Social Work: A Case Worker's View." *Social Service Review,* **43** (September 1969).

Herman, Melvin, and Michael Munk, *Decisionmaking in Poverty Programs: Case Studies from Youth Work Agencies,* New York: Columbia University Press, 1968.

Higginson, M. V., *Managing with E.D.P.,* New York: American Management Association, 1965.

Hofstadter, Richard, *The American Political Tradition,* New York: Vintage, 1960.

Intergovernmental Board on Electronic Data Processing of the State of California, *Survey of EDP Activities in State and Local Government,* Sacramento, 1970 (mimeo).

Kaysen, Carl, "Data Banks and Dossiers," *Public Interest,* Spring 1967.

Kibbee, J. M., and V. V. Almendinger. "The Bay Area Transportation Study Commission Information System Data Description and Documentation," Santa Monica, Calif.: Systems Development Corporation, December 1965.

Kramer, S. N., *History Begins at Sumer,* Garden City, N.Y.: Doubleday, 1959.

Levin, Melvin, *Community and Regional Planning,* New York: Praeger, 1969.

Mann, Floyd L., and Lawrence K. Williams, "Observations on the Dynamics of Change to Electronic Data Processing Equipment," *Administrative Science Quarterly,* **5** (1960), pp. 217–256.

Marx, Gary T., *Protest and Prejudice,* New York: Harper & Row, 1969.

McLaughlin, John, *Information Technology and Survival of the Firm,* Homewood, Ill.: Dow Jones-Irwin, 1966.

Merton, Robert K., "Social Problems and Sociological Theory," in Robert K. Merton and Robert A. Nisbet (eds.), *Contemporary Social Problems,* New York: Harcourt Brace Jovanovich, 1966.

Merton, Robert K., *Social Theory and Social Structure,* New York: Free Press, 1957.

Meyer, Marshall, "Automation and Bureaucratic Structure," *American Sociological Review,* **74** (1968), pp. 108–116.

Miller, Herman I., "Is the Income Gap Closed? 'No,' " *New York Times Magazine Section,* November 11, 1962.

Montijo, R. E., Jr., "California D.M.V. Goes On Line," *Datamation,* **13** (May 1967), pp. 31–36.

"More Job Banks," *Public Automation,* December 1969.

Parker, J. K., "Operating a City Data Bank," *Public Automation,* June 1965.

"Proposals for Municipal Information Systems Asked," *Datamation,* November 1969.

Ragan, L., "Chicago's Police E.D.P. System," *Datamation,* **13** (July 1967), pp. 52–53.

Ramo, Simon, *Cure For Chaos*, New York: McKay, 1969.

Read, Conyers, *Mr. Secretary Walsingham and the Policy of Queen Elizabeth*, Oxford: Clarendon, 1925.

Rogers, Clark D., and Claude D. Peters, "Directory of the Status of State and Local Systems," *AIP Survey of Automated Information Systems: Part I*, Pittsburgh, Pa.: American Institute of Planners, 1967.

Rose, Michael, *Computers, Managers, and Society*, Baltimore: Penguin, 1969.

Santa Clara County, *The LOGIC Information System—Local Government Information Control*. Santa Clara County, Calif.: Data Processing Center, General Services Agency, 1969.

Schmandt, Henry J., *The Milwaukee Metropolitan Study Commission*, Bloomington: Indiana University Press, 1965.

"SCOPE Completes First Year of Fighting Crime in Nevada," *Computer World*, December 1968.

Seigman, Jack, and Bernard Karsh, "Some Organizational Correlates of White Collar Automation," *Sociological Inquiry*, **32** (1962), pp. 108–116.

Smelser, Neil, *Theory of Collective Behavior*, New York: Free Press, 1963.

Sofen, Edward, *The Miami Metropolitan Experiment*, Bloomington: Indiana Universtiy Press, 1965.

Solomon, Barbara M., *Ancestors and Immigrants*, Cambridge, Mass.: Harvard University Press, 1956.

Squire, P. S., *The Third Department*, London: Cambridge University Press, 1968.

Stenton, Doris M., *English Justice Between the Norman Conquest and the Great Charter, 1066–1215*, Philadelphia: American Philosophical Society, 1964.

Tamaru, Takuji, "Prospects in Municipal Information Systems: the Example of Los Angeles," *Computers and Automation*, January 1968, pp. 15–18.

"Traffic Safety—A National Data Center." *Systems Development Corporation Magazine*, **11** (May 1968).

Tri-State Transportation Commission, *Annual Report, 1967*, New York: Tri-State Transportation Commission, 1967.

T.R.W. Systems Group, *Systems Technology in Service of Society*, T.R.W. Inc., 1969.

U.S. Advisory Commission on Inter-Governmental Relations, *Fatcors Affecting Voter Reactions to Governmental Reorganization in Metropolitan Areas*, Washington, D.C.: Government Printing Office, May 1962.

U.S. Bureau of the Budget, "Inventory of Automatic Data Processing Equipment in the Federal Government," Washington, D.C.: Government Printing Office, June 1965.

U.S. Congress, House of Representatives No. 858, "Use of Electronic Data Processing in the Federal Government," Committee on Post Office and Civil Service, 88th Congress, 1st Session, 1963.

U.S. Department of Housing and Urban Development, *Urban and Regional Information Systems: Support for Planning in Metropolitan Areas*, Washington, D.C.: Department of Housing and Urban Development, 1968.

U.S. Office of Economic Opportunity, "Establishment of OEO Planning-Programming-Budgeting System (PPBS)," Washington, D.C.: Office of Economic Opportunity, 1966.

U.S. Senate, 90th Congress, *Hearings Before the Subcommittee on Administrative Practice and Procedure of the Committee on the Judiciary,* U.S. Senate, 90th Congress, 1st Session, 1967.

Valentine, Charles A., *The Culture of Poverty—A Critique and Counter Proposals,* Chicago: University of Chicago Press, 1968.

Walker, Charles R., *Toward the Automated Factory,* New Haven, Conn.: Yale University Press, 1957.

Westin, Alan F., "Civil Liberties and Computerized Data Systems," Presentation before the Johns Hopkins–Brookings Institution Lecture Series on Computers, Communications, and the Public Interest, Washington, D.C.: January 8, 1970.

Westin, Alan F. (ed.), *Information Technology in a Democracy,* Cambridge, Mass.: Harvard University Press, 1971.

Westin, Alan F., "Legal Safeguards to Insure Privacy in a Computer Society," *Communications of the Association for Computing Machinery,* **10** (September 1967), pp. 533–537.

Whisler, Thomas L., and George P. Schultz, "Automation and the Management Process," *Annals of the American Academy of Political Science,* **340** (March 1962), pp. 81–89.

Wilson, James Q., "Politics and Reform in American Cities," in Ivan Hinderaker, (ed.), *American Government Annual 1962–1963,* New York: Holt, Rinehart, & Winston, 1962.

Woodward, Joan, *Industrial Organization: Theory and Practice,* London: Oxford University Press, 1965.

Zweig, Stefan, *Joseph Fouché: The Portrait of a Politician,* Eden and Cedar Paul (transls.), New York: Viking, 1930.

Chapter 6

Awa, Eme O., *Federal Government in Nigeria,* Berkeley: University of California Press, 1964.

Alinsky, Saul, *Reveille for Radicals,* Chicago: University of Chicago Press, 1967.

Altshuler, Alvin, *The City Planning Process,* Ithaca, N.Y.: Cornell University Press, 1967.

Banfield, Edward C., and James Q. Wilson, *City Politics,* New York: Vintage, 1963.

Banton, M., "Adaption and Integration in the Social Systems of Temne Immigrants in Freetown," in Immanuel Wallerstein, (ed.), *Social Change: The Colonial Situation,* New York: Wiley, 1966.

Berelson, Bernard, Paul Lazarsfeld, and William McPhee, *Voting,* Chicago: University of Chicago Press, 1954.

Blau, Peter M., and Richard W. Scott, *Formal Organizations,* San Francisco: Chandler, 1962.

Brzezinski, Zbigniew, "The American Transition," *The New Republic,* **157** (December 23, 1967), pp. 18–21.

Burns, Tom, and G. M. Stalker, *The Management of Innovation,* London: Tavistock, 1961.

Campbell, Ronald F., Cunningham, L. Luvern and Roderick F. McPhee, *The Organization and Control of American Schools,* Columbus, Ohio: Merrill, 1965.

Charters, W. W., Jr., and Theodore M. Newcomb, "Some Attitudinal Effects of Experimentally Increased Salience of Group Membership," in Eleanor Maccoby, Theodore M. Newcomb, and Eugene L. Hartley (eds.), *Readings in Social Psychology,* New York: Holt, Rinehart, & Winston, 1958.

Coleman, James S., and Elihu Katz, *Medical Innovation: A Diffusion Study,* Indianapolis, Ind.: Bobbs-Merrill, 1966.

Crozier, Michel, *The Bureaucratic Phenomenon,* Chicago: University of Chicago Press, 1964.

Cruse, Harold, *Rebellion or Revolution,* New York: Morrow, 1969.

Cruse, Harold, "Revolutionary Nationalism and the Afro-American," *Studies on the Left,* **2** (1962).

Dahl, Robert, *Modern Political Analysis,* Englewood Cliffs, N.J.: Prentice-Hall, 1963.

Deutsch, Karl, *Nationalism and Social Communication,* Cambridge, Mass.: M.I.T. Press, 1953.

Deutsch, Karl, "Transaction Flows as Indicators of Political Cohesion," in Philip E. Jacobs and James Toscano (eds.), *The Integration of Political Communities,* Philadelphia: Lippincott, 1964.

Deutsch, Morton, and Robert M. Krauss, "Studies in Interpersonal Bargaining," *Journal of Conflict Resolution,* **6** (1962), pp. 52–76.

Downs, Anthony, "A Realistic Look at the Final Payoffs from Urban Data Systems," *Public Administration Review,* **27** (September 1967), pp. 204–209.

Durkheim, Emile, *The Division of Labor in Society,* New York: Free Press, 1960.

Emerson, Rupert, *From Empire to Nation,* Cambridge, Mass.: Harvard University Press, 1960.

Etzioni, Amitai, *Political Unification,* New York: Holt, Rinehart, & Winston, 1965.

Etzioni, Amitai, "Two Approaches to Organizational Analysis: A Critique and a Suggestion," *Adminstrative Science Quarterly,* **5** (1960), pp. 257–278.

Feshbach, Norma D., "Non-Conformity to Experimentally Induced Group Norms of High Status Versus Low Status," *Journal of Personality and Social Psychology,* **6** (1967), pp. 55–63.

Galbraith, John Kenneth, *American Capitalism: The Concept of Counter Vailing Power.* Boston: Houghton Mifflin, 1956.

Gerlach, Luther, and Virginia Hines, *People, Power, Chance: Movements of Social Transformation.* Indianapolis, Ind., Bobbs-Merrill, 1970.

Glazer, Nathan, and Daniel P. Moynihan, *Beyond the Melting Pot,* Cambridge, Mass.: M.I.T. Press, 1970.

Green, A. D., "The Professional Social Worker and the Bureaucracy," *Social Service Review,* **40** (1967), pp. 71–83.

Harvard Law Review Editors, "The Administration of Complaints by Civilians Against the Police," *Harvard Law Review,* **77** (January 1964), pp. 499–519.

Hillman, Arthur, *Community Organization and Planning,* New York: Macmillan, 1950.

Homans, George C., *The Human Group,* New York: Harcourt Brace Jovanovich, 1950.

Horstein, Harvey, "The Effects of Different Magnitudes of Threat upon Interpersonal Bargaining," *Dissertation Abstracts,* **26** (1966), pp. 4852–4853.

Hunter, Floyd, *Community Power Structure,* Chapel Hill: University of North Carolina Press, 1953.

Jacobs, Philip E., and James Toscano (eds.), *The Integration of Political Communities,* Philadelphia: Lippincott, 1964.

Kornhauser, William, *The Politics of Mass Society,* New York: Free Press, 1959.

Lazarsfeld, Paul F., and Herbert Menzel, "On the Relation Between Individual and Collective Properties," in Amitai Etzioni (ed.), *Complex Organizations: A Sociological Reader,* New York: Holt, Rinehart, & Winston, 1961, pp. 422–440.

Levine, Sol, and Paul E. White, "Exchange as a Conceptual Framework for the Study of Interorganizational Relationships," *Administrative Science Quarterly,* **5** (1960), pp. 583–601.

Lipset, Seymour M., *The First New Nation,* New York: Basic Books, 1963.

Litwak, Eugene, and Lydia F. Hylton, "Interorganizational Analysis: A Hypothesis on Coordinating Agencies," *Alministrative Science Quarterly,* 6 (1962), pp. 395–415.

Locke, John, *Two Treatises on Government,* edited by Peter Laslett, Cambridge: Cambridge University Press, 1961.

Longabaugh, Richard. "A Category System for Coding Interpersonal Behavior as Social Exchange," *Sociometry,* **26** (1963), pp. 319–344.

Lowi, Theodore J., "Machine Politics—Old and New," *Public Interest,* 9 (Fall 1967), pp. 83–92.

MacBride, Robert, *The Automated State,* Philadelphia: Chilton, 1967.

Maccoby, Eleanor, Theodore M. Newcomb, and Eugene L. Hartley (eds.), *Readings in Social Psychology,* New York: Holt, Rinehart, & Winston, 1958.

March, James G., and Herbert A. Simon, *Organizations,* New York: Wiley, 1958.

Marris, Peter, and Martin Rein, *Dilemmas of Social Reform,* New York: Atherton, 1967.

Moore, Barrington, Jr., *The Social Origins of Dictatorship and Democracy.* Boston: Becon Press, 1967.

Moynihan, Daniel Patrick, *Maximum Feasible Misunderstanding,* New York: Free Press, 1969.

Mulder, M., et al., "Illegitimacy of Power and Positive Attitude Towards the Power Person," *Human Relations,* **19** (1966), pp. 21–37.

Murdoch, Peter H., "The Development of Contractual Norms in the Interdependent Dyad with Power Differentiation," *Dissertation Abstracts,* **27** (1966).

Parsons, Talcott, *The Social System,* New York: Free Press, 1951.

Robinson, Joan, *Economics of Imperfect Competition,* London: Macmillan, 1969.

Rosen, George, *Democracy and Social Change in India,* Berkeley: University of California Press, 1966.

Scalapino, Robert, *Parties and Politics in Contemporary Japan,* Berkeley: University of California Press, 1962.

Schurman, Franz, *The Attack of the Cultural Revolution on Ideology and Organiza- tion,* Berkeley: Center for Chinese Studies, University of California at Berkeley, 1967 (mimeo).

Seeman, Melvin, "On the Meaning of Alienation," *American Sociological Review,* **24** (December 1959), pp. 783–791.

Selznick, Philip, *TVA and the Grass Roots,* Berkeley: University of California Press, 1949.

Skolnick, Jerome, *Justice Without Trial,* New York: Wiley, 1967.

Smith, W., "Power Structure and Authoritarianism in the Use of Power in the Trial," *Journal of Personality,* **35** (1967), pp. 65–89.

Stouffer, Samuel, et al., *The American Soldier,* Vol. 1, Princeton, N.J.: Princeton University Press, 1949.

Thomas, Edwin J., "Effects of Facilitative Role Interdependence on Group Func- tioning," *Human Relations,* **19** (1957), pp. 347–366.

Thompson, James D., *Organizations in Action,* New York: McGraw-Hill, 1967.

Townsend, Harry, *Scale, Innovation, Merger, and Monopoly,* New York: Oxford University Press, 1968.

Van Velson, J., "Labour Migration as a Positive Factor in the Continuity of Tonga Tribal Society," in Immanuel Wallerstein (ed.), *Social Change: The Colonial Situation,* New York: Holt, Rinehart, & Winston, 1966.

Von de Mehden, Fred R., *Religion and Nationalism in South East Asia,* Madison: University of Wisconsin Press, 1963.

Wallace, Anthony F. C., "Revitalization Movements," *American Anthropologist,* **58** (1965), pp. 264–281.

Weber, Max, *The Theory of Social and Economic Organization* (transls.), A. M. Henderson and Talcott Parsons. New York: Free Press, 1947.

Wheaton, William L. C., "Integration at the Urban Level: Political Influence and the Decision Process," in Philip E. Jacobs and James Toscano (eds.), *The Integra- tion of Political Communities,* Philadelphia: Lippincott, 1964.

Wildavsky, Aaron, "The Political Economy of Efficiency," *Public Interest,* Summer 1967, pp. 30–48.

Wilensky, Harold, and Charles N. Lebaux, *Industrial Society and Social Welfare,* New York: Free Press, 1968.

Woodward, Joan, *Industrial Organization: Theory and Practice,* London: Oxford Uni- versity Press, 1965.

Chapter 7

Ackoff, Russell, and Patrick Rivett, *A Manager's Guide to Operations Research,* New York: Wiley, 1963.

Alexander, Tom, "Computers Can't Solve Everything," *Fortune* (October 1969).

Anderson, Martin, *The Federal Bulldozer,* Cambridge, Mass.: M.I.T. Press, 1964.

Bollens, John C., *American County Government,* Beverly Hills, Calif.: Sage, 1969.

Beckett, J. A., "The Total Systems Concept: Its Implications for Management," in *The Impact of Computers on Management,* Cambridge, Mass.: M.I.T. Press, 1967. Editor: Charles A. Myers

Bendix, Reinhard, *Nation-Building and Citizenship,* Garden City, N. Y.: Doubleday, 1969.

Bergst, George L., and Robert Donati, *County Aspects of the State Information Study,* Sunnyvale, Calif.: Lockheed Missiles and Space Co., 1965.

Bucher, Rue, and Anselm Strauss, "Professions in Process: An Emergent Approach," *American Journal of Sociology,* **66** (1967), pp. 325–334.

Burck, Gilbert, "Management Will Never Be the Same Again," *Fortune,* July 1969.

Burck, Gilbert, "Will the Computer Outwit Man?" *Fortune,* October 1969.

Corwin, R. G., "A Study of Conflict in Nursing Role," *American Journal of Sociology,* **66** (1967), pp. 604–615.

Galbraith, John Kenneth, *The New Industrial State,* Boston: Houghton Mifflin, 1967.

Gamson, William A., *Power and Discontent,* Homewood, Ill.: Dorsey, 1968.

Gans, Herbert J., "The Failure of Urban Renewal," in Herbert J. Gans (ed.), *People and Plans,* New York: Basic Books, 1968.

Goode, W. J., "Encroachment, Charlatanism, and the Emerging Professions: Psychology, Sociology, and Medicine," *American Sociological Review,* **25**, pp. 902–914.

Green, A. D., "The Professional Social Worker in the Bureaucracy," *Social Service Review,* **40** (1967), pp. 71–83.

Greenburger, Martin. "The Uses of Computers in Organizations," *Scientific American,* September 1966.

Hall, Richard, "Professionals in Bureaucracy: Alienation Among Industrial Scientists," *American Sociological Review,* **32**, pp. 755–789. 1967.

Hearle, Edward, and R. J. Mason, *A Data Processing System for State and Local Government,* Englewood Cliffs, N.J.: Prentice-Hall, 1962.

Hofstadter, Richard, *The Age of Reform,* New York: Random House, 1955.

Key, V. O., *Southern Politics in State and Nation,* New York: Knopf, 1949.

Lee, Eugene C., *The Politics of Non-Partisanship,* Berkeley: University of California Press, 1960.

Milliman, Gordon, "Real Time Information Retrieval—Social Service Files," Report to the California Association of County Data Processors, Fall 1965.

National Municipal League, *The County Manager Plan,* New York: National Municipal League, 1945.

Ortega, Milton E., *A Critical Analysis of the Spanish Surname Population—HEW 701 Survey of 1966,* Spanish Speaking Information Center, 1968 (mimeo).

Stone, Harold, Don K. Price, and Kathryn Stone, *City Manager Government in the United States,* Chicago: Public Administration Service, 1940.

"Law Enforcement Is Everybody's Business," Presentation to the 7th Annual Institute on Police-Community Relations, February 6, 1964 (mimeo).

U.S. Department of Commerce, Bureau of the Census, *United States Census of Population 1960, State Economic Areas.* Vol. 6.

Weidner, Edward W., "Review of the Controversy over County Executives," *Public Administration Review,* **11** (1948), pp. 90–110.

Westin, Alan F., *Privacy and Freedom,* New York: Atheneum, 1967.

Wilson, James Q., *Varieties of Police Behavior,* Cambridge, Mass.: Harvard University Press, 1968.

Chapter 8

Banton, Michael, *The Policeman and the Community,* London: Tavistock, 1964.

Cicourel, Aaron, *The Social Organization of Juvenile Justice,* New York: Wiley, 1968.

Columbia Law Review Editors, "The Right to Nondiscriminatory Enforcement of State Penal Laws," *Columbia Law Review,* **82** (1967), pp. 730–735.

Fosdick, Raymond B., *American Police Systems,* New York: Century, 1920.

Hoover, J. Edgar, *Should You Go Into Law Enforcement?* New York: New York Life Insurance Company, 1961.

IIT Research Institute, *A Socio-Economic Valuation Study for the Automatic License Plate Scanning System,* Annapolis, Md.: IIT Research Institute, 1969.

Kaplan, John, *Marijuana—The New Prohibition,* New York: World, 1970.

Lane, Roger, *Policing the City—Boston 1822–1885,* Cambridge, Mass.: Harvard University Press, 1967.

Klimkowski, Harold, "The Police Budget: The Mistake of Using the $OSQ + CI = MPP$ Formula," *The Police Yearbook,* **50** (1966).

Matarazzo, Joseph D., et al., "Characteristics of Successful Policemen and Firemen Applicants," *Journal of Applied Psychology,* **48** (1964).

Morris, Orval, and Morris Hawkins, *The Honest Politician's Guide to Crime Control,* Chicago: University of Chicago Press, 1969.

President's Commission on Law Enforcement and Administration of Justice, *The Challenge of Crime in a Free Society, Task Force Report: The Police,* Washington, D.C.: Government Printing Office, 1967.

Schur, E. M., *Crimes Without Victims,* Englewood Cliffs, N.J., Prentice-Hall, 1965.

Shoup, Carl, "Standards for Distributing a Free Government Service: Crime Prevention." *Public Finance,* **19** (1964).

Skolnick, Jerome, *Justice Without Trial.* New York: Wiley, 1967.

U.S. Department of Justice, Federal Bureau of Investigation, *Crime in the United States—Uniform Crime Reports 1967,* Washington, D.C.: Government Printing Office, 1968.

Walton, Frank E., "Selective Distribution of Police Patrol Force," *Journal of Criminal Law, Criminology, and Police Science,* **49** (1958).

Westley, William A., "Secrecy and the Police," *Social Forces,* **34** (1956).

Westley, William A., *Violence and the Police,* Cambridge, Mass.: M.I.T. Press, 1971.

Wildavsky, Aaron, *The Politics of the Budgetary Process,* Boston: Little, Brown, 1964.

Wilson, O. W., "Selective Distribution of Police Patrol Force," *Journal of Criminal Law, Criminology, and Police Science,* **49** (1958).

Whitaker, Ben, *The Police,* Middlesex, England: Penguin, 1964.

Yale Law Journal Editors, "Program Budgeting for Police Department," *Yale Law Journal,* **76** (Marhc 1967).

Chapter 9

Cook, Fred J., *The F.B.I. Nobody Knows,* New York: Macmillan, 1964.

Cressey, Donald, *Theft of a Nation,* New York: Harper & Row, 1969.

Downs, Anthony, *Inside Bureaucracy,* Boston: Little, Brown, 1967.

Federal Bureau of Investigation, "A National Crime Information Center, *FBI Law Enforcement Bulletin,* Washington, D.C.: Government Printing Office, 1968.

Hodge, Robert W., Paul M. Siegel, and Peter H. Rossi, "Occupational Prestige in the United States: 1925-1963," in Reinhard Bendix and Seymour M. Lipset (eds.), *Class, Status, and Power,* New York: Free Press, 1966.

Kadushin, Alfred, "Prestige of Social Work," *Social Work,* **3** (April 1958).

Niederhoffer, Arthur, *Behind the Shield,* Garden City, N. Y.: Anchor, 1969.

Pound, Roscoe, *The Development of Constitutional Guarantees of Liberty,* New Haven, Conn.: Yale University Press, 1967.

President's Commission on Law Enforcement and Administration of Justice, *The Challenge of Crime in a Free Society,* Washington, D.C.: Government Printing Office, 1967.

President's Commission on Law Enforcement and Administration of Justice, *The Challenge of Crime in a Free Society. Task Force Report: Science and Technology,* Washington, D.C.: Government Printing Office, 1967.

Smith, Bruce. *Police Systems in the United States,* New York: Harper & Row, 1960.

World News, February 20, 1971.

Chapter 10

Elazar, Daniel, *The American Partnership,* Chicago: University of Chicago Press, 1962.

Lipset, Seymour M., *The First New Nation,* Garden City, N.Y.: Anchor, 1967.

Chapter 11

Bell, Daniel, *The End of Ideology,* New York: Free Press, 1962.

Ellul, Jacques, *The Technological Society,* New York: Random House, 1967.

Gouldner, Alvin, *Patterns of Industrial Bureaucracy,* Glencoe, Ill.: Free Press, 1954.

Lipset, Seymour M., et al., *Union Democracy,* Garden City, N. Y.: Doubleday, 1962.

Michels, Robert, *Political Parties,* New York: Free Press, 1962.

Index